MW00508594

HURLBUT'S LIFE OF CHRIST

FOR YOUNG AND OLD

A COMPLETE LIFE OF CHRIST WRITTEN IN SIMPLE LANGUAGE, BASED ON THE GOSPEL NARRATIVE

BY REV. JESSE LYMAN HURLBUT, D.D.

Author of "Hurlbut's Story of the Bible"
Former Editor International Sunday-School Lessons

ILLUSTRATED

With Colored Plates and Full Page Halftone Reproductions from the Paintings of WILLIAM HOLE, R.S.A., R.E., and other artists. Also including Maps and Photographs of the Holy Land.

PHILADELPHIA
THE JOHN C. WINSTON COMPANY
PUBLISHERS

Coming to Jerusalem these strangers asked of every one whom they met: "Can you tell us where to find the little child who is born to be the King of the Jews?"

Preface

IN the preparation of this volume the aim in view has been to tell the story of Jesus Christ in a manner that will be attractive to both young and old, to children and their teachers. While the purpose of the writer has been to adapt the narrative to the understanding of a child of ten years, so that he will not need to ask the meaning of a sentence or a word: yet it has also been his desire to make it not childish, but simple, so that older readers may find it interesting and profitable.

In order that this book may not lead its younger readers or listeners away from the Bible, but directly toward it, no imaginary scenes or conversations have been introduced. The design has been to write the biography of Jesus, not a romance founded upon his life.

The order of events has been carefully considered; and follows that of the best authorities, accepting as historical *all* the four gospels and *all* their contents; raising no questions concerning miracles or the relative values of different portions of the record. The first purpose of every student or reader of the Bible, whether young or old, should be to become thoroughly familiar with its contents. Without a full knowledge of the Scriptures as they are, he is absolutely unfit to cope with the questions of authorship or the credibility of the sacred writings.

Preface

No attempt has been made to formulate from the record of Christ's life a doctrinal system. Theology is the loftiest study for the human intellect; but it belongs to the mature mind, not to the realm of childhood. Nor has it been the writer's aim to find in this story moral lessons for the young. The works and words of Jesus will make their own application to their reader, whether they be children or adults.

The typography, the illustrations, and the mechanical execution of such a work as this are of almost equal importance with its literary material. All that diligent effort, artistic taste, and abundant resources can do to make this book attractive and helpful to its readers, has been done by the Publishers.

That this volume may awaken a new interest in that Life of lives, which has brought the light of life to untold millions since it was lived upon the earth: that the children of this generation, who are to become the pillars of the coming years, may learn to love and follow Him who is the Elder Brother and Saviour of us all, is the prayer of the author of these pages.

Jesse Lyman Hurlbut

August 28, 1915.

Contents

Contents

Contents

Contents

Why Everybody Should Know the Life of Christ

THERE HAVE been many famous men in this world, and every one wishes to know who they were and why they are called great. In almost every city in America may be seen a statue of George Washington, or Abraham Lincoln, or Benjamin Franklin, or General Lee, or General Grant. Whenever you see one of these statues, you ask—if you do not know already—who this man was and why his statue has been set up. In Canada, every house has on the wall a portrait of the great and good Queen Victoria, and when a child sees it he wishes to know something of her life and her greatness. You see pictures of a man standing on the deck of a ship, or going ashore under palm trees on an island, and are told that he is Christopher Columbus—and every child in America knows something of his story. Men like Napoleon Bonaparte, and Julius Caesar, and Alexander the Great, are written about, and talked about; and every child should know who these men were and why they are famous.

Did you ever think that there is one man who has been talked about, and written about, and sung about, more than any other man in all the world; and that man is Jesus? For one book telling of Washington, or Napoleon, or Columbus, there are hundreds of books telling of Jesus. Every year at least fifteen million copies of the Bible are printed and sent out into the world, in every language spoken on this earth. Why does everybody wish to have a Bible in his house? It is because that book tells of Jesus. If the pages that tell of Jesus should be torn out of the Bible, few people would care to have it or to read it.

There are more portraits of Jesus Christ, painted and drawn and printed, than of any other man who has ever lived. Everybody knows the picture of Jesus as soon as he sees it, whether it be of the baby Jesus in his mother's arms, or the boy Jesus in the Temple, or the Saviour teaching, or dying upon the cross. You do not need to be told which one in any picture is Jesus—his face is so well known that you know it at once. No other face among all the men who have ever lived from Adam the first man down to today, is known to as many people as the face of Jesus. Then, too, look in the hymn books of the churches and the song books of the Sunday-schools, and see how many of the hymns and songs are in praise of Jesus Christ. You do not find songs in praise of Julius Caesar, nor of Christopher Columbus, nor even of George Washington. No one who gives it thought doubts that the most famous man in all the world is Jesus Christ; and because he is so famous and so great, every one should know something of his life.

Then, too, everybody likes to hear stories of wonderful things. Even though we know that they are not true stories, every one listens to fairy tales and the stories of the "Arabian Nights." But how often, when the story is ended, the child looks up to the story-teller's face and says, "Is it all true?" Now, the story of Jesus is full of wonders. You read of his turning water into wine when the guests at the feast needed it, of his touching the eyes of a blind man and giving him sight, of his speaking to the storm and bringing peace, of his walking upon the waters in another storm to help his friends in danger, and, most wonderful of all, of his coming out of his own tomb living, after he had died. Wonderful indeed are the stories told of Jesus; and the greatest wonder is that they are all true. You would like to hear those stories, I am sure; and every child should know them and be able to tell them to others.

Let me give you another reason why every one should know the story of Jesus. He came to show us who God is, what God is to us, and how God feels toward us. Every one, even every child, thinks of God and in his heart wishes to know about God. How terribly some people have mistaken God! They have thought of him as an enemy, not as a friend. You can see in some countries images of a person with forty arms, and on every hand something to kill a man with—a sword, a spear, an arrow, a club, a cup of poison, or some other fearful thing—and that is the thought of God in that land: a mighty being who hates men! In old times, many people thought that their gods were pleased when men killed their own children and burned their bodies on an altar as an offering to God. God saw all over the earth that men had wrong and cruel thoughts of him; and he sent his Son Jesus Christ to teach men by his words, and to show men in his life what God is, how God feels toward us, and how we should feel toward God. If Jesus had done no more for us than to teach us the Lord's Prayer, beginning with the words "Our Father who art in heaven," he would have done enough to make us love him. He showed people that God is their Father, the Father of every one in all the world, and that as a Father we may call upon him, just as any child can go to his father for whatever he needs.

There was once an artist who was called upon to paint the portrait of a good man. But the man had died ten years before; the artist had never seen him, and there was no picture of him to be used as a copy. At first the artist did not know what to do. Then a thought occurred to him.

"Is there no one," he said, "who looks like this man, so that I can see him and know something of the man's face?"

"Why, yes," they answered. "He has left a son, a man grown, who looks exactly like his father."

The artist studied the face of the son, and from it painted a likeness of the father, whom he had never seen. No one has ever seen God, but if we would know, not his face, which we cannot know, but his nature, how kind, and loving, and helpful, and willing God is, we have only to think of Christ; and if we know Christ, the Son of God, we know God, his Father and our Father. For this reason, because in Jesus we may know God, everybody should know about Jesus.

But Jesus came to this world, not only to show us what God is, but to show us what we should be and how we should live. Whatever his work may be, every one needs a copy which he can look at and follow. The child who is learning to write must have a copy, so that he may know how to shape his letters. The boy or girl learning to draw has a copy or a model to guide him in his drawing. When a man is about to build a ship, he first makes a model and then shapes his great ship exactly like it. Perhaps you have heard the lines in Longfellow's poem, "The Building of the Ship."

> "In the shipyard stood the Master,
> With the model of the vessel
> That should laugh at all disaster,
> And with wave and whirlwind wrestle."

Well, we are all builders. Each one of us, boy or girl, man or woman, is building for himself what no one else can build for him: his character, what he is to be, whether good or bad, whether wise or ignorant, whether noble or selfish. And in building up ourselves we need a model, one perfect man, on whom we can look and whose life we can copy. That model we can find in Jesus. He lived our life, and in living showed us how we should live. Even a little child may say, "Jesus was once a little child; and I will try my best to be just such a child as he was." A boy of twelve may think of Jesus as a boy and resolve to live as Jesus lived. The young man, working in a shop, or office, or in the field, may take Jesus the workingman for his pattern. When Jesus was on the earth, he said many times, and to different people, "Follow me!" He says it to every one of us. But if we are to follow Jesus and to be like him, the best man that ever lived, we must study him, must know about his life, must have every story of him in our mind and in our heart; and that is another reason why every one should know the story of Jesus.

It is now almost two thousand years since Jesus lived on the earth and walked among men. Since he came, the world has become a different world, just as far as they have heard the story of Jesus and have learned to follow him. People have become less selfish and more thoughtful of others, more willing to help others, more generous in giving to others. Think of all the homes for the poor, of all the hospitals for the sick, of all the places where little children are cared for, of the playgrounds, of the love shown at Christmas time, of ten thousand ways in which the world is better. And then remember that all these good things come from Jesus Christ and his love in the hearts of men. But for Jesus, this would have been a dark world. The proof of this is that these good things are to be seen only in the lands where Jesus is known and loved and followed. Look at the lands where Christ is unknown and you find them dark and sad. There is still much to be done to make this a perfect world. We see terrible wars, and the poor still suffering wrong, and many people still selfish and cruel to their fellow-men. What can we do to make this a better and a brighter world? We can do as Jesus did. It was said of him, "He went about doing good"; and that may be said of us if we will follow Christ. But to make this world good, we must know him who is its power for goodness; and that is another reason why every one should know the story of Jesus.

Let me name only one reason more why we should know the story of Jesus: through him we have what we need most of all—the forgiveness of our sins. Suppose that someone who watches us all the time should keep a list of every wrong-doing, of every fiery temper, of every angry word, of every blow struck, of every time that one of us failed to do what is right, of every time that one let pass a chance to do some good act to another—what a long list it would be! There is such a list kept. An eye that never sleeps sees every act, the eye of God; and he remembers all our deeds, and the things left undone which we ought to have done. Is there any way to have that list against us taken away, blotted out and forgotten? Yes, there is one who can take our sins away and make the black story of our life as white as snow. That one is Jesus Christ, the Son of God. He can forgive our sins, as he forgave the sins of men while he was on the earth; and he longs to have us ask him for forgiveness. Should we not love him for this? And should we not wish to hear about him and to know all the tender story of his love?

These, then, are some of the reasons why we should all seek to know the story of Jesus: because he is the greatest and most famous man that ever lived; because his story is full of interest and full of wonders, and is true; because he came to show us how kind and loving God is, and how willing to have us call upon him; because his life shows us a pattern of what we may be and tells us how we may be like him; because Jesus has made and is still making the world better, and brighter, and happier, wherever he is known; and best of all, because through Jesus our Saviour our sins may be forgiven and taken away, and we may be pure and holy as Jesus was upon the earth.

With these thoughts and aims, this Story of Jesus has been written. May it help many, young and old, to know Jesus better, to love him more, and to follow him more closely!

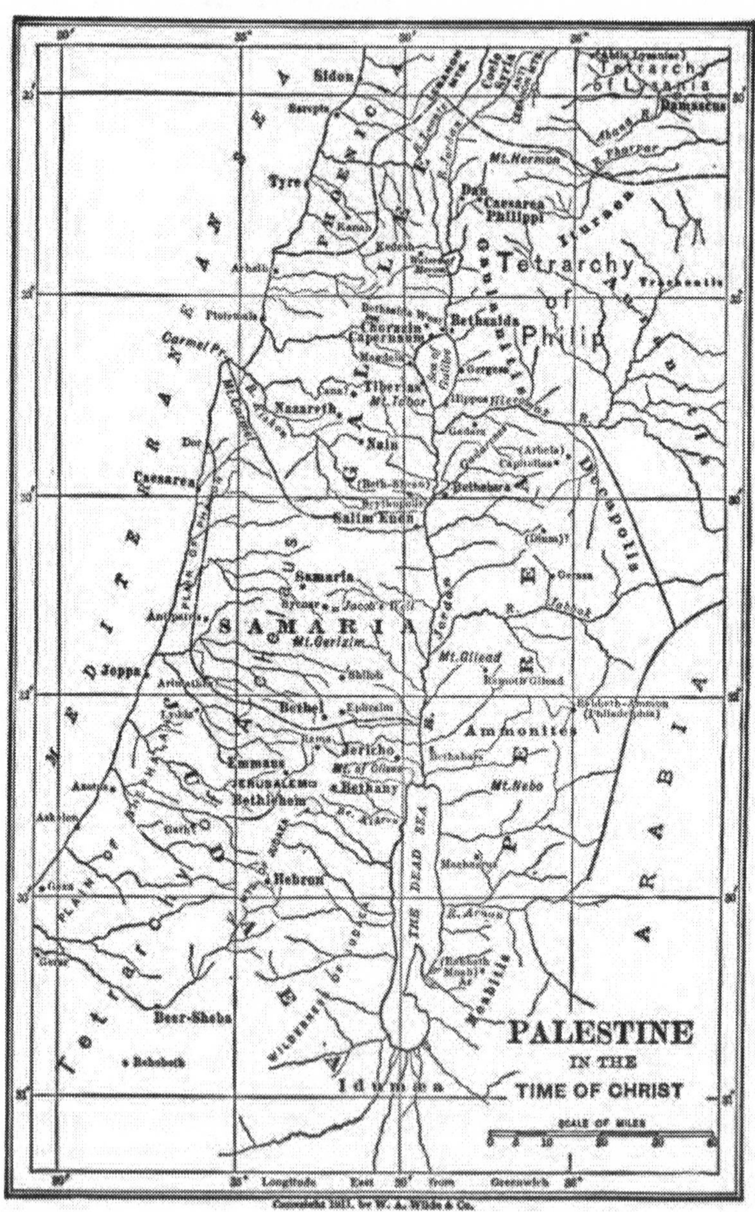
PALESTINE
IN THE
TIME OF CHRIST
Sidon
Tyre
Damascus
Mt.Hermon
Caesarea Philippi
Tetrarchy of Philip
Bethsaida
Capernaum
Tiberias
Nazareth
Nain
Caesarea
Joppa
SAMARIA
Samaria
Mt.Gerizim
Mt.Gilead
Bethel
Jericho
Emmaus
JERUSALEM
Bethlehem
Bethany
Ammonites
Mt.Nebo
Hebron
Beer-Sheba
THE DEAD SEA
Decapolis
ARABIA
Idumea
Longitude East from Greenwich
SCALE OF MILES

The Lord's Land

CHAPTER I

FIRST OF ALL, let us take a journey to the land where Jesus lived. We will sail in one of the big ocean steamers across the Atlantic, heading our prow a little to the south, and in eight days will pause at the Rock of Gibraltar, which stands on guard at the gate of the Mediterranean Sea. Do you know what "Mediterranean" means? It means, "among the lands"; and when you look at this sea on the map, you see that it has lands around it on every side, with only a narrow opening at Gibraltar, where its blue waters pour into the Atlantic Ocean.

We will enter the Mediterranean Sea, and sail its entire length, past Spain and France and Italy on the left. We just miss touching the toe of Italy, for you know Italy runs into the sea like a great leg with a high-heeled boot upon its foot. And just beyond Italy we sail by Greece, which looks somewhat like a hand with fingers wide apart.

While we are passing by these lands on the left, we are also sailing past Morocco and Algiers, and Tunis and Tripoli on the right. We stop at Alexandria in Egypt, at one of the mouths of the river Nile, and soon after we leave the big steamer at Port Said, where the great Suez Canal begins.

There in the afternoon about ten days after our leaving America, we go on board a smaller ship, and sail northward past the eastern shore of the Mediterranean Sea. The next morning we awake to find our ship at anchor in front of a city on a hillside, rising up in terraces from the water.

That city is now called Jaffa, or Yafa; and it is the place where the steamers stop to send ashore those who are about to visit the Holy Land, for that is the name given to the land where Jesus lived. Do you remember in the Old Testament the story of Jonah, the prophet who tried to run away from God's call to preach in the city of Nineveh? Well, it was from this city of Jaffa, then called Joppa, that Jonah started on his voyage, which ended inside the big fish. Perhaps you remember also the story of Dorcas, in the New Testa-

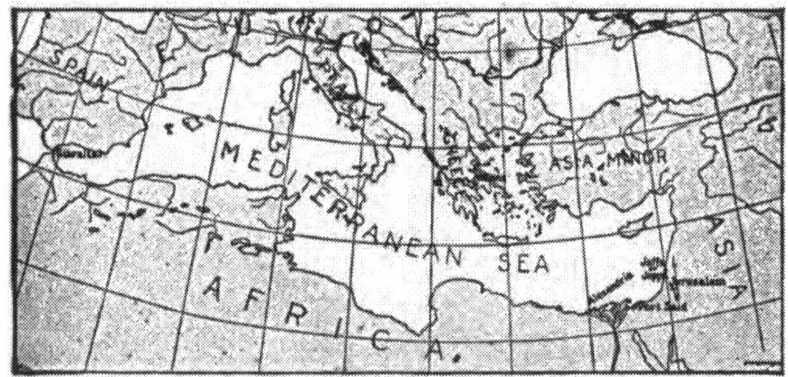

The Mediterranean Sea

ment, that good woman who helped the poor; and after dying was raised to life through the prayer of the Apostle Peter. Dorcas too lived at Joppa; and they show the house where, it is said, Peter stayed while he was visiting in that city.

Here at Jaffa or Joppa we end our long sea-voyage of about six thousand miles. We go ashore in a small boat, tossing up and down on the waves, for there is no wharf where a steamer can land its passengers. And now we are standing on the soil of the Holy Land, where Jesus lived. In Christ's time this land was called Judea. In our day its name is Palestine.

It is a small country. If you will turn to the map of the United States, and look at New Hampshire, you will see a state in form quite like Palestine, and only a little smaller in size; for Palestine, or the Holy Land, contains about twelve thousand square miles, and New Hampshire a little more than nine thousand.

There is no real harbor at Jaffa. Steamers must anchor some distance out, and passengers are landed by rowboats

From Joppa we must go across Palestine if we would look at the part of the land among the mountains where Jesus lived. We can now ride in a railroad train, something that Jesus never saw while he lived on the earth; or we can go in a carriage, or on a horse, or on the back of a camel, as you will see some people riding, or in what they call "a palankeen," which is something like a coach-body set not on wheels, but between two pair of shafts, one in front, the other behind, and a mule harnessed in each pair, so that the rider has one mule in front and the other back of him.

As we ride over the land we notice that at first it is very level. This part of the country is called "the Sea Coast Plain," and a plain it surely is, almost as level as a floor. All around, you see gardens and farms, orange trees and fig trees. If you could pluck one of these golden oranges and taste it, you would find that it is one of the sweetest and richest and juiciest that you have ever eaten, for the Jaffa oranges are famous

House of Simon, the tanner, in Joppa, where Peter stayed while visiting in that city

for their flavor. You ride between great fields of wheat and rye and barley, for this Sea Coast Plain is a rich farming land.

But after a few miles, ten or fifteen, we notice that we have left the plain and are winding and climbing among hills. In place of the farm-lands, we see here and there flocks of sheep with shepherds guarding them, just as the boy David watched over his flock three thousand years ago. Indeed, in our journey we might pass over the very brook where David found the round, smooth stones, one of which he hurled with a sling into the giant Goliath's forehead. This is the region of low hills, the foothills of the higher mountains beyond. It is called "the Shephelah," a name not easy to remember. In the Old Testament days, many battles were fought on these hills between the Israelites and the Philistines, their fierce enemies.

These foothills of the Shephelah are not many miles wide; and beyond them we come to the real Mountain Region of Palestine. Mountains rise on every hand, bare, stony, with scarcely any soil upon their steep sides, and with not a tree to be seen for miles. They are rocky crags, with here and there a village perched on their summits or clinging to their walls. This mountain land, more than the hills and plains below, was the home of the Israelites, the people from whom Jesus came. We wonder how they could ever have found a living in such a desolate land; but everywhere we see the ruins of old cities, showing that once the land was filled with people. In those times, two thousand and more years ago, all these mountain-sides, now bleak and rock-bound, were covered with terraces, where grew olive trees, fig trees and vineyards; where gardens blossomed and great crops were raised to feed the people. Even now in the spring and early summer, the valleys between these mountains are covered with flowers of every color. Scarcely another land on earth has as many wild flowers as this land of Pal-

A saddled camel

estine. This mountain-belt, running from the north to the south throughout the land was the part of Palestine where nearly all the great men of Israel lived and died. Here among the mountains in the south is Bethlehem, where Jesus was born. In a mountain village in the north, Nazareth, was the home of Jesus during nearly all his life; and over these mountains everywhere in the land, Jesus walked in the three years of his preaching and teaching.

We pass over these mountains from east to west, and then from the heights we look down to a valley which runs north and south, the deepest in all the world, where we can see a little river with many windings, and rapids and falls, rolling onward to drop at last into a blue lake in the south. This river, as you know, is the Jordan, crossed by the Israelites when they first came to this land; the river where Naaman washed away his leprosy, where Elijah struck the waves with his mantle and parted them, and in whose water Jesus was baptized.

We journey across this Jordan valley, from ten to twenty miles wide, and then we climb again high and steep mountains. This region is called the Eastern Table Land, because the mountains gradually sink down to a great desert plain on the east. Here we see the ruins of once great cities, where now only a few wandering Arabs pitch their tents.

We have now crossed the land of Palestine, and we have found that it contains five parts lying in a line: first, the Sea Coast Plain; second, the Shephelah, or foothills; third, the Mountain Region; fourth, the Jordan valley; and fifth, the Eastern Table Land.

But we must keep in mind that the land when Jesus lived there was very different from the land as we see it. Now it is a poor land; then it was rich.

Now its villages are made of miserable mud-houses, where live people who look half starved; then it was a land of well-built towns and happy people. Now we find roads that are mere tracks over the stones; then there were good roads everywhere. Now the hills rise bare and rocky; then they were covered with gardens. Now scarcely a tree can be seen in miles of travel; then the olive and the vine and the palm grew everywhere. We see the land in its ruin; Jesus saw it in its riches.

The valley of Gehenna, to the east of Jerusalem

The People in the Lord's Land

CHAPTER 2

NEARLY ALL the people living in Palestine in the time of Jesus were of the Jewish race. Two thousand years before Jesus came, a great man was living in that land, named Abraham. To this man, God gave a promise that his children and their children after them for many ages should live in that land and own it. Abraham's son was named Isaac, and Isaac's son was named Jacob. All the people of Palestine had sprung from the family of Jacob, and by the time Jesus came, these descendants of Jacob, as they were called, were in number many millions, and were to be found in other lands besides Palestine; although more of them lived in Palestine than in any other land.

Jacob, Abraham's grandson, was also named Israel; and on that account all the people sprung from him were called the Israelites. Jacob or Israel had twelve sons, from whom came the twelve tribes of Israel. But one son, named Judah, had more descendants or people springing from him than any other; and as most of the people in Palestine were of Judah's family, all of them were spoken of as Jews, a word which means sprung or descended from Judah. So the people to whom Jesus belonged were sometimes called Israelites, but more often Jews. They had another name, "Hebrews," but that was not used as often as the two names, Israelites and Jews.

For many years, long before Jesus came, the Jews were rulers in the land of Palestine, with kings of their own race, as David and Solomon in the early times, and King Jeroboam and King Hezekiah later. But in the time of Jesus, the Jews were no longer rulers in their own land. Palestine was then a small part of the vast Roman Empire, which ruled all the lands around the Mediterranean Sea. Its chief was an emperor, who lived at Rome in Italy. At the time when Jesus was born the emperor was Augustus. He was then an old man, and died very soon after the birth of Jesus. The

Tiberias, on the Sea of Galilee, where Herod lived

emperor who followed him was named Tiberius, and he ruled most of the years that Jesus was living in Palestine.

But there was another king ruling the land of Palestine under the Roman emperor, at the time when Jesus came. His name was Herod, and because he was a very wise and strong man, although a very wicked man, he was called Herod the Great. He ruled the land of Palestine, but in his turn obeyed the orders of the emperor Augustus at Rome. Herod also was a very old man at the time of Jesus' birth, and died soon afterward.

When Herod the Great died, his kingdom was divided into four parts. Each of these parts had a king of its own, and three of these kings were Herod's sons. Herod Antipas ruled over Galilee in the northwest, and Perea in the southeast; Herod Philip was over the country in the northeast; and Herod Archelaus ruled the largest portion, in the south. None of these little kings were good men. They had their father's wickedness, but did not have his ability to rule. One of them, Archelaus, was so bad that all the people asked the emperor at Rome to take his rule away. This the emperor did, and sent a man from Rome to govern the land in his place. You have heard of the Roman governor who was over this part of the land while Jesus was teaching. His name was Pontius Pilate; and he it was, you remember, who sent Jesus to die upon the cross.

The land of Palestine at that time was divided into five parts, which were called "provinces." The largest of these provinces was Judea, the one on the south, between the Dead Sea and the river Jordan on the east, and the Mediterranean Sea on the west. North of Judea was a small province called Samaria, where lived a people who were not Jews but Samaritans. The Jews hated the Samaritans, and the Samaritans, in turn, hated the Jews. Samaria was governed as a part of Judea, not with a separate ruler. These were the two provinces at first under Archelaus and then under the Roman governor.

In the north of Palestine, west of the river Jordan and the Sea of Galilee, was the province of Galilee, a country full of mountains, where Jesus dwelt for nearly all his life. The ruler of this province was Herod Antipas. He lived most of the time at a city which he had built beside the Sea of Galilee, and had named Tiberias, after the Roman emperor Tiberius.

Samuel anointing Saul to be the first king of Israel

Across the Jordan, on the east, opposite to Galilee was another province. In the Old Testament times, this land had been called Bashan, which means "woodland," because it was a land of many forests. In the New Testament time it was generally spoken of as "Philip's province," because its ruler was Herod Philip, the best of Herod's sons, and none too good, either.

South of Philip's province, and east of the river Jordan, was a province named Perea, a word meaning "beyond," because this region was beyond or across the river Jordan. At the time of Jesus' life, Perea was like Galilee, ruled by Herod Antipas. Once at least Jesus visited this province; and here he told the Parable of the Prodigal Son, which everybody has heard.

A heathen idol

Although the mighty Roman empire gave to the Jews in Palestine a government that was just and fair, it was not a Jewish rule; and the Jews were not contented under the power of foreigners. They felt that they more than other nations were the people of God, and that they had a right to rule themselves, under kings of their own race. Also they read in their Bible the promises of the prophets that from Israel should come forth a king, out of David's line, who should rule the world.

This great King, whom the Jews hoped for and looked for, they called "Messiah," a word in the Jews' language meaning the same as the word "Christ," which is a Greek word, meaning "the Anointed One," that is, "the King." You remember that in the Old Testament story the prophet

Samuel anointed Saul to be the first king of Israel, that is, he poured oil on his head; and that afterward he chose the boy David to be the next king by the same sign. When we say "Jesus Christ," Jesus is his name and "Christ" is his title; and we mean "Jesus the King."

We know that this promised King whom the Jews called Messiah was Jesus Christ who rules over the hearts of men everywhere; but the Jews thought that it meant a king like Herod or the emperor Tiberius, only better and wiser, who should live in a palace at Jerusalem, their chief city, and make all lands obey his will. This hope made the Jews very restless and unhappy under the Roman power. They were always looking for the coming of this mighty King of the Jews, who should lead them to conquer the earth.

Interior of Jewish synagogue in Palestine

In their worship the Jews were different from all the rest of the world. Every other people had gods of wood and stone, images before which they bowed and to which they gave offerings. In all the cities of that world were temples and altars to these idols, made by the hands of men. But in the land of the Jews were no images, no idol-temples, and no offerings to man-made gods. The Jews, whether in Palestine or in other lands, worshipped the One God who was unseen, the God to whom we also pray. In their chief city, Jerusalem, was a splendid temple where God was worshipped; and in every Jewish city and town were churches, where the people met to read the Bible, to sing the psalms of David, to offer prayer to God, and to talk together about God's laws. These churches were called "synagogues," and wherever Jews lived, synagogues were to be found. The Jews looked with great contempt upon the idol-worship of other nations, and were proud of the fact that ever since the days of their father Abraham, they had worshipped only the Lord God.

Ruins of ancient synagogue at Kefr Birim, in Galilee

The Stranger by the Golden Altar

CHAPTER 3

IN THE land of Palestine one city was loved by the Jews above all other places. That was Jerusalem, the largest city in the land in the province of Judea. It was to the Jews everywhere, not only in Palestine but over all the earth, wherever Jews lived, "the holy city." From all parts of the land the people came at least once in every year, and many families, three times each year, to worship God in Jerusalem. At these great feasts, as they were called, all the roads leading to Jerusalem were thronged with travelers going up to Jerusalem for worship. And the Jews in other lands, many hundreds of miles away, even as far as Rome itself, tried at least once in their lives to visit the city. They sang about Jerusalem songs such as:

> "If I forget thee, O Jerusalem,
> Let my right hand forget her cunning;
> Let my tongue cleave to the roof of my mouth
> If I remember thee not,
> If I prefer not Jerusalem
> Above my chief joy."

That which made Jerusalem a holy city was its Temple, a magnificent building on Mount Moriah, just across a valley from Mount Zion, where the larger part of the city stood. The Temple they called "The House of God," for in it the Jews believed their God made his home. In front of this Temple stood an altar, which was like a great box made of stone, hollow inside, and covered with a metal grating. Upon his altar a fire was kept burning night and day, and on the fire the priests who led in the worship of God, laid offerings of sheep and oxen, which were burned as gifts to God; while around the altar the people stood and prayed to God as the offering, which they called "a sacrifice," was burning.

Inside the Temple building were two rooms. The room in front was called "the holy place," and in it stood on one side a table covered with gold, on which lay twelve loaves of bread as an offering to God; one loaf for each of the twelve tribes of Israel. On the other side of the room stood a golden lamp-stand, with seven branches, called "the golden candlestick." At the farther end of the room stood another altar, made of gold, smaller than the great altar in front of the Temple. On this golden altar the priest offered twice each day a bowl of incense, which was made by mixing some sweet-smelling gums, frankincense and myrrh, and burning them, so that they formed a fragrant white cloud, filling the Holy Place.

Looking up the Kedron Valley toward Mt. Moriah

Beyond the Holy Place was another room called "The Holy of Holies." Into this room no one entered except the high priest, and he on only one day in the year; for this inner room was set apart for the dwelling-place of God; and the Jews believed that in this room the light of God was shining so brightly that no one could endure it. In the first Temple built by King Solomon, the Ark of the Covenant stood in the Holy of Holies. This was a chest covered with gold, within which lay the two stone tables on which the Ten Commandments were written. But the Ark of the Covenant

The Mosque of Omar, now on the place where the Temple once stood

had been lost, and in the time of which we are speaking, nothing was in the Holy of Holies except a block of marble.

One day an old priest named Zacharias was offering incense upon the golden altar in the Holy Place. He had filled the bowl, which they called a censer, with the frankincense and myrrh, and had placed in it some coals of fire from the great altar in front of the Temple.

He had come into the Holy Place, bringing his censer of incense, which sent its white cloud into the air, and was just about to lay it upon the altar, when he was startled at suddenly seeing someone standing by the golden altar on the right side.

Zacharias was surprised to see anyone in the room, for he knew that no one but himself had a right to be there. But he was still more surprised and filled with

High Priest, altar of incense, table for shew bread, and Ark of the Covenant

fear when he looked at this stranger standing by the altar. He seemed like a young man, and his face and body and clothes were bright and shining like the sun, so glorious that the old priest could not bear to look upon him.

At once Zacharias knew that this glorious person was an angel sent from God. He trembled with fear; his knees shook, and he could scarcely keep from falling on the floor. The angel spoke to him, gently and kindly:

"Zacharias, do not be frightened. You have nothing to fear. I have come to you with good news. God has heard the prayers that you and your good wife Elizabeth have been sending up to heaven for these many years. You shall have a son, and shall call his name John. Your son when he becomes a man will bring joy and gladness to many people; for he shall be great in the sight of the Lord; and it shall be his work to make his people ready for the coming of the King for whom they have been looking so long. You must see that your son never drinks any wine or strong drink, for he is to be set apart for God, to serve God only, and to speak the word of God to the people, telling them that their King and Saviour is at hand."

The golden candlestick

The priest was so filled with surprise and fear that he could scarcely believe what he heard.

"How can these wonderful words be true?" he said. "I am an old man, and my wife is also old. We are too old now to have children. How can I believe all this?"

The angel was not pleased when he saw that Zacharias doubted his word, and he said:

"I am the angel Gabriel, that stands before God; and I have been sent from God to speak to you and to bring you this good news. Now, because you did not believe God's word, you shall be stricken dumb, and shall not be able to speak until my words come true and your child is born."

And then the angel vanished out of sight as suddenly as he had come, and Zacharias was left alone.

All this time a great crowd of people was standing outside the Temple, worshipping God while the offering was made. They wondered that Zacharias was waiting so long in the Temple; and they wondered more when he came out and they found that he could not speak. He made signs to them, trying to show them he had seen an angel, but he did not tell them what the angel had said, for that was meant for himself only and not for others.

Each priest stayed for one week in the Temple and then went to his house; so after a few days Zacharias left Jerusalem and returned to his house in the southern part of the land, not far from the old city of Hebron, the place where Abraham, Isaac and Jacob, the early fathers of the Israelites, were buried.

How happy Elizabeth was when her husband, by signs and by writing, told her of the angel and his promise that she should be the mother of one who was to bear the word of the Lord to the people. Such men, to whom God spoke and who spoke for God, were called "prophets." Many great prophets in past years had spoken the word of God to the Israelites, men like Samuel and Elijah and Isaiah. But more than four hundred years had passed away since the voice of a prophet had been heard in the land. Their promised son was to rise up and speak once more God's will to his people. Zacharias and Elizabeth might not live long enough to hear his voice as a prophet, but they had God's promise, and in that promise they were happy, waiting for their child to come and grow up to his great work.

The Angel Visits Nazareth

CHAPTER 4

FOR OUR next story we visit Nazareth, a village in Galilee, nearly seventy miles north of Jerusalem. Galilee, as we have seen, was the northern province or division of the land, lying between the river Jordan and the Great Sea. The lower part of Galilee is a great plain, called "the plain of Esdraelon," or "the plain of Jezreel," where many battles have been fought in past times. The upper part of Galilee is everywhere mountains and valleys, with villages perched on the mountain tops or clinging to their sides, and sometimes nestled in the valleys. Just where the plain ends and the mountains begin, we find a long range of steep hills. If we climb to the top of this range, on one side we see the plain stretched out, and far in the distance the Mediterranean Sea; and on the other, or northern slope of the hills, we come to the city of Nazareth. There the mother of Jesus lived as a young girl before her son was born, and there Jesus lived during most of his life.

Nazareth is there still, although many of the old towns in that land have passed away; and now it is quite a city, but in the time of which we are telling it was only a village. All around it are hills. One can stand in the town and count fifteen hills and mountains, all in sight.

Its narrow streets climb the hills between rows of one-story white houses, many of them having a little dome on the roof. Around each roof in those times of which we are telling was a rail with posts on the corners,

Nazareth from the road to Cana

to prevent any one on the roof from falling off, for the flat roof was used as a place of visiting and of rest, since the house inside was dark, having no glass windows, but instead only one small hole in the wall. None of these houses had a door opening upon the street. Beside the road was a high wall, and in it a gate leading to an open court, at one end of which stood the house.

In the village was one fountain, to which all the women went for water. There were no wells or pumps or pipes with water in the houses; and around the fountain might be seen in the morning a crowd of women bringing water-jars empty, and carrying them home full of water, balanced on their heads. No one often saw a man carrying a jar of water, for this was looked upon as a woman's work.

In one of those small white houses of Nazareth lived a young Jewish girl named Mary. We do not know how she looked, for although many artists have made pictures of her, all have drawn or painted her as they imagined her to be, not as she was. All that we really know of Mary, we read in two of the four gospels, Matthew and Luke; and neither of these tell us anything about her early life or her family. It has been said that her father's name was Joachim and her mother's was Anna; but this is not found in either of the gospels, and we do not know whether it is true.

We do know, however, that she was a pure-hearted, lovely girl, who served the God of Israel with all her heart and lived a holy life. She knew her Bible well, we are sure, for its words came readily to her lips; and she was a girl who thought much and talked but little. In those years she might have been seen often going with the other girls of the village to the fountain for water, or sitting in the women's gallery in the church, listening thoughtfully to the reading from the Bible, and with her rich young voice joining in the chanting of David's psalms.

In that land girls are promised in marriage while very young, and Mary was at this time promised to be married to a man named Joseph, who was a carpenter, or, as he is called in the gospels, a worker in

The well of the Virgin Mary, at Nazareth

wood. The two families, Joseph's and Mary's, were not rich. They belonged to the working class of people, but they were not like many, wretchedly poor. They were just plain, honest, working people, able to earn a comfortable living.

Although Joseph and Mary were of the common people, they came from the noblest blood in all the land. Both were sprung from the royal line of David,

Mary beheld the angel Gabriel suddenly beaming upon her.

the greatest of the kings of Israel, and the singer of many beautiful psalms. They lived in little one-room houses, and their hands were hard from work, but they could trace their line back to the palace where David the founder of their family dwelt.

On one day Mary was alone. It may have been in her own little home, or upon its roof, where she often went for prayer, or perhaps under a tree on the hillside near the village. Just as Zacharias a few months before had seen a heavenly, gloriously-shining being in the Temple, so now Mary beheld the same angel Gabriel suddenly beaming upon her. In a sweet voice he said:

"Peace be with you, Mary! You are in high favor and love, for the Lord is with you!"

The voice was gentle, but the sight of this shining form filled the young girl with alarm. She knew not what to think, nor why this glorious being had come to her. But after a moment the angel went on speaking, and said:

"Do not be afraid, Mary, for God has chosen you among all women for his special favor. You shall have a son; and you shall give him the name Jesus, because he shall save his people from their sins. He shall be great, and shall be called the Son of the Highest God. God shall give to him the throne and the kingdom of his father David. He shall reign forever over the people of Israel, and of his kingdom there shall be no end."

The angel paused and Mary found words to speak, tremblingly and with fear:

"How can all this come to me? I do not understand what it all means!"

Then the angel spoke again to the troubled and frightened girl:

"The Holy Spirit of God shall come to you, and the power of God shall be upon you; and therefore that holy child that is to be given you shall be called "The Son of God." Also, let me tell you that your cousin Elizabeth is soon to have a son in her old age. This may seem strange to you; but no word of God is without power. Every promise of God shall surely come to pass."

Then Mary said:

"I am the Lord's servant, and I can trust him. Let it be to me as you have spoken. I will rest without fear in the will of the Lord."

Then, as suddenly as he had come, the angel vanished out of sight, and Mary was left alone. She was filled with wonder at what she had seen and heard. Any young Jewish girl to whom came the news that the words of the prophets in the Bible were now to come true, that the long-promised King of Israel was soon to be born, and that she should be his mother, would be amazed and perhaps alarmed at the message.

Some girls would have talked about it, and might even be proud at such an expectation. But Mary's was a quiet nature, not apt to speak of her deepest thoughts. She felt in some way that there was no one in her home or in her village with whom she could speak of these things. She hid them silently in her heart, but thought about them day and night.

Elizabeth greeting Mary: "Blessed, most blessed are you among women!"

A Young Girl's Journey

CHAPTER 5

AFTER THE visit of the angel and the message which he had brought, Mary's mind was filled with many thoughts and her heart was full. She was only a young girl, not older than sixteen years, perhaps as young as fifteen; for if she were older she should have been already married. In that land nearly all young women are married as soon as they are sixteen years old; and very few stay unmarried.

Mary felt that she must talk with somebody of all these wonderful things that had been spoken to her. We would think that her mother was the one with whom she could open her heart most freely, but we are not sure that her mother was living. And is it not true that a young girl can sometimes tell to a dear grandmother, or some other old lady who is her friend, the deep things of the heart that she may hesitate to mention even to her own mother?

She thought of one who was not her grandmother, but who from her age and sweetness seemed like one. Her mind turned to Elizabeth, living far away in the south. The angel, you know, had told her that Elizabeth was also to have a child, and perhaps she would be able to understand Mary's feelings better than any other woman.

Elizabeth was related to Mary. She is named in the gospel of St. Luke as Mary's cousin, though very likely they were not near, but distant relatives. Mary knew that she was wise and good, that she loved her, and being old, could give her advice. Mary made up her mind to visit Elizabeth and open her heart with her fully about what the angel had spoken to her. From Nazareth to Elizabeth's house was a long distance, in a straight line more than eighty miles, but much farther by the road which travelers from Galilee generally followed in going from the north to the south of the land.

Very soon after the angel's visit, Mary left her home and began her journey southward. Of course, a young girl could not take a journey so long alone. But there were always caravans or parties going from Galilee to Jerusalem, and Mary would travel with one of those companies. A soldier would ride on a horse, a general in his chariot, and an Arab on his camel; but most men in those times walked, even on long journeys. A woman would ride on an ass, which was the animal preferred by the Jews for travel.

We may think of Mary with a beating heart leaving her home in Nazareth in company with a caravan or party of people journeying to Jerusalem to attend one of the great feasts held every year in that city. Their most direct way would be over the mountains; but it would be rough and stony; up one mountain, down another, and around a third mountain, nearly all the way. Besides, this way would lead them through the country of the Samaritans, which lay between Galilee and Judea, and such was the hatred between Jews and Samaritans that it was scarcely safe for a company of Jews to go through their land. A large company would need to stop by night at some inn, and the Samaritans often shut their inns against those who were going to Jerusalem.

The line of travel from Nazareth would be to go over the steep hill on the south of their village, then follow a well-trodden way eastward down to the river

Jordan. There they would find a very good road built by the Romans, straight down the Jordan Valley, with mountains on either side. This they would follow about sixty miles until they came to Jericho. There they might rest for a few days; and then climb the steep path up the mountains to Jerusalem. This Jericho road was a hiding place for robbers, and it was never safe for anyone to travel it alone. But in a large company, with many men, and often a guard of soldiers, the travelers need not fear. They would easily reach Jerusalem in a week or ten days after leaving Nazareth, and might make the journey in five days if they were in haste.

In Jerusalem Mary would visit with some friend. All the families in the land had friends in Jerusalem with whom they stayed while attending the great feasts, of which three were held each year; and the dwellers in Jerusalem opened their houses to the same families year after year. After the feast, Mary would find another caravan or party going home to Hebron and the villages near it, and she would travel the rest of her journey, about twenty miles, with this party. Altogether, Mary's journey, from Nazareth to Hebron, was nearly one hundred and twenty miles long. Although many people were with her all the way, she was alone in spirit, for she could speak to no one of the great thoughts which burdened her mind and her heart.

At last her long journey was over. She stopped at the door of the house of Zacharias; and in a moment was clasped in the arms of Elizabeth. In some strange way God had given to Elizabeth to know all that had come to Mary. In a loud voice she said:

"Blessed, most blessed are you among women! And blessed among men shall be the son born to you! High indeed is the honor mine today when the mother of my Lord comes to my home! Blessed is she that believed the angel's word, for that word shall surely come true!"

In that moment Mary's feelings, long held in, broke out into song. For this young woman's soul was not only pure and tender and devout, it was the soul of a poet whose thoughts shape themselves into verse. Mary spoke and sung a song which has become famous. Someone wrote it down, and Saint Luke, who wrote the gospel, found a copy of it and gave it to the world. Everyone should read it. We give it here.

MARY'S SONG

My soul beholds the greatness of the Lord,
And my spirit hath rejoiced in God my Saviour.
For he hath looked upon his servant in my lowly state;
And from this time people in all ages shall call me blessed.

For he that is mighty hath done to me great things;
And holy is his name.
And his mercy is from age to age
On those who fear him.

He hath showed strength with his arm;
He hath scattered the proud in the vain thoughts of their heart.
He hath put down princes from their thrones,
And hath lifted up those of humble state.

The hungry he hath filled with good things;
And the rich he hath sent empty away.
He hath given help to Israel his servant
That he might remember mercy
As he spoke to our fathers,
Toward Abraham and his children forever.

For three months Mary stayed with Elisabeth in that quiet home, the old woman and the young woman, both soon to be mothers, talked together day after day. Perhaps by this time people were going to another feast in Jerusalem, and Mary found again a party of pilgrims —for that was the name that they gave to people going to Jerusalem to worship—who were returning to Galilee. She went home, comforted in spirit and made strong by her visit with Elizabeth.

It was either while Mary was visiting with Elizabeth, or soon after her return to her home, that Joseph, her promised husband, began to question in his mind whether he ought to marry her. There was a strange look in her face, and he saw that she had thoughts in her mind of which she could not speak to him. He loved her deeply, and it was with sorrow that he asked himself whether they would be happy together.

But one night, while he was sleeping, a dream came to Joseph. In his dream he saw an angel standing by his side. The angel said to him:

"Joseph, son of David, do not be afraid to take Mary for your wife. She shall have a son; and his name shall be Jesus, for it is he that shall save his people from their sins."

The word Jesus, in the language of that people, means "Saviour," and often Jesus is spoken of as "Our Saviour" because he came to take away our sins.

After this message, Joseph hesitated no longer. He did as the angel had bidden him. He was married to Mary, and led her to his own home, in which was also the shop where he followed his trade as a carpenter.

The Boy Who Never Tasted Wine

CHAPTER 6

NOT LONG after Mary's visit, the child promised to Zacharias and Elizabeth was born. In Jewish families the coming of a child into the home was always the cause of great gladness; and the gladness was greater at the birth of this baby, because this was the first child, and the father and mother were old. All the friends of Zacharias and Elizabeth came to see them and to rejoice with them over the boy whom God had given them.

"He must be named Zacharias after his father," said the visitors.

"Not so," answered the mother; "he shall be named John."

"Why should you give him that name?" they said. "None of your family has ever been called John."

But Elizabeth insisted that her boy should bear the name John.

You remember that Zacharias had been stricken dumb at the time when the angel spoke to him in the Temple. In all the months since he had not spoken a word. Nor could he hear what was said; for now they made signs, to ask him what should be the child's name. They brought him a writing table, and on it he wrote, "His name is John." So that was the name of this child of promise, just as the angel Gabriel had said.

You may ask, what was a writing table? In those times paper was very scarce and high in its cost. It was used only for writing down matters that were important. For common uses, each family had a writing table, which was a board over which was spread a thin layer of wax. On this wax they marked what they wished to write, with a sharp-pointed pen of iron or steel. This kind of a pen was called a stylus. The other end of the pen was flat, like an ivory paper-cutter. After writing, they could smooth it all out again; and the wax was then ready to be used once more.

Just as soon as Zacharias had written the words "His name is John," the power to hear and to speak came back to him. He began to praise God in a loud voice, and gave forth a song of rejoicing. This song was afterward written, and may be read in the gospel by St. Luke, near the end of the first chapter.

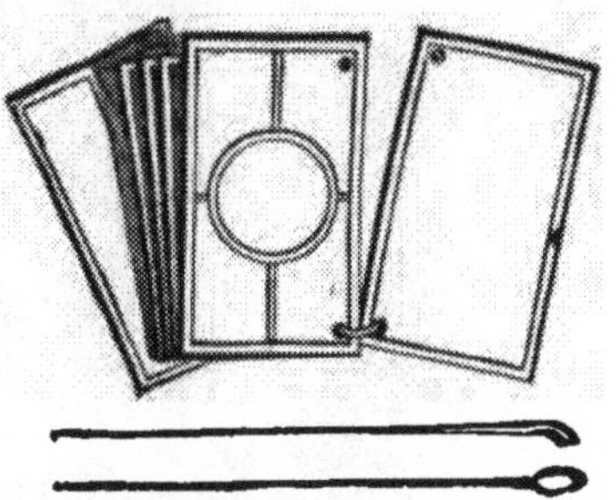

Writing tablets

In this song, Zacharias gave thanks to God for having blessed his people and kept the promises that had been made in God's name by all the prophets of old time. The prophets, as you may know, were the good men who listened to God's words and then gave them to the people, speaking with God's power; and sometimes telling, long before the time, of great events that were to take place. They were men like Moses, who saw God face to face, and Samuel the wise ruler, and Elijah the prophet of fire, and Isaiah, who declared Christ's coming long before his day. In the Old Testament times there was always a prophet to tell the people the will of God. But since the Old Testament had been finished, almost five hundred years before this time, no prophet had stood up in Israel with the word of the Lord.

Zacharias knew that this newly-born child should

grow up to give God's message to the people. He said in his song:

"And you, O child, shall be called the prophet of God;
For you shall go before the Lord Christ, to make ready a way for him;
You shall give to his people the good news of a Saviour,
And the forgiveness of their sins
Because of the tender mercy of God."

In the home of Zacharias and Elizabeth the baby John grew up a strong, noble boy. Very early they

John the Baptist in the desert

told him of the angel's visit, and of the command that throughout his life he was not to taste wine nor any strong drink. He was under a vow or pledge of special service for God; and one sign of his pledge was to be his not tasting wine nor even eating grapes. Another sign was in leaving his hair to grow long and never cutting it. Everyone who saw him would know by these signs that he was pledged to a life of peculiar service to God.

When John became a young man he went away from his home and lived in the desert, alone with his own thoughts and with God. Very likely, his father and mother died before he went to live alone, for at the time of his birth they were old people and could not live many years.

John lived upon the plainest of food, the locusts that could be gathered in the field, and were boiled, to be eaten by the poorest people. He ate also the honey made by the wild bees and stored by them in hollow trees and holes in the rocks. All those years of his young manhood, John was thinking upon the work to which God had called him, talking with God and learning God's will; so that when the time came, he could give God's message to the people.

Plowing in Bible time

They sought out the inn at Bethlehem but Joseph found within its walls no place where his wife could rest after her long and wearisome ride.

The Child-King in His Cradle

CHAPTER 7

FOR A FEW months after their marriage, Joseph and Mary lived in their little house at Nazareth. Joseph worked at his trade as a carpenter, while Mary cared for the home and carried the water for the needs of the house from the well in the middle of the village, walking with her jar full of water on her head.

One day Joseph came home and told his wife that he had been called to go on a journey to Bethlehem, which was the town from which their family had come. Both Joseph and Mary, as we have seen, had sprung from the line of the great King David, who had been born in Bethlehem more than a thousand years before. Every one who belonged to the line of David, wherever he might be living, looked upon Bethlehem as the home-town of his family.

The Emperor Augustus at Rome, who ruled over all the lands and was above Herod, the king of Judea, had given orders that a list should be made of all the families in his wide empire. He wished to lay a tax upon every family; that is, to call upon every family to pay money for the support of his officers, his army, his court; and in order to fix this tax, he must have written down the names of all the people.

In our land such a list is made every ten years, and is called a census. With us, men are chosen in every city and town to go to the people where they live and make the list of their names. From all the states throughout the land, these lists are sent to one office, and there the names are arranged in order.

But the Romans who were ruling the world at that time chose a plan for making this great list which would give themselves the least trouble, even though it gave to the people under them much more trouble, and compelled them to make long journeys. Instead of appointing in each place an officer to take the names of the people at the places where they were living, they

Church of the Nativity, Bethlehem, said to enclose the birthplace of the Saviour

made a law that every family must go to the city or town from which they or their fathers had come, and there give their names to the officers who were making the roll of the people. Those who were living in Jerusalem, and had come from Shechem or Joppa or Caesarea, must journey to one of these places and there make their report; those who were living in Nazareth and had come, or their parents before them had come, from

The shepherds came to the stable, opened the door and found just what the angel said they would see, a tiny babe lying in the manger.

any other place, must go to their home-town, however far it might be, and in that place be enrolled or written upon the list of names.

There is no reason to suppose that Mary, although herself sprung from the family of David, was compelled to make this journey to Bethlehem with her husband. The Roman laws took very little notice of women, unless they were rich women who could be taxed. Joseph could go alone to Bethlehem, and there have both their names written upon the list. But at once a thought came to Mary, and she said to her husband:

"You shall not make the journey to Bethlehem alone. I will go with you."

We are not told why the young wife was resolved to go with her husband on the long journey, but the reason may have been this: Mary knew that she was to have a son, and the time for his coming was now near at hand. She knew, too, that her child should be the Son of David and the King of Israel, that he was to sit on David's throne. She wished him to be born, not in the village of Nazareth in Galilee, but in David's own town of Bethlehem. He was to spring from the royal line, and she was willing to endure a hard, trying journey, and even to suffer, that her son might come from the royal city where David lived. Mary had read the books of the Old Testament, and she knew that in those books it had been written by the prophets, to whom God had spoken, that this king, whom they called Messiah and Christ, should be born in Bethlehem. These were the reasons that made Mary decide so quickly to go with her husband on his journey to Bethlehem, the city of their fathers.

So Joseph locked up his carpenter's shop and set his wife upon an ass, and with a staff walked beside her, over the mountain and down the valley to the river

Jordan, and thence following the river, over the Roman road, the same long road that Mary had taken in the caravan or company of pilgrims some months before. Joseph had been over that road many times, going up every year to the feasts at Jerusalem, so that he knew all the places which they passed, and could tell Mary stories of their people and the great events which had taken place on the mountains or in the cities as they came into view in their journey.

They stopped at Jericho, near the head of the Dead Sea, and there turned westward, climbing the mountains over the robber-haunted road, and reaching Jerusalem. Perhaps they rested a day or two in this city and then went over to the mount of Olives, past the village of Bethany; and six miles south of Jerusalem they entered the gate of Bethlehem.

They had no friends with whom they could stay in Bethlehem, and so they sought out the inn, or the khan, as it was called. This was a large building with rooms around an open court. In this court the animals and the baggage were placed, and the guests of the inn were in the rooms around it. But Joseph and Mary were not the only people who had come to Bethlehem to have their names enrolled or written upon the lists for the taxing. Others had reached the inn or khan before them. When they came the courtyard was filled with asses and camels and chariots and baggage, and all the rooms around the court were crowded with visitors. Joseph found within the walls of the khan no place where his wife could rest after her long and wearisome ride.

But at last Joseph learned of a place where they might stay through the night and for a few days. It was only a cave, hollowed out in the hillside, used as a stable for cattle; but miserable as it was, Mary was glad to lie down upon the straw and rest. And in that cave-stable Mary's child was born. She wrapped her little baby in such clothes as she could find at hand, and laid him for his first sleep in the manger where the oxen had fed. This was the lowly cradle of the Son of David, the King who was to rule over all the earth! King Herod in his palace did not know, and the Emperor Augustus at Rome did not dream, that in the humble stable at Bethlehem was lying a Prince who should reign over a realm vastly greater than Judea or the Roman Empire; that all the world should date their years from the year when that baby was born; and that his name would be praised long after their names had been forgotten.

Main street in Bethlehem

But although neither King Herod, nor the Emperor Augustus, nor the high-priest and rulers in Jerusalem were there to welcome their new-born King, there were some visitors at his manger-cradle. In the open fields around Bethlehem were shepherds, watching at night over their flocks of sheep, just as, a thousand years before in the same fields, the young shepherd David had cared for his sheep, guarding them from wild beasts of the wilderness and from robbers.

Suddenly a great, dazzling light flashed upon these shepherds, and they saw, as Zacharias had seen by the altar, and as Mary had seen in Nazareth, a glorious angel standing before them. The shepherds were filled with fear and fell upon their faces on the ground, not daring to look up at the shining form. But the angel spoke to them kindly and graciously, saying:

"Do not be afraid, for I come with good news, which will make you glad; news for all God's people. On this very night is born in yonder city of David, one who shall be the Saviour, even Christ your Lord and King. Would you wish to go and see this child? I will tell you how you can find him. Look for a newly-born baby wrapped in such clothes as babies wear, and lying, not in a cradle in a house, but in the manger of a stable, where the oxen and the asses are kept. There you will find the child who is to be the King of all the earth!"

While shepherds were listening to the words of this angel, they saw that the entire midnight sky over them was filled with a multitude of heavenly beings. The shepherds heard them sing:

"Glory to God in the highest,
And on earth peace among men in whom God is well pleased."

Then the vision faded away, the angelic host passed out of sight, and in the dark sky only the stars were shining above them. Then the shepherds said to each other:

"Let us leave our sheep here for a little while, and go to the village and see this wonderful thing that has come to pass. How good it is that the Lord has given this word to us, that we may be the first to look upon our King!"

It did not take the shepherds a long time to find the right stable and the manger, for Bethlehem was then only a small village. They came, opened the door, and found just what the angel had said they would see, a tiny baby lying in the manger, his mother hovering near, and Joseph watching over them both in tenderness.

They saw the royal little one, and bowed low around his manger cradle, then went again to their flocks in the field, praising God for his goodness in sending the long-promised King. The people to whom the shepherds told this story, wondered at it, hardly knowing whether to believe it or not; for this was not the way in which they looked for the King of Israel to come. They were expecting a prince to be born in a palace, not a working-woman's child in a dark cave where cattle were kept.

But Mary, happy with her little one, clasped him to her heart and said nothing to anyone of the angel that had come to her in Nazareth, and of the promises given her about this child. When the day came to name the child, she simply said, "His name shall be Jesus," but she told no one why the name was given. It was a common name among the Jews, so no one was surprised at the name. But no word could tell better than his name "Jesus" what this child should become, for the word Jesus means "Saviour."

Simeon came forward and took the infant Jesus into his arms, and lifting up his eyes to heaven gave thanks that he had seen the Saviour.

The Baby Brought to the Temple

CHAPTER 8

ALTHOUGH JESUS was born in a stable and slept in a manger, he did not stay in that place long. After a few days Joseph was able to find a more comfortable home, where the young mother and her baby were taken. The Jews were very kind to strangers of their own people, and welcomed them to their houses when passing through their towns.

Joseph and his family were in Bethlehem for some weeks, perhaps for some months. It may have been their purpose to make Bethlehem their home, and to bring up this child, the Son of David, in David's own city, where he could have a better training for his coming life, whatever that life might be, than in the country village of Nazareth.

On the day when Jesus was forty days old, he was brought with his mother to Jerusalem, which was only six miles from Bethlehem. There he was taken to the Temple for a service which showed that he was given to God and to be brought up as God's child. It was the rule of the Jews that after the first child had come to a family, an offering should be made on the altar in the Temple for him and prayers should be said. A family that was rich would offer for their first child a sheep, which was killed and burned on the altar as a gift to God in place of the child. If the family was poor, or of the working class of people, the parents offered a pair of doves or pigeons. Joseph and Mary brought a pair of doves, and stood by while these were burned on the altar, Mary holding her baby in her arms.

At that moment there was in the Temple an old man named Simeon. He was a good man and very earnest in his prayers to God that he might live to see the Messiah-King of Israel, the Christ of God, who had been promised through the prophets of old. And God had said to Simeon that he should not die until he had seen Christ. On that morning a voice had seemed to say to him, "Go to the Temple." He obeyed it, not knowing why he had been sent to that place on that day.

Mary and the doves

As Joseph and Mary brought the baby Jesus into the Temple, the voice of the Lord spoke again to Simeon, saying:

"This child is David's Son, the King of Israel."

The old man came forward, held out his arms, and took the child into them, folded him to his bosom, and lifting up his eyes to heaven, said in Hebrew verse:

"Now, Lord, thou mayest let thy servant go
According to thy word, in peace.
For these eyes of mine have seen thy Saviour
Whom thou hast sent to all the people.
A light to shine upon the nations,
And the glory of thine own people Israel."

Joseph and Mary were filled with wonder at the

act and words of the old man, whom they had never seen before and did not know. But as he placed the child in their arms again, he prayed for God's blessing upon both Joseph and Mary.

"Listen," he said, "this child will become a cause for many to fall and to rise again in Israel. He shall be God's sign of mercy, but many shall speak against him. Also, sorrow like a sword shall pierce through your soul, O mother; and the thoughts out of many hearts shall be made known."

Those words seemed very strange at the time; but long afterward, when Jesus had grown to be a man, Mary found how true they were, as she saw enemies gathered against her son, and at last looked at him dying upon the cross. Then, indeed, a sword went through Mary's soul.

Just at that moment a woman came up to the little group. She was very old, more than ninety years of age; and being a widow and a devout worshipper of God she stayed nearly all her days in the Temple praying. God had spoken to her also with the promise of a coming Christ, the Saviour and King. She too saw in this little baby the promised Messiah, and in a loud voice gave thanks and praise to God. All who heard her wondered at her words, and wondered all the more as they looked on this plainly-clad father and mother with their baby, all evidently from the country, and the speech of Joseph and Mary showing they had come from Galilee in the far north.

Thus even while Jesus was a very young baby, only forty days old, here in Jerusalem a few people had looked upon him and spoken of him as the coming King of Israel.

Joseph and Mary carried the child back to their new home in Bethlehem; and Mary had more thoughts to hide within her silent heart long after that day in the Temple.

The Followers of the Star

CHAPTER 9

WHILE JOSEPH and Mary with the child Jesus were still staying in Bethlehem, the city of Jerusalem was stirred by the coming of some men from a land far away, with a strange question. These men were not Jews, but were Gentiles, which was the name that the Jews gave to all people except themselves. All Romans and Greeks and Egyptians and all others who were not of their own race, the Jews called by the name "Gentiles." These Gentile strangers who came to Jerusalem were asking of everybody whom they met this question:

"Can you tell us where is to be found the little child who is born to be the King of the Jews? We have seen his star in the east, and we have come to do him honor?"

Who were these men, and what was the star that they had seen?

We are not certain as to their land, but it is generally thought to have been the country now called Persia, then known as Parthia, a land about a thousand miles to the east of Judea. Although some Jews lived in that land—for Jews were to be found then as now in all lands, especially in large cities—the people of Parthia were not Jews, but, as the Jews called them, Gentiles. Although not of the Jewish race, these people were like the Jews in one respect—they never bowed down to worship images which men had made. They worshipped the One God of all the earth; and they prayed with their faces toward the sun. They said that they did not worship the sun, but the One God who was like the sun, the light of the world.

Among these Parthian people were many men who at night studied the stars in the sky. They did not have telescopes, as those who look at the stars now have, to bring the heavenly bodies, the moon, the planets, and the stars nearer to them; they could only use their own eyes, but by long study they had learned much about

The Wise Men on their Journey

the stars, could tell of their movements and where in the sky to find each one of them. The men who gave their lives to this study of the stars were called Magi, a word meaning "Wise Men"; and these strangers who were seeking the child-king in Jerusalem are sometimes spoken of as "the Wise Men," sometimes as "the Magi."

The people of that time believed that when great kings were born, or before they died, strange stars suddenly appeared in the heavens, shone for a time and then as suddenly passed out of sight. A year or perhaps two years before Jesus was born in Bethlehem, such a star, very bright, that had never before been seen, began to shine. In some way it came to the minds of these men that this star pointed to the coming of a great king who was to rule over all the lands, and who was to be found in the land of Judea.

These Wise Men at once made up their minds to go to the land of Judea and see this child-king. It was a long and hard journey of more than a thousand miles. They must pass from the high plains of Parthia down to the lowlands of Babylonia, must find some way to cross two great rivers, the Tigris and the Euphrates. Then they would come to a vast trackless desert, where nothing grew and there was no water. If they went around this desert they must follow up the Euphrates River far to the north, and then traveling southward under the shadow of lofty mountains, they would come at last to Judea, and to Jerusalem, its largest city. Through all that long and trying journey, which would last a year, traveling most of the way on camels, they saw the wonderful star in the sky seeming to lead the way.

From the story as told in the Gospel by St. Matthew it appears that when these men came to Jerusalem the star was no longer shining. However, the loss of the star would not matter so much, now that they were in the King's own land, for they supposed that everybody in that country, and especially in the city of Jerusalem, would know that their Prince was born. But to their surprise, nobody seemed to have heard about the newly-born King. They did not meet the shepherds of Bethlehem, who had seen the angel on the night of Jesus' birth, nor did they hear of old Simeon and Anna who a month or more before had seen the Christ-child. Very, very few were those who knew that the King had come, and none of these few people did these strangers chance to meet.

They thought that at one place they could surely learn where to look for this young Prince. That was the king's palace in Jerusalem. Herod was still living, although old and very feeble, yet as fierce and cruel as ever. Perhaps they thought that this Prince for whom they were looking might be a son or a grandson of the king. Herod did not live in Jerusalem, for he did not like its people and he knew how greatly its people hated him; but he had a palace in the city and he came to it often for short visits. He may have been in Jerusalem when the Wise Men came; or they may have sought Herod down at Jericho, twenty miles away, where most of the time he lived.

As soon as the old king heard the question of these strangers, and learned that they had been led by a star to his land, he was filled with alarm. A child born to be king of the Jews—if there was such a child, what would become of Herod's own throne and crown? If he could find where this child was, he would send his soldiers to the place and soon kill him, as he had killed many others whom he suspected of seeking to take away his kingdom. But Herod hid his cruel purpose, and spoke kindly to these strangers about their errand. He asked them when the star appeared, how it looked, and how they knew that it showed that a king had been born.

Then Herod sent for the wisest men in his land, the teachers of the law who lived in Jerusalem. He knew that all the people were looking for the coming of their Messiah-king, whom they also called the Christ.

"Can you tell me," asked Herod, "in what place this great King, the Messiah or Christ, is to be born?"

The scholars were ready with their answer. They said:

"In Bethlehem of Judea, the city of David, this King who springs from David's line shall be born. This is what the old prophets have said."

And they read to him one of the promises of the prophets that the King should come out of Bethlehem.

Then Herod sent again for the Wise Men, and asked them to give him the exact time when they first saw the star. When he had learned the time, he thought at once that this long-looked-for King must have been born in Bethlehem less than two years before.

"Go to Bethlehem," said Herod to the Wise Men, "and search through the town until you find this child; and when you have found him, come and tell me, for I wish to do honor to this King."

That was what Herod said; but what he meant to do was a very different thing, as we shall see.

The Wise Men at once started for Bethlehem, which was only six miles from Jerusalem. They went over one of the mountains, and then one said to another:

"Look, there is the star once more! See it in the sky just before us!"

The star stood over the road leading to Bethlehem, and again they followed it rejoicing. It led them straight to the city, and then to a house, over which it seemed to pause. They knocked at the door, and when it was opened they went into a room, where they found a baby lying in its young mother's arms.

These Wise Men knew at once that here was the King for whom they had sought so long and traveled so far. They bowed before him to the ground to show the high honor in which they held him. Then they opened the treasures which they had brought from their own land, and gave to him rich gifts, such as were presented to kings. They gave him gold, and frankincense and myrrh, the fragrant gums that were used in offerings and were very costly. Thus, while in his own land only a few people showed their gladness at the coming of their king, the strangers from a distant country came to pay him honor. We would have thought that some of the learned Jews, who could tell King Herod where the King was born, might have come with the Wise Men to see him. But these great scholars really cared very little about Jesus. They stayed at home and soon forgot the men of the east, their journey, and their question.

The well of the Wise Men, near Bethlehem

Joseph and Mary taking the child Jesus with them set out on their journey to the land of Judea

Safe in Egypt

CHAPTER 10

ON THE night after their visit to Mary and her child, the Wise Men had a dream. In their dream they heard the voice of God saying to them:

"Do not go to meet King Herod again. He is no friend to this princely child. Return to your own land by some other way, and do not let Herod know it."

The Wise Men obeyed the voice of the Lord. They left Bethlehem very quietly, telling no one the road that they were taking; and without going through Herod's city, went back to their own land, far-distant Parthia.

As soon as the Wise Men had left, on that night Joseph also had a dream. He saw an angel by his bed, who said to Joseph:

"Rise up at once; take the little child and his mother, and go as quickly as you can down to the land of Egypt, stay in that country until I tell you to leave it, for very soon King Herod will try to kill this child."

Without waiting a moment, Joseph awaked Mary from her sleep, and in the night they left the house, taking the sleeping baby with them. They passed silently through the dark streets of Bethlehem and found the road that would lead them to Egypt. At times Mary rode upon an ass, holding her precious child; at others she walked while Joseph guided the animal which carried their possessions. It was a journey of more than a hundred miles to Egypt, but they went in safety, unknown to King Herod.

In Egypt they could dwell safely, for that land was not a part of Herod's kingdom. Many Jews were dwelling there, and among them Joseph could live by his trade, for he was a skilful worker in wood. How long they stayed in Egypt we do not know. It may have been either a few months or a few years.

Herod waited for some time to see the Wise Men again, and to find where the child-king was living. But

Joseph and Mary with Jesus in Egypt

as the days passed and he heard nothing from them, and finally learned that they had left for their home-land without obeying his command to come and see him, he was very angry. But he was resolved to kill this child, who if he should live might take the kingdom from him or from his family.

Herod planned and carried out a fearfully wicked

deed, but not more wicked than many deeds that he had already done. He sent a troop of his soldiers to Bethlehem, with orders to go into every house in the village, to find every child that was two years old or under that age, and to kill them all. This terrible thing the soldiers did, and a great cry went up to heaven from the mothers and fathers whose little ones had been slain by the wicked king's command.

But Herod's slaughter of the little children was all in vain, as must be every attempt to fight against God. Herod thought that surely this royal child must be among those little dead bodies in Bethlehem, and that his throne was safe. But by that time the little Jesus was in Egypt, sleeping under one of its palm trees beside the river Nile, or looking with wide-open baby eyes upon the pyramids and the Sphinx, the wonderful works of ancient time, carved in stone.

Herod did not live long after this. He died full of years, full of wickedness, and suffering great pain. Then Joseph in Egypt dreamed again. The angel whom he had seen so many times before came once more and said to him:

"Joseph, you may now take the young child and his mother and go back to the land of the Jews, for those who sought to kill the child are dead and can do him no harm."

Then Joseph as before fastened a saddle on the ass and placed their possessions upon its back. The little family then set out upon its journey back to the land of Judea. The purpose of Joseph and Mary was to go back to Bethlehem, David's city, and there bring up this child whom they expected one day to sit on David's throne as King of Israel. But on the way they met other travelers and asked them:

"Who is now the King in Judea, since Herod is dead?" They said to Joseph:

"The king over Jerusalem and Judea is now Archelaus, the son of the old King Herod, and he is as wicked and as cruel as his father was before him."

This news made Joseph and Mary afraid to go to Bethlehem. They thought, "Perhaps King Archelaus may have heard of the child Jesus, and is watching for the chance to kill him."

They made up their mind not to go near Bethlehem or Jerusalem, but keeping away from the land ruled by Archelaus, to return to Nazareth, where both had lived before their marriage. So it came to pass that Jesus who was born in Bethlehem of Judea was brought up in Nazareth of Galilee.

Bronze coin of Herod Agrippa I

Large bronze coin of Agrippa II

A Child's Life in Nazareth

CHAPTER II

THE LITTLE Jesus must have been between two and five years old when he was brought to Nazareth, just coming out of babyhood and growing into a little boy; and Nazareth was his home for at least twenty-five years, all through his childhood, his boyhood and his young manhood.

Jesus was not the only child living in that little white house of one story and one room on the side of the hill. Soon another baby boy came, who was named James, who grew up to become a great man, and many years after wrote one of the books in the Bible, the Epistle of James. Then, one after another, came three more boys, Joseph and Simon and Judas. When we read that name "Judas" we are apt to think of the wicked Judas, who sold the Lord Jesus for a few pieces of silver. But that was a different Judas. This Judas, like his brother James, long afterward wrote another book in the New Testament, the Epistle of Jude. Somewhere in the list of children were two girls—there may have been more than two, but the number and names of the girls have not been kept

After a few years that little house must often have been crowded, with children coming one after another, and always a baby to be cared for. And much of the time it was the shop where father Joseph did his work as a carpenter. The floor of brick or of clay was often littered with shavings and the workman's tools were on the table.

The house had very little furniture; no chairs, no bedstead with a mattress upon it, no stove and no pictures

The child Jesus loved outdoor life, he knew the flowers that grew in the fields and the birds flying in the air.

upon the walls. In one corner a little fire was lighted for cooking the meals, and the smoke went up through a hole in the roof, unless the wind blew it back into the room. They never made a fire to keep the house warm in winter, but when it was cold just waited for the sun to come out. Sometimes a snowstorm came, but the snow seldom stayed more than two or three days. The

Jesus as a boy at the house of his father and mother

children of Joseph never took a sleigh-ride and never coasted on sleds down the steep hills.

If there was a table for their meals, it was very low, less than two feet high; and they sat around it on little cushions, dipping their hands or pieces of bread into one common dish for food. Sometimes the table was just a round measure turned upside down; and sometimes the meal was served on the floor, as we serve meals on the grass at a picnic.

When night came, they unrolled some mats, which through the day were rolled up and stood against the wall, spread them on the floor and lay down upon them to sleep, throwing over themselves the long mantle which had been their outside garment through the day. When the door was shut, the house was dark, for its only window was a little hole in the wall; and they

Women grinding grain in Bible times

lighted it by an oil lamp, which stood either on a tall stand or on a little shelf.

But the house was used little in the daytime, for everybody lived out of doors, in the open court in front, in the streets and on the hills around. On pleasant days Joseph took his tools in the court and worked in wood. We are apt to think of Joseph as building houses, as in our time that is the chief work of a carpenter. But the houses were made of clay or rough stone, and the carpenter did very little work upon them. His chief business was in making wooden plows, yokes for the oxen, the little tables, and the peck or bushel measure, which was to be found in every house, and was also used in place of a table.

One very useful article was either in the house or in the court—the hand mill for grinding grain, made of two round flat stones. Our flour comes to us from great factories, but in that land each family had its own little mill. They poured the grain into a hole in the upper millstone, and then turned the stone round and round by a handle until the grain was ground into flour. This was hard work, but it was always done by the women. Often two women helped each other to turn the handle of the upper millstone. Mary's arms often ached in making the flour needed for her large family. When her daughters grew strong, they helped her in this work.

When Jesus became a boy six years old, he was sent to school with the other boys. There were no schools for girls among the Jews, so far as we know. The school was held in the village church, which they called the synagogue. The teacher was always a man, and he was generally the janitor of the church, who kept the building in order.

The Jews had a pretty name for the village school. They called it "The Vineyard," as though the children were bunches of little grapes, growing up to ripen in the sun. In this vineyard-school there was only one book for study. That was the Bible. The Jews had only the Old Testament, for the New Testament had not yet been written. Each of the larger books was in a separate volume in the form of a long roll of parchment; that is, a sheet made of sheepskin which had been made smooth, on which the words were written. Several of the smaller books were written on one roll. In the school there was only one copy of the Bible for all the scholars, but each boy had a board and a piece of chalk, with which he wrote sentences from the Bible and then learned them by heart. When his text had been learned, each pupil cleaned off his board like a slate and wrote on it a new lesson. All the teaching in a Jewish school was in the Old Testament.

The copy of the Bible in the school was generally one that had been used in the church until it had grown old and worn out. When they obtained a new set of the books for the service in the church, they gave the old copies to the school.

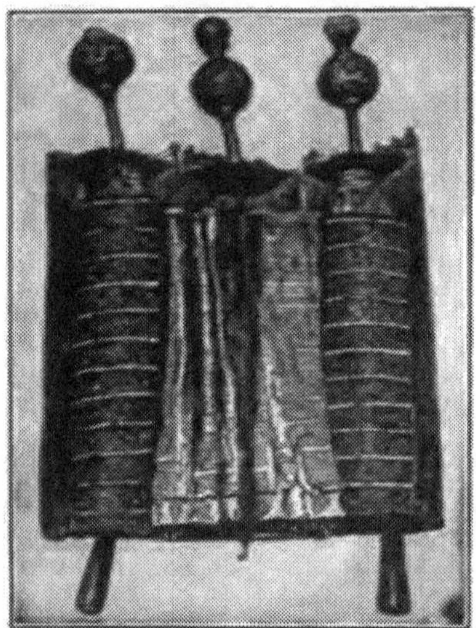

Roll of book

You can see in that same land now a school of children just like those in the time when Jesus was a boy. The children sit on the floor in a circle, the teacher being one of the ring. When they repeat their verses in learning them, all are talking aloud at the same time, so that the school is very noisy. We could not study in such a din, but they do not seem to mind it.

School was not very hard in that country. Our children have one holiday in each week, free from school; but in the school where Jesus was taught, they had two holidays in every week, besides the sabbath. In addition to these holidays there was a long recess of three hours in the middle of each day, and no school at all if the day was very hot.

When Jesus was a small boy he was taken by father Joseph to the church, which you remember they called the synagogue. The men and boys sat on the floor upon rugs or mats, while the women and girls were in a gallery, looking down upon them. All the men and boys wore their hats in the church. Their hats were turbans of cloth wrapped around their heads. But each one as he entered the door slipped off his shoes or slippers, and was barefooted in the church at the hour of worship. If at the hour of worship you go to a Mohammedan church in that country—which they call a mosque—you will see all the shoes standing outside the door.

In the church they had no minister to lead the service and to preach a sermon. The men took turns in charge of the worship. One read from one part of the Old Testament, another from another part. If they found a boy who was a good reader he was often called upon to read the Bible in the church service. They had prayers, always read from a book; they sang together from the Psalms; and whoever wished to speak could do so.

But we are not to think of the child Jesus as always at school or at church. He was a strong, hearty, healthy boy. He loved outdoor life, he knew the flowers that grew in the fields and the birds flying in the air. He played with other boys and knew all their games. Two of these games he once happened to mention long after, while he was teaching. One game was the wedding, when they sang and danced; the other was the funeral, when they cried with loud voices, making a mournful wail. We know, too, that in those times the boys played ball and marbles, and a game somewhat like ten-pins.

Jesus was not a lonely boy, living apart. He was always fond of having others around him. When he was a man, traveling and teaching over all the land, he had his twelve chosen friends who were always with him, and we may be sure that as a boy he liked to be with other boys, and in turn was liked by the boys of his village.

We may be sure, too, that he grew up a good boy; one who always tried to do right, at home, at school, or in play. At home he would help Joseph in his shop and his mother in her work or in caring for the smaller children; in school we know that he learned his verses in the Bible, because in after years he could always call them to his mind and speak them; and in play he was always fair and good-hearted and willing. We are told that he grew in knowledge and in the favor of God and of all people. In other words, he was a boy that everybody liked.

The citadel of ancient Bethshean, in the Jordan valley, twelve miles south of sea of Galilee

The Boy Lost and Found

CHAPTER 12

JESUS STAYED at the school in the village church until he was twelve years old. By that time he could read and write and could also repeat many verses. But as his reading book and spelling book and copy book and memory verses were all in the Bible, and as he heard long readings from its books at the church service, we may be sure that he knew quite well all the best things in that best of all books, the Bible. One proof of this is that in later years, when anyone tried to puzzle him with a hard question, he often answered promptly with a sentence from the Bible.

A Jewish boy generally left school at the age of twelve, unless he wished to become a rabbi, which was the name among the Jews for a teacher of their law. If that was his wish or the purpose of his parents, he was sent up to Jerusalem to study in the college held by the scribes or teachers in the Temple. Saul of Tarsus, a boy about four years younger than Jesus, whom we know as Paul the Apostle, was a student in the Temple college, but Jesus was not. While the young Saul was studying in Jerusalem, Jesus as a young man was working in the carpenter shop at Nazareth.

When Jesus was twelve years old he was taken on his first journey from Nazareth up to Jerusalem to attend the great feast of the Passover. Three great feasts were held during the year. The feast of the Passover was in the early spring, and kept in mind the great day when the Israelites went out of Egypt, no longer slaves but free men. The feast of the Pentecost was held in the late spring, just fifty days after the Passover—the word "pentecost" meaning "fifty days"—and reminded the people that fifty days after their fathers went out of Egypt, God gave them their law amid lightning and thunder on Mount Sinai. The feast of the Tabernacles, or "feast of tents" (for that is the meaning of the word tabernacles), was held in the fall; and at this time the people built for themselves huts of green branches, ate in them and slept in them for a week, to show the outdoor life of the early days in the wilderness, while they were marching to Canaan, the Promised Land. These three great feasts were held in Jerusalem, and from every part of the land the people came up to the city to attend them.

It was a great event when the boy Jesus for the first time went on this journey to Jerusalem. The younger children were left at home, under the care of some friend, for a boy did not begin attending these feasts until he was twelve years old. Of course, Joseph and Mary knew all about this journey, for they had made it many times. They went in the caravan or company from Nazareth, following the road that Joseph and Mary had taken on their way to Bethlehem, twelve years before. As they journeyed, Mary seated on the ass, Joseph and the boy Jesus walking beside her, they would talk about the places which they passed, and the stories of old times told about them. Jesus knew all those stories, for every Jewish boy had heard them, over and over.

As they paused on the top of the hill beside Nazareth, below them was spread out the great plain of Esdraelon, and they would say, "That mountain by the Great Sea on the west is Mount Carmel, where Elijah built his altar and made his great offering, when in answer to his prayer the fire came down from heaven and burned up the bullock laid on the altar. Do you see that road running across the plain? On that road Elijah ran in front of King Ahab's chariot, after the long drought, when the rain was coming. And then, this plain! Over it from Mount Tabor, there on the left, Deborah and Barak chased the flying Canaanites across the plain. Do you see that second mountain beyond Tabor? That is Mount Gilboa; and at its foot Gideon with his brave

Mount Tabor and the plain of Esdraelon

three hundred frightened at night the Midianite host and won a great victory."

They went down into the Jordan valley and walked southward by the Roman road, following the Jordan River. At one place the mountains on either side came down close to the river, and there was barely room for the road between the foaming stream on one side and the steep rocks on the other.

"Look," said Joseph, "this is the place where the waters rose up and stood in a heap when our fathers under Joshua were about to cross the river, thirty miles below."

They crossed a brook which fell into the river; and Joseph said, "Do you see this brook? Up there among the mountains was the place where the prophet Elijah was fed by the ravens; for this is the brook Cherith."

They came to the place just above Jericho where under Joshua the Israelites walked across the dry bed of the river, the holy ark carried by the priests in front and the people following in a long procession. There

The Temple of Herod—restored by Fergusson. The covered portico on the left is the royal porch extending along the southern side of the Temple area. The colonnade running from left to right is Solomon's porch extending across the eastern side of the area. The courts were much larger than as here shown.

the river is very wide and quite shallow, so that people walk across, except in the early spring, when it is swollen by the rains and the melting snow on the high mountains far to the north.

There they would point out across the river Mount Nebo, where Moses stood looking upon the land and then all alone lay down and died. They stopped for a rest at Jericho, where were stories to tell of the walls that fell down when the Israelites marched around them, and

At last his parents found Jesus in the Temple, the center of a company of learned scholars; he was asking questions of them and they were asking questions of him, while all around were people listening and wondering at this boy's deep knowledge of the truth.

the priests blew their ram's-horn trumpets. Perhaps they stopped and drank at the great spring near Jericho where the water was made pure by Elisha the prophet. And after a climb up to the mountains, at the end of six days or a week, they came to Jerusalem, the end of their journey, and the place called by the people "the holy city."

And then, there was the splendid Temple of God! How the boy's heart was stirred as he walked over the bridge leading from Mount Zion to Mount Moriah! They went into the great outside court, the court of the Gentiles, the only place in the Temple where foreigners were allowed to enter; and the boy Jesus was shocked to see that it had been turned into a market, where cattle and sheep and doves were sold, and where tables stood around for the men who changed foreign money into Jewish shekels.

Over the eastern wall and the Golden Gate, they saw the Mount of Olives, then covered to the top with vineyards and olive trees and gardens. They climbed up a flight of steps and passed through a gate called "the Beautiful Gate," into a smaller court, like the outer court open to the sky. This was named "The Court of the Women" because from its lattice-covered gallery the women looked down on the altar and the services of worship. Jesus noticed that in this Court of the Women were many classes of young men studying, seated in a circle, listening to their teachers. How he longed to sit down among them and listen to these wise scholars; for though only a boy, he had thought deeply on many things which he had read, and many questions had come to his mind which he greatly desired to have answered. He saw the sacrifice offerings laid on the altar and burned, while trumpets sounded and censers of incense were waved and the priests chanted the psalms of David.

While the family were in Jerusalem they found friends with whom they stayed, and in their house the Passover feast was eaten. It was a very simple meal, just a roasted lamb, some vegetables and bread made without yeast, in thin cakes, like soda biscuit, only larger. They ate the meal lying down on couches around the table, their heads toward the table, their feet away from it. It was the custom or rule of the Jews, at this feast, to have the story of the first Passover. Perhaps Joseph said to Jesus:

David street, Jerusalem, looking toward Olivet

"My son, you know what took place when this passover was eaten for the first time. Tell us the story."

Then the boy Jesus told of the terrible plagues that fell upon the land of Egypt; of the last and greatest sorrow, the death of the oldest son in every house; how the Israelites sprinkled their door-posts with the blood of the slain lamb and were passed over by this death-angel; how they ate the lamb on that night, dressed for their journey; and how they went out of Egypt and marched through the Red Sea.

The family were in Jerusalem for a week, and every day Jesus went up to the Temple to worship in its services and to learn what he could from its teachers. The last day of their visit came, and at its close the families going to Galilee met together for their homeward journey. A horn was blown and the caravan or company started northward. Mary missed her son, but thought that he was somewhere in the crowd, talking with other boys of his own age. But when night came, the company stopped to rest and Jesus did not appear. Mary was alarmed. They looked through all the crowd, but no Jesus was to be found.

Then in great trouble, Joseph and Mary hastened back to Jerusalem, looking for their boy. They asked for him among the friends at whose house they had stayed, but he had not been there. They wandered up and down the narrow streets, but while they saw many groups of boys, their boy was not among them. At last, on the third day, they looked for him in the Temple. In one of its courts a crowd of people were listening to the teachers who seemed to be talking with someone. They drew near, and Mary's heart began to beat as she suddenly heard a boy's voice sounding from the middle of the throng. She knew that voice, in its clear, rich, honest tone! She pressed her way in; and there stood her boy, the center of a company of the learned scholars. He was asking questions of these men, and they in their answers were asking him questions in turn, while all around were people listening and wondering at this boy's deep knowledge of the truth.

Mary hastily rushed up to Jesus, and said:

"My son, why have you treated us so unkindly? Your father and I have been looking for you, in great trouble, for three days!"

Jesus looked up at his mother's face, with surprise, and said:

"Why should you look for me? Did you not know that I would be in my Father's house?"

Evidently on the last day of their stay, he had slipped away for one more visit to the Temple; and once there his mind and heart had been so full that no thought of the home-going had come to him. He had just stayed there in the courts of the Lord's house without a thought of the outside world.

Where had he slept on those two nights? Who had given him food during those three days? He might have lain down, as thousands did during the feast, under the olive trees on the Mount of Olives. Some stranger may have seen him and invited him to a meal. But it would not be strange if in his deep, whole-souled interest, he had never thought of food and had eaten nothing during those three days.

But without a word he took his mother's hand and walked out of the Temple. He made the journey home to Nazareth, saying little but thinking much of all that he had seen and heard. One great, precious truth at least had come home to his heart. He felt that the Lord God of Israel was his own Father and he could trust fully the Father God.

The Young Woodworker

CHAPTER 13

FOR EIGHTEEN years after the visit to the Temple, Jesus was living in Nazareth, growing up from a boy to a young man. A Jewish boy generally left his school at about thirteen years of age, and began working at some trade or business. Jesus went into Joseph's shop and helped in the work, making plows and ax-handles and rakes and the plain furniture for the houses. Whatever Jesus did was done well, and we cannot doubt that in his trade he soon became a skilful worker. His ax-handles and plows were as good as the best; and if he made a bushel measure, it was a true one, for Jesus was a boy that could be trusted.

As a boy, he was like other boys, playing happily in play-time and working heartily in work-time. Some boys like to be alone, reading and thinking and dreaming; but Jesus was not one of that kind. All through his life he liked to have people around him, and as a boy we may be sure he had many friends among other boys. He was strong, in good health, could run and jump and climb trees. With his boy friends he wandered among the mountains and upon the great plain just over the hills from his town. The Sea of Galilee was only twenty miles away, and we do not doubt that Jesus with his friends went fishing in its blue waters and brought home to his mother the fish which he had caught.

After a time, Joseph, the husband of Mary, died, and Jesus was left to care for his mother and her large family of children. It is no light load for one just coming out of boyhood and just beginning to be a man,

Jesus went into Joseph's shop and helped in the work, making plows and ax-handles and the plain furniture for the houses.

to have laid upon him the earning of enough money to buy food for a mother and at least six younger brothers and sisters; and this was the load which the young Jesus took up. But although Joseph who had been a father to him was gone, Jesus knew that his heavenly Father was still with him, and he could call upon him for help in every need.

Jesus worked hard all the long days, but when the Sabbath day came, which among the Jews was Saturday, his shop was shut up and he sat on the floor of the village church, listening to the reading of the Old Testament and joining in the songs of praise. He took his turn as the reader at the desk, and as he read the lesson in Isaiah or Micah or Hosea, he saw meanings in the verses that others could not see, for in the long hours of the workshop he was thinking and praying and listening to the voice of God.

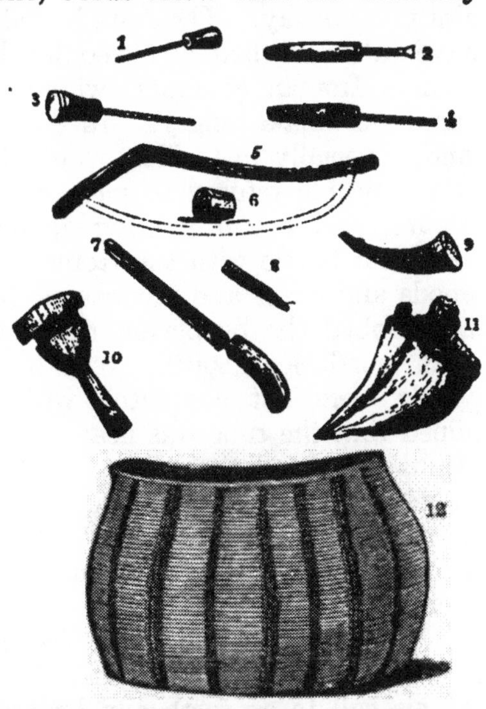

Tools of an oriental carpenter. 1, 3, 4. Drills. 2. Chisel. 5. Handle of a drill. 6. Nut held in the hand while the drill revolves. 7. Saw. 8. Punch. 9. Horn of oil. 10. Mallet. 11. Bag for nails. 11. Basket to hold tools.

While Jesus was living this quiet life in the home and the shop some changes were going on in the land. The ruler in Galilee was Herod Antipas, the son of that wicked

Herod who killed all the babies in Bethlehem; and he was very little better than his father. In Judea, the part of the land around Jerusalem, Archelaus, another son of Herod, ruled so badly that all the people sent to the Emperor Tiberius at Rome asking to have him taken away. The Jews hoped that they might then have rulers of their own people; but the Emperor sent them a Roman governor, whom they did not like but dared not make angry. In many places through the land, especially in Galilee, where Jesus was living, some of the people refused tc pay their taxes to the Roman empire, and began fighting against the rulers. They could not battle with the Roman armies, and hid in the woods and caves and mountains, but came out in bands and robbed the people on the roads. All through the land, north and south, were fear and trouble. The people were not contented with their rulers, and all hoped that the time was near when the Kingdom of God would come and their Roman officers and tax-gatherers would be driven away. They looked for a kingdom like the one over which David reigned a thousand years before, a kingdom with armies and victories over its enemies and a palace for the king.

But they did not know that in that little one-room house on the hillside of Nazareth, the King was waiting for his call to go forth and bring in the true Kingdom of God.

The Voice by the River

CHAPTER 14

WHILE JESUS was still living in Nazareth and working in his carpenter shop, suddenly the news went through all the land that a strange man was preaching in the desert country of Judea, not far from Jerusalem; and that all the people were going out of the cities and villages to hear him.

This man was John, the son of the old priest Zacharias and his wife Elizabeth. You remember that an angel came to Zacharias while he was standing by the altar in the Temple, and told him that he should have a son, and that his name should be John. John had now grown up and was a young man about thirty years old. He had lived out in the desert places away from the cities and their crowds, so that he could be alone and think and pray and listen to the voice of God. And God had spoken to him in the desert and he had told him to preach to the people and tell them how to get ready for the Kingdom of God, which was soon to come.

John was preaching beside the river Jordan, at the foot of the mountains; and from the cities and villages everywhere the people went to listen to his words. John did not look like the men of his time. He had never cut his hair, and it hung upon his shoulders in a long black mass. His black beard, too, was very long, for it had never been trimmed. His clothing was a skin torn from a beast or a mantle woven from the rough, shaggy hair of the camel, fastened by a leather belt around the waist. He had lived out of doors in the sun and the winds and the rain, so that his face and arms and legs

John the Baptist preaching in the wilderness

and his bare feet were all brown and hard. He ate for his food the locusts which he could pick up in the fields and the woods and the honey to be found in the hollow trees. When the people looked at him, they thought of the great prophet Elijah, who many hundred years before had gone up to heaven in a chariot of fire near that very place where John was preaching, and they said wonderingly to each other:

"This must be Elijah, the fiery prophet, who has come back to earth."

A prophet among the Israelites was a man who brought to the people the word which God had given him to speak. The books of the Old Testament, which all the people knew almost by heart, told of many prophets, such as Moses, who brought water for his people by striking the rock; Samuel, whose prayers saved the people from their enemies; Nathan, who spoke bold words to David the king; and Elisha, who had made the bitter waters of a spring sweet, had cured the leper Naaman and wrought many wonderful works. Of all the prophets, they thought Elijah the greatest, and they remembered that in the last book of the Old Testament, the book of the prophet Malachi, it was written:

"Behold, I will send you Elijah the prophet before the great day of the Lord shall come."

And when the people looked at this strange man who was preaching by the river, they thought that the day of the Lord was surely coming, and that here was the prophet Elijah as had been promised.

John said to the people, in his preaching, that the Kingdom of God was near at hand and that every man must be ready for it. To make themselves ready, they were to confess their sins, to stop doing wrong and to begin to do right. As a sign of their willingness to cease from evil and to serve the Lord, they were baptized by John in the river Jordan. John said to them:

"I baptize you with water, but there is one among you, of your own people, one whom you do not know, who is greater than I, so much above me that I am not worthy to stoop down and tie his shoestrings. He will come soon; and when he comes, he will not baptize with water as I do. He will baptize you with fire and with the Spirit of God."

The river Jordan

He spoke further about this Greater One who was coming so soon, and said:

"He shall deal with the people as the farmer deals with his grain on the threshing floor. He will sweep the floor most carefully; the wheat he will put in his barn and the chaff he will burn up with a fire that cannot be put out."

The people came to John and said to him:

"What shall we do to make ready for the coming of this Great King?"

John answered them:

"Let everyone do what he can to help those who are in need. If any of you have two coats, give one of them to some poor man that has no garments; and those of you who have wheat and barley, give to those who are hungry something to eat."

Some of the men who gathered the taxes from the people for the Roman rulers came to John and said:

"What would you have us do to make ready for the coming of the King? Shall we tell the people that they are to pay no more taxes?"

"No," answered John. "Let the people pay their taxes as before; but see that you do not make them pay more than is right, and do not rob them."

For many of these tax-collectors (who were called publicans) took from the people more than they had a right to take, and used the people's money for themselves. They made themselves rich by robbing the people. Everywhere the people hated these tax-collectors, and called them "sinners."

The soldiers and policemen came to John and said, "And what shall we do?"

John said to them:

"Do not be harsh and rough with the people. Treat everyone kindly. Be contented with your pay, and do not make the people give you money that you have no right to ask."

These were some of the many things that John said to the people. All his words came to this: "If you are doing wrong, stop it and begin to do right. Do not be selfish, but love your fellow men and do good to them. And be ready when the King comes to obey him."

John was called "John the Baptist" because he baptized in the river Jordan all those who promised to follow his teachings.

The leaders of the people in Jerusalem did not believe the words of John and were not baptized by him. They did not know exactly what to think of him, and they sent some priests and others to see him. These men came and asked him:

"Who are you? Are you the Christ, the promised King?"

"No," answered John, "I am not the Christ."

"What then?" said they. "Are you Elijah the prophet come to earth again, as some people say you are?"

"No," answered John again, "I am not Elijah."

"Well, then," they said, "tell us who you are, so that we can give an answer to the rulers who have sent us."

And John said:

"In the book of the prophet Isaiah it is written, 'The Voice of him that cries in the desert: prepare ye the way of the Lord, make a straight path before him.' I am that voice to speak to the people and make them ready for the King, who is even now among you, although you do not know him, and who will soon make himself known."

The Carpenter Leaves His Shop

CHAPTER 15

AFTER SOME months the news was brought to Nazareth that John the Baptist had come up the river Jordan and was now preaching at a place about twelve miles south of the Sea of Galilee. The place where John was preaching had two names. It was called "Bethany beyond Jordan," there being another Bethany quite near Jerusalem; and it was also called "Bethabara," a word which means "the place where one can walk across the river"; for there the river Jordan was so shallow that people waded across it. John had chosen this place because the sloping shore beside the river was fitted for the crowds to listen to his preaching, and the shallow water was near at hand for baptizing the people.

Bethabara or Bethany was about twenty-five miles from Nazareth; and over the plain just across the hill was a road leading down to the river at that place, where people used to cross the Jordan on their way to the land of Decapolis and Perea beyond. Nearly all the people had heard John preach, and most of them had been baptized by him as a sign that they promised to turn from evil and do good and look for the King who was soon to come.

Jesus felt that the time had now come for him to begin the work to which God had called him. He had told no one of his purpose, not even his mother; but one day he left his carpenter shop to his younger brothers, who were now young men and able to care for their mother. He walked down the valleys, came to the river Jordan, waded the stream, and at Bethabara, in front of a crowd of people from every part of the land, for the first time he saw John the Baptist. No doubt Mary had told her son all the story of the angel by the altar, of John's birth and of his early life; but in all the years Jesus and John had never met.

Jesus listened to the words of John, and then with the others he came forward to be baptized. John looked at this strange young man who was drawing near, and as he looked the voice within him said:

The Jordan. At the supposed place of Christ's baptism.

"The long-promised King has come! This Man is He!"

John felt that here was one who needed no baptism; for he knew that this man had no sins to give up, and was already doing God's will perfectly. He felt unwilling to baptize him, and said:

"It is not fitting that I should baptize one so good and so great in the sight of God as you are. I need to be baptized by you, and do you come to me?"

But Jesus answered him:

"It is best that it should be so. Whatever is right for other men is right also for me. Let me do this as my duty to God."

Then John yielded to the will of Jesus and baptized him. Just as Jesus rose out of the water a strange thing happened. While he was praying a light flashed from the sky and seemed to rest upon the head of Jesus like a white, shining dove coming down upon him; and

As Jesus rose out of the water, a light flashed from the sky, resting on his head, and the voice of God was heard saying: "This is my Son, my Beloved, in whom I am well pleased."

a voice was heard somewhat like a peal of thunder. Those standing on the shore felt that some words were spoken, but they could not understand them. John alone heard and understood. It was the voice of God, and John afterward told the people that these were the words spoken:

"This is my Son, my Beloved, in whom I am well pleased."

At that instant a mighty Power came upon Jesus. The Spirit of God had always been with him and had caused him to feel that the Lord was fitting him to do some great work. But in that moment when the light from heaven fell upon him and the voice of God was heard, Jesus was filled with the Spirit of God as no man, not even the greatest of the prophets, had been filled before. He knew now that he was not only a prophet, one who hears God's voice and speaks God's words; but more than a prophet, he himself was the Son of God. He saw as in a flash what was God's plan for his kingdom on the earth; and that it was a kingdom far different from that expected by the Jewish people. He knew that he, who up to that moment had been the woodworker of Nazareth, was from that hour to be the Prince of the heavenly kingdom. He was to lead the people to God and to show in his own life how men should live. He was to bring God down to men and to bring men to God. All this and more that we cannot understand came to the soul of Jesus as he stood on the brink of Jordan with the light of God upon his face.

Alone in the Desert

CHAPTER 16

AFTER HIS baptism Jesus felt that for a time he must be alone to think over the great change that had come upon him. Only yesterday he had been the carpenter in Nazareth, and now he knew that he was the Son of God and the King of Israel! So sudden and mighty a change as this made him feel that he must go to some quiet, lonely place, where he could think and pray and find out his Father's will for himself and the work that he was to do.

Without speaking even a word with John, Jesus slipped out of the crowd upon the bank of the river. He walked toward the south, not following the well-known road beside the Jordan, over which he had walked many times while attending the feasts in Jerusalem, but choosing the paths along the mountain-side where he would not meet people, for he wished not to talk with men but with God.

He came at last to a very lonely place, between Jericho and Jerusalem; a place where no man lived and where even the Arabs of the desert scarcely ever wandered. The only living creatures in the desolate land were the wild beasts, the wolves and the foxes, whose howls could be heard at night. There upon the top of a hill, with rocks all around, he sat down to rest. His mind had been in such a whirl of excitement, and his heart was beating with such strong feeling, that he had never thought of taking with him any food to eat. For many days and nights he was alone, praying and talking with God and never once thinking of eating. More than

Jesus chose the paths along the mountainside where he would not meet people, for he wished not to talk with men but with God.

a month passed away, even forty days, before the feeling of hunger came upon him.

Then suddenly he felt a sharp gnawing in his body, and he knew that he was famishing for food. He felt that he must have something to eat or he would die there in the desert, with the great work to which God had called him all left undone. Around him were the rough stones of the wilderness, and as he looked on them, this thought came to his mind:

"There is no need for me to starve in this desert. If I am the Son of God, as the voice from heaven said, then I need only to speak a word and these stones will be turned to bread!"

Then Jesus thought again, and said to himself, "Yes, I am the Son of God, and I have the power to make these stones turn into bread for me to eat. But that power was given me by my heavenly Father; and it was given, not that I should use it for myself, but for the help of others who are in need. It is not God's will that I should make bread out of stones for myself."

And then a sentence out of the Bible came to the mind of Jesus, and he said, "It is written, Man shall not live by bread alone, but by every word that comes out of the mouth of God."

Jesus seemed to be alone in the desert, but there was one who was watching him, all unseen. That one was the evil spirit, Satan, who hated Jesus, knowing that he was the Son of God and the Saviour of the world. He had put into the mind of Jesus the thought of turning stones to bread and using the power which God had given him for himself alone. Jesus was quick to see the purpose of Satan and to turn away from it.

Then another thought came to the mind of Jesus. He said to himself, "I know that I am the King of Israel, the Messiah whom the people have been looking for so

When Satan, the wicked spirit, found that he could not persuade Jesus to do his will, he left him.

long. But how shall I cause the people to know that I am their King? What can I do to make them believe in me?"

At that moment, while Jesus was trying to think out the best plan for beginning his work and making himself, as the Son of God, known to the people, Satan, the evil spirit, was ready with another word. He said, "Here is a good plan. Go to the Temple in Jerusalem at some feast-time when it is crowded with people, and in the sight of all the crowd, leap off one of the towers. You will not fall to the ground, but will come sailing down through the air, for all power is yours. And when the people see you, they will fall on their faces before you and will believe in you as the King so long promised. You know that you are the Son of God and that God will take care of you. Don't you remember that in one of the psalms it is written, 'He shall give his angels charge over thee, and in their hands they shall bear thee up so that thou shalt not dash thy foot against a stone?' "

Jesus saw at once that this was not God's plan, but Satan's plan. It would not be trusting God, but would be putting God's power and God's care to a trial to show what Jesus himself could do. He would not perform this foolish act, nor anything like it, of his own accord. He would wait until God told him what to do, and would do nothing until he was sure that it was the will of God. Again a sentence out of the Bible came to his mind, and he said:

"It is written again, 'Thou shall not put the Lord thy God to trial.' "

That means that we should never make a show of our trust in God or let others see by some act that is not needed what God can do to help us. We must not venture into danger to show how God can bring us out of danger.

Jesus had now settled two great questions. He would not use his wonder-working powers for himself, even to save his own life; and he would do nothing merely as a show, but would in all things work only the will of his Father. There was one more question to be met: he was to become the King of Israel, but what kind of a kingdom would he have?

He knew well that all the Israelite people, not only in Judea and Galilee, but in all the lands, were looking for a king who should rule in Jerusalem, somewhat as the Emperor Tiberius was ruling in Rome. They hoped for a king who should gather an army, should drive out the Romans, should fight battles, win victories and make his kingdom the ruling power in the world. They looked for the time when the Romans should be under their feet, and when all other lands should pay taxes and serve their king in Jerusalem.

All this Jesus knew, and Satan, the wicked spirit, was at his side, though unseen, to say to him:

"Take my advice, and I will give you all the kingdoms of the world; for they are mine and I can give them to whom I please."

Jesus knew that what the people wanted was just what Satan wanted, a worldly, wicked kingdom, built out of war and blood and the killing of all who would not submit to it. But that would not be the Kingdom of God. It would be the Kingdom of Satan, as so many kingdoms and nations have been in the past. To do as Satan wished him to do would be just the same as if he bowed down before Satan and worshipped him as his Lord and Master. This he would not do; and his last words to the tempter were:

"Go away from me, Satan! It is written, 'Thou shalt worship the Lord thy God, and him only shalt thou serve!'"

Jesus saw plainly that in making this great choice to please God, he would not please his own people, the Jews. He knew that the rulers and the priests and the scribes, those who were the leading men of the time, would be against him, would refuse to follow him, would try to stir up the people against him and would try to kill him. But Jesus was ready to die in serving God, rather than to live in doing the will of Satan.

When Satan, the wicked spirit, found that he could not persuade Jesus to do his will, he left him. And afterward, angels from heaven, sent by his Father, came to him in the desert and gave him all the food that he needed.

The gospels of Matthew and Luke, which tell the story of this meeting with Satan and of Jesus' victory, do not say just where it took place. All we know is that it was in the "desert" or the "wilderness." But near Jericho stands a mountain where it is thought by some that Jesus stayed during those forty days. This mountain on that account is called by a name which means "fortv davs"—Mount Quarantania.

Mount Quarantania. Believed by some to be the mount where Jesus was tempted.

Andrew brought his brother Simon to Jesus, who gave him a new name, "The Rock," or Peter.

The Earliest Followers of Jesus

CHAPTER 17

AFTER HIS forty days in the desert, Jesus began his work of winning men to the Kingdom of God. This plan was, at first, to talk to men one by one, until he could gather around him a little company of those who would believe in his words as a teacher, and follow him as their leader. The men who would be best fitted to become his first followers were some of those who had been already taught by John the Baptist. So from the wilderness Jesus turned his steps northward once more, and walked up the well-trodden road toward Bethabara, where nearly two months ago he had been baptized.

At Bethabara with John the Baptist was a group or company of young men, who were known as John's "disciples," that is, men who stayed with him to learn his teachings after the crowds had gone home. Some of these were fishermen from the Sea of Galilee who had left their nets and their work that they might listen to John.

John was standing with some of these men around him, when at some distance a stranger was seen walking up the road. These disciples of John did not know who this man was, but John remembered him, for the light flashing from the sky upon his face at the moment of his baptism and the voice from the heavens, had stamped Jesus upon his memory. He pointed to Jesus and said:

"Look! Yonder is the Lamb of God, who takes away the sin of the world! This is the one of whom I spoke when I said, 'After me shall come a man who is greater than I, and who shall baptize not in water but in the Holy

Spirit.' Upon this man I saw the Spirit coming down like a dove and resting upon him. And I tell you all that this man is the Son of God."

While John was speaking these words, Jesus passed out of sight, and John and his disciples saw no more of him that day. But on the next day, when John was standing with two of his followers, Jesus again walked by, and John again looked at him and said to the young men:

"Look! The Lamb of God!"

The two young men when they heard these words at once left John and walked toward Jesus. As they drew near, Jesus turned and said to them:

"Why do you follow me? What is it that you wish?"

They said to him: "Teacher, we wish to know where you are staying, so that we can see you and talk with you."

"Come and see," said Jesus; and he led them to the house where he was staying as a guest. In those times the Jews welcomed to their homes those who were on a journey and for a few days needed a resting place. It was about ten o'clock in the morning when those two men sat down in the house with Jesus, and they stayed with him all the rest of the day until the sun went down, listening as he talked to them about the Kingdom of God. His words went straight to their hearts, and on that day those two young men believed in Jesus as their Messiah-Christ; that is, the King of Israel, long promised by the prophets of the Old Testament and long looked for by the Israelite people. The two words Messiah and Christ mean the same. One is in the Hebrew language; the other in the Greek, and both words mean "The Anointed One," or "the King of Israel."

Thus, on the first day of his teaching Jesus found two followers. Both of these men were fishermen from the Sea of Galilee, not many miles away. One was a man named John, who was afterward called "the disciple whom Jesus loved," for of all his followers, John was the one nearest to Jesus. Long afterward, John wrote one of the most precious books in the Bible, "the Gospel according to John," which shows us, more than any other book, the inmost heart of Jesus.

The other young man was named Andrew. He thought at once of his older brother, Simon, who was also a follower of John the Baptist. He went to find Simon, and said to him:

"We have found the Messiah, of whom the prophets have spoken!"

He spoke in the Hebrew tongue, which was the language of his people. If he had spoken in Greek, the tongue in which the New Testament was first written, he would have said, "We have found the Christ;" that is, the King. Andrew brought his brother Simon to Jesus; and as soon as Jesus looked at him, before Andrew had spoken his name, he said:

"Your name is Simon, and you are the son of Jonas. But I will give you a new name. In the time to come you shall be called "the Rock."

In the Hebrew language the word meaning "rock" is "Cephas" or "Kephas." In Greek it is "Peter." After this Simon was sometimes called Cephas, but more often Peter. He became a leader among the followers of Jesus, and many years later wrote one, perhaps two, of the books in the New Testament.

Jesus had now three followers who believed in him as their Lord and King; and the next day he found a fourth. This man was named Philip, and he came from a place called Bethsaida, on the northern shore of the Sea of Galilee. Jesus said to Philip:

"Follow me."

And he too joined the little company of the disciples or followers of Jesus. Philip at once thought of a friend of his own, a very good and pure man, who he thought would be glad to join him as a follower of Jesus. He went to look for him and found him standing under a fig tree. He said:

"We have found him of whom Moses wrote in the law, and of whom the prophets spoke, the Christ. His name is Jesus, the son of Joseph; and he comes from the town of Nazareth."

Now Nathanael's home-town was Cana, only a few miles from Nazareth. Nathanael thought of Nazareth as a mean place. He could not believe that the great King of Israel, the Christ, should spring from such a village. He looked for him to come from some great city, like Jerusalem, or from Bethlehem, David's town. He did not know that Jesus had been born in Bethlehem; in fact he had never heard of Jesus, and he said:

"Do you tell me that anything good can come out of Nazareth?"

Now, Philip was not wise enough to tell Nathanael the reasons why he believed in Jesus. It is hard to put into words some of our deepest thoughts. But he gave to Nathanael a very wise answer.

"Well," said Philip, "come and see Jesus for yourself."

Jesus had never seen Nathanael before, but as he drew near, Jesus said to those who were standing by:

"Look! here comes a true Israelite, a man of God, one whose heart has in it nothing evil."

Nathanael was greatly surprised at these words of Jesus. He said,

"How is it that you know me?"

"Before Philip spoke to you," answered Jesus, "while you were standing under the fig tree, I saw you."

"Teacher," said Nathanael, "you are the Son of God; you are the King of Israel."

Jesus said:

"Do you believe because I said, 'I saw you underneath the fig tree?' You will yet see greater things than these. In truth, I say to you that you shall see the heaven opened and the angels of God going up and coming down upon the Son of Man."

By "the Son of Man," Jesus meant himself. He used those words to show that while he was "the Son of God," he was also a man among men.

Jesus had been preaching or talking to a few men about the Kingdom of God, and already he had gained five followers. There may have been others, for not long afterwards we find James, the brother of John, among his disciples.

The village of Bethphage, on the Mount of Olives

Jesus, with his first followers, John, Andrew, Philip and Nathanael, left the river Jordan and walked to the village of Cana in Galilee.

The Water Turned to Wine

CHAPTER 18

SOON AFTER Jesus met the men who became his first followers he left the river Jordan, and with these men walked to the land of Galilee, to the village of Cana, about six miles north of Nazareth. This was the town where Nathanael, one of the first five followers of Jesus, lived.

At Cana a marriage was to be held, and Jesus with all his followers was invited. In that land, at a marriage, a feast was always given, and all the friends of the newly-married couple, with their friends also, and almost everybody in the village, were expected to come. The feasting and dancing and merry-making often lasted through a whole week.

Before the feast was over they found that the wine, which in those times everybody drank freely, was used up, and those who were giving the feast had no wine to set before their guests. This filled them with alarm, for at such times the wine was expected to flow freely, and not to have wine for the company at a feast was considered almost a disgrace.

The mother of Jesus was there as a friend of the family. She thought of a way to help those who were giving the feast, and called her son aside from the crowd, and said to him very quietly:

"They have no wine."

She knew what very few knew, that Jesus was the Son of God, and that all power was in his hands. He had not yet done any of those wonderful works of curing the sick, making the blind to see and making the deaf to hear, which he did so often afterward; but Mary believed that he could do them if he chose. She thought that perhaps he would use his power to give the wine that was needed. It was with this hope that she said to him, “They have no wine.”

Cana, and its well

The answer that Jesus gave was not such in its words as to encourage her.

“Woman,” said he, “what have you to do with me in this matter? My time is not yet come.”

His speaking to his mother as “Woman,” instead of saying “Mother,” as a young man would among us, was not lacking in respect. It was the usage of that time for a son to say “Woman,” and not “Mother.” She saw in his face a look showing her that she had not spoken in vain. So she turned to the servants who were standing near. “Whatever he tells you to do,” she said, “do it.”

One of the usages of the Jews was to wash their hands before they sat down to a meal. This washing was not merely to make their hands clean; it was a sort of religious service, and the Jews were very strict in doing it. When so large a company met for a feast, a great deal of water was needed. In the hall were standing six large jars for water, each jar of a size to hold nearly twenty gallons. They were nearly empty, because all the guests had washed their hands before sitting down at the feast. Jesus pointed to these jars and said to the servants:

"Fill all those jars with water."

They obeyed him and filled all the jars up to the brim. Then Jesus said again:

"Now draw out from the jars, and carry what you take out to the ruler of the feast."

Wondering, the servants dipped their pitchers into the great jars which only a few moments before they had filled with water. How surprised they were to find each pitcher as it came out full of red wine! They carried it to the ruler of the feast. He tasted it and saw that it was wine of the very best kind. He did not know how it had been made, but supposed that it had been brought suddenly from some wine merchant. He called the young man who had been married, and in whose honor the feast was being held, and said to him:

Stone water-jars

"Everybody serves his best wine at the beginning of his feast; and afterward, when people have been drinking some time, he brings wine that is poorer; but you have kept your best wine until now!"

The only ones who knew whence the new wine had come were the servants. But they soon told others, and the word was passed around the company that Jesus of Nazareth, Mary's son, had wrought this wonderful work. His followers, the five or more disciples who had come with Jesus to the wedding feast, now believed more fully

The mother of Jesus called her son aside and said to him quietly: "They have no wine."

than before that their teacher was more than a mere man, that the power of God was upon him and that whatever he should say was the word of God.

Such a work as that of turning the water into wine, a work that no man could do without God's power, was called "a miracle." It showed that the one who wrought it was a man sent from God, doing God's will and speaking God's word. This was the first miracle or work of wonder that Jesus wrought; but after this we shall read of many miracles.

From the wedding feast Jesus went down the mountains of Galilee to the city of Capernaum, which stood on the shore of the Sea of Galilee on the northwest. With Jesus on this visit to Capernaum were his mother, some of his younger brothers and his followers.

Oriental basin, ewer, etc.

Nicodemus sought Jesus quietly one night to talk with him and learn more of his teachings.

The Lord in His Temple

CHAPTER 19

THE SPRING-TIME of the year came, when the people from all parts of the land went up to Jerusalem to attend the great feast of the Passover.

You remember that this feast was held to keep in mind how more than a thousand years before God had led the Israelite people out of Egypt, where they had been slaves. It was called the feast of the Passover because on the night of their going-out the angel of death had "passed over" the houses of the Israelites when he brought death to the Egyptian homes. On that night, too, they went out of Egypt in such haste that the women did not have time to wait for the bread to rise before baking it, and all the bread eaten at that time was "unleavened bread," or bread made without yeast.

To keep in mind that great day, the day when Israel became a nation, ruling itself, in the spring of every year all the people gathered in Jerusalem, and for one week ate unleavened bread, that is, bread made without yeast. Great services were held in the Temple on every day of this feast; and on one evening a special dinner of a roasted lamb was eaten by everybody, to keep in mind the last meal which the Israelites ate in the land of Egypt, with their hats on their heads and their cloaks on their shoulders and their shoes on their feet, all ready to march away.

Jesus and the little company of his disciples or followers went up to Jerusalem, walking, as many times before, down the Jordan valley to Jericho, and then climbing the hills to the holy city. For many years

Jesus had been coming to the feast of the Passover; but never before had he come as he came now, in the power of the Spirit, as the Son of God.

Around the House of God was a great open court, called the Court of the Gentiles, where foreign people who were not Jews came to pray; since none but Jews or Israelites could enter the inner courts. But the Jews held all Gentiles or foreign people in contempt. They did not look upon the part of the Temple buildings where foreigners prayed as holy; and they had turned this court, the Court of the Gentiles, into a market place. Here Jesus found everywhere sheep and oxen brought there for sale; cages full of doves, which were sold to the poorer people for offerings upon the altar; counters where sat men changing the money of people from other lands into the coins of Judea. There was nothing of the quiet and peace which should be in a place of prayer; all was noise and confusion; the lowing of oxen, the voices of men buying and selling, the jingling of silver on the tables.

These sights and sounds stirred the heart of Jesus. He felt that such work as went on around him was unfit and was wicked in a place set apart for the worship of God. He picked up a piece of rope from the floor and untwisted its cords until it seemed like a whip. Then standing before the buyers and the sellers, he called upon them to stop their trading. They looked up amazed at this stranger whose face glowed with power as though he were a king.

Alone, without help from anyone, he drove all these people out of the court. He bade them lead away the sheep and the oxen; he commanded those who sold the doves to carry out their cages; he overturned the tables of the money-changers and sent their silver rolling upon the floor.

Standing before the buyers and the sellers, he called upon them to stop their trading; he overturned the tables of the money changers and sent their silver rolling upon the floor.

where men cheated and did evil deeds, Jesus himself was the house of God. The rulers said:

"This Temple has taken forty-six years to build, and it is not finished yet; and will you raise it up in three days?"

Nearly fifty years before, King Herod had begun to rebuild the Temple, which in his time had become old and decayed. The repairs were made very slowly, and in the time of Jesus the building was still far from being finished. It was not finished until more than twenty years afterward.

We know what Jesus meant by those words; that three years afterward, those very men would cause him, the Son of God, whose body was God's dwelling place, to be put to death; and within three days after his death he would rise from his tomb, to be the Temple of God again and forever. The disciples of Jesus heard these words, but at that time did not know what they meant.

Jesus stayed for some time in Jerusalem and talked to the people about the Kingdom of God. He also did some wonderful works, such as curing the sick; and the people who saw these acts believed his words, as from one whom God had sent to men. But the priests and the rulers hated Jesus, because he spoke against their wicked lives, and they did all that they could to turn the people away from him.

Among the rulers, however, were a few men who listened to Jesus and believed his words. One of these was a man named Nicodemus. He wished to have a talk with Jesus and learn more of his teachings. But he was afraid to be seen with Jesus in the day-time, knowing that the other rulers were so strongly against Jesus. So he went quietly one night, unknown to everybody, and had a meeting with Jesus. Nicodemus began by saying:

"Teacher, we all know that you have been sent by God to speak to us, because no one could do these wonderful things that you are doing unless God were with him to give him power."

Jesus said to him:

"Let me tell you and all your people one thing. No man can have any part in the Kingdom of God unless he is born again from God."

Nicodemus did not know what this meant, and he said, "How can a man be born again after he is grown up?"

"Every man," said Jesus, "must become a new man and have the Spirit of God dwelling in him, if he is to come into the Kingdom of God. Do not be surprised that I say to you, 'You must be born anew.' There are many things that you cannot understand. Listen to the wind blowing! You can hear it, but you cannot tell from what place it comes nor to what place it goes. Just so is it with every one who is born of God's spirit."

What Jesus meant in these words was that every one who would be a follower of Christ needs to have a new heart and to live a new life; and this new heart and new life God alone can give to him.

One great sentence was spoken by Jesus at this time. Here it is.

"God so loved the world that he gave his only Son, that whosoever believeth on him should not perish, but have eternal life."

At the Old Well

CHAPTER 20

AFTER THE Passover, Jesus went teaching through the villages in Judea, the province or part of the land around Jerusalem. As Judea was the largest of the five provinces, it gave its name also to the whole land, which was called both "Judea" and "the land of Israel." John the Baptist was still preaching and baptizing, although the crowds which now came to hear him were not so great as before. While John was near the Sea of Galilee, Jesus stayed in Judea, so that none might think that he was trying to draw the people away from John.

But after a time Jesus heard that John the Baptist had been put in prison by Herod Antipas, the wicked ruler of Galilee and Perea. Herod had stolen from his brother Philip his wife, named Herodias, and was living with her. John said to him:

"It is against the law of Moses and of God for you to take away your brother's wife."

This made Herod angry with John, and Herodias even more angry. She wished to have John put to death for his bold words, but Herod, though he was not a good man, was unwilling to have John slain, and partly to keep him safe from the hate of his wife, he ordered that he should be put into prison. To a man like John, used to the free life of the wilderness, and not even willing to live in town or village, it must have been hard to be shut up in a prison cell, within four walls, and to be able only to see the outside world through grated windows.

As soon as Jesus learned that John the Baptist was shut up in prison, he ended his work in Judea, and with his disciples started for Galilee, his old home in the north. On this journey he did not go the way of the river Jordan, but took the most direct road, which would lead him through the land of Samaria. He knew that the Samaritan people who lived in that land hated the Jews and often robbed them when they traveled through

John the Baptist rebuking Herod

their country. Still, Jesus made up his mind to go through Samaria.

Leading the little company of his followers, he walked northward from Jerusalem, past Bethel, where long before Jacob lying on his pillow of stone had his wonderful dream of the ladder reaching up to heaven; past Shiloh, where once the holy Ark of God had been kept in the Tabernacle in the days of Samuel; and over mountains where battles had been fought and victories won.

Early one morning, after walking in the night, Jesus and his disciples came to an old well, about two miles from the city of Shechem. Nearby was a little village, named Sychar, which could be seen from the well, and although it was a Samaritan village the followers of Jesus went to it to buy some food. This well was very old. It had been dug by Jacob, the early father of all the Israelite people, more than eighteen hundred years before Jesus came to that place. And it is still there, a well dug out of the solid rock nearly one hundred feet deep, and even now having water in it ten months of the year, but apt to be dry in the summer. That well is now nearly four thousand years old, yet every traveler who visits it may look down into its depths, may see a bucket of water drawn and may have a drink from it.

In that time a well did not have with it a pump for bringing up the water, nor was there even a rope to let down into it; but each one who came to draw water—and it was generally a woman—brought a rope and a water-jar. As Jesus sat beside the well, very tired and hungry and thirsty, he had nothing with which to draw water. As the Son of God upon the earth, he could have made the water come to him, but he would not, for you remember that in the desert Jesus would do no wonderful work, no miracle, merely for his own need.

Suddenly Jesus heard the sound of someone coming. He looked up and saw a woman, with her water-jar and rope, standing by the well. From her dress he knew that she was not a Jewish but a Samaritan woman, and being the Son of God, he saw more. He knew at once all her life, which had not been a good life. But he looked into her heart and saw that she had a longing after God and after good. He said to her:

"Will you give me a drink of water from this well?"

The woman glanced at Jesus, and knowing from his dress and his manner of speaking that he was a Jew, said to him:

"How is it that you, who are a Jew, ask drink from me, a Samaritan woman?"

The Jews looked down upon the Samaritans, never asked any favors of them, and would not drink from a cup or pitcher that a Samaritan had handled. The woman knew this, and was greatly surprised that this strange young man of the Jewish race should speak to her. Jesus answered her:

"If you knew what God's free gift is, and who he is that is asking you for a drink, you would have asked him instead, and he would have given you living water."

As Jesus said these words, very thoughtfully, the woman looking and listening felt that this was no common man. She thought that he might be a prophet, a man whom God had sent to do mighty works and speak the words of God. She said, very respectfully:

"Sir, you have nothing to draw water with, and the well is very deep. Where can you get your living water? Are you a greater man than our father Jacob, who dug this well and gave it to us, and drank of its water himself, with his sons and his sheep and oxen?"

Jesus answered her:

"Anyone who drinks this water will be thirsty again, but anyone who drinks the water that I will give him will never thirst any more. The water that I will give him will turn into a well of water springing up to everlasting life."

"Oh, sir," said the woman, "give me some of your

living water, so that I need not be thirsty nor come all this road to draw water."

Jesus looked earnestly at the woman's face, and then said to her:

"Go home; call your husband, and come here again."

The woman's face clouded, her eyes dropped, and she looked as if she felt ashamed, while she answered in a low voice, "I have no husband."

Jesus looked at her steadily, and said:

"You have spoken the truth. You have no husband. But you have had five husbands, and the man with whom you are living now is not your husband. You spoke the truth in those words."

The woman was filled with wonder as she heard the stranger speak. She saw at once that here was a man who knew everything. She was sure that God had spoken to this man and given him this knowledge of her. "Sir," said she, "I see that you are a prophet of God. Tell me, then, whether our people or the Jews are right. Our fathers have worshipped God on this mountain; but the Jews say that Jerusalem is the place where all should go to worship God."

As she spoke, she pointed to the mountain that was standing near, Mount Gerizim, on the top of which was the temple of the Samaritans.

"Woman, believe me, answered Jesus, "there is coming a time when men shall worship God in other places besides this mountain and Jerusalem. The time is near, it has even now come, when the true worshippers everywhere shall pray to the Father in spirit and in truth. God is a Spirit, dwelling everywhere, and those who worship him, must worship in spirit and in truth."

The woman said to Jesus:

"I know that Messiah is coming, the Christ sent

Jesus sat beside the well, very tired and thirsty, but he had nothing with which to draw water. Suddenly he heard the sound of someone coming, and looking up saw a Samaritan woman with her water jar.

from God to be our King. When he comes he will explain everything to us."

Then Jesus said to her, "I who am now speaking to you am he, the Christ!"

Just at that moment the followers of Jesus, John and Peter, and the others, came back from the village with the food which they had bought. They were surprised to find their Master talking with a woman, but they said nothing.

The woman had come to the well to draw water, but in her interest in this wonderful stranger she forgot all about her errand. Leaving her water-jar she ran back to the village and said to everybody whom she met:

"Come with me and meet a man who told me everything I have done in all my life! Is not this man the Christ whom we are looking for?"

After the woman went away toward her home, the disciples urged Jesus to eat some of the food which they had brought. A little while before Jesus had been hungry, but now in talking with the woman and leading her mind to the truth, he had forgotten his own needs.

"I have food to eat," said he, "that you know nothing of."

They looked at each other and said:

"Can it be that someone has brought him something to eat?"

But Jesus said to them, "My food is to do the will of my Father who sent me into the world, and to finish the work that he gave me to do. . Do you say that there are four months before the harvest time will come? I tell you to look on the fields, and find them already white for the harvest. You shall reap and gain a rich harvest, gathering grain for everlasting life."

Jesus meant that this woman, bad though she may have been before, was now eager to hear his words and to come to God. So his disciples would soon find the hearts of men everywhere, like a field of ripe grain, ready to be won and to be saved.

Soon the woman came back to the well with many of her people. They all asked Jesus to come to their village and teach them. He went to the town of Sychar and stayed there two days, talking to the people about the Kingdom of God and showing them how they might enter into it. Many of the people in that place and near it believed in Jesus as the Christ, the King sent from God, and they said:

"Now we have heard for ourselves and we know that this is really the Saviour of the world."

Scene in Damascus, showing houses on the walls

The Nobleman's Boy

CHAPTER 21

AFTER STAYING two days in Sychar, the village near Jacob's well, Jesus and his disciples went on their way northward to the land of Galilee. They walked across the great plain where so many battles had

Jacob's well as it is at the present time

been fought in the old times, and climbed the mountains beyond it. Nazareth, where Jesus had lived for so many years, was on his way, but Jesus did not at this time stop there, for he had in his mind to visit it a few weeks later. With his followers, Jesus came for the second time to Cana, the place where a few months before he had turned the water into wine.

When Jesus was at Cana at his first visit, very few people had heard his name. But now everybody was talking about him, for all the people who had come home from the Feast of the Passover told their friends and neighbors of the wonderful young Prophet who had been preaching in Jerusalem, and had driven the men buying and selling out of the Temple, and had wrought wonders in curing the sick.

In the court of a village home in Cana of Galilee

About twenty miles from Cana was the city of Capernaum, on the shore of the Sea of Galilee. At Capernaum was living a man of high rank, an official of King Herod Antipas. This nobleman was in deep trouble, for his son was very ill with a great fever and lying at the point of death. The news that Jesus was again in Galilee, and only twenty miles away, brought to the nobleman a hope that perhaps this Prophet might be willing to come down from Cana to Capernaum and cure his son.

At once he made up his mind to go to Jesus and ask him to come and help him. It was a hard journey from Capernaum to Cana, twenty miles of mountain climbing; but this anxious father started very early in the morning, and came to Cana at about one o'clock in the afternoon. He found Jesus, told him how ill his son was, and begged him to come to Capernaum and cure him. Jesus did not seem very willing to go. He said to the nobleman:

Site of Capernaum

"Unless you people are always seeing me do wonderful works you will not believe in me."

"Oh, sir," pleaded the troubled father, "do come down quickly or my son will die!"

"There is no need for me to come," said Jesus. "You may go home, for your son will live and will get well."

These words would make a heavy trial to this man's faith in Jesus. For how could he know that his son would be well, without any sign given him by Jesus? And how could he understand that Jesus by a word could cure someone who he had not seen and who was twenty miles away? But the father at once believed the promise of Jesus. He did not even hurry home to see if his boy was cured, but waited until evening before starting upon his journey.

The next day, as he was nearing home, his servants met him with the glad news:

"Your son is living and is very much better."

"At what time," said the nobleman, "did he begin to improve?"

"It was yesterday," they told him, "at about one o'clock when the fever left him."

The man was not surprised, for it was just as he had expected. That hour, one o'clock, was the very time that Jesus had said to him, "Your son will live."

This miracle, or work of wonder, was much talked about and led not only this nobleman, but all his family with him, to believe that Jesus was the Saviour and the King of Israel who had been promised so long.

The Carpenter in His Home-town

CHAPTER 22

SOON AFTER the visit to Cana, and the cure of the nobleman's son, Jesus walked over to his old home at Nazareth, which was only six miles away. He thought of his sisters in that city, who were now grown women with children of their own, and he longed to see them. He thought, too, of the boys with whom in other days he had played and had sat in the school, now men with families; of his former neighbors, whom he had not seen for nearly a year. His heart was full of love for his own people, and he felt that out of the power God had given him he could speak to them words that would do them good.

Of course, the people of Nazareth had heard wonderful stories about their former townsman; that he had suddenly come forth as a great teacher, speaking truths such as never had been heard before; and especially, that he had done wondrous works of curing the sick at Cana and at Capernaum. All these reports were surprising to the people of Nazareth, because among them Jesus had never shown any signs of greatness. He had sat in his seat in the church, but had never spoken from the pulpit; and they had known him as a good young man, kind and gentle toward all, and an honest, skilful workman at his trade. But they had never thought of him as a teacher, or a prophet bearing a message from God, or as a worker of wonders, such as they had heard of his doing in Cana and Capernaum.

It was expected that Jesus on the Sabbath day would speak in the church at Nazareth (they called

The people in the synagogue at Nazareth did not care for the words of Jesus. In their rage and fury they leaped from their seats and dragged him out of doors.

their church "the synagogue," a word that means "a meeting of the people"); and everybody was present to see him and to hear him. In a gallery on one side were his sisters, looking and listening, but unseen, because the women's gallery in all Jewish churches was covered with a lattice-work. There on the floor, seated on rugs or mats, were his neighbors and the people who had seen him grow up from a boy to a man. They were present, not to learn, but to listen and judge his words, and especially to see what great things he might do.

Jesus walked up to the platform, and the officer in charge handed him the rolls on which were written the lessons for the day. This officer was at the same time the janitor or keeper of the building and the teacher of the school held there during the week. This man may have been the teacher who had taught Jesus as a boy to read. One of the lessons for that day was in the sixty-first chapter of the book of Isaiah the prophet. A part of it read thus:

"The Spirit of the Lord is upon me,
Because he hath set me apart to preach the gospel to the poor.
He has sent me to say that the prisoners shall be set free,
That the blind shall have their sight again,
That the poor and suffering shall be given freedom,
That the time of favor from God has come."

While Jesus was reading from the Bible, he stood up, and all who were present also stood, for the Jews showed their respect for the Bible by standing whenever it was read. When he had finished the reading, he folded up the roll, handed it back to the officer, and sat down, and the people also sat down likewise. Often the man who preached in the synagogue or church was seated while speaking. Jesus began by saying:

"Today this word of the prophet has come to pass in your hearing."

And he went on to tell in simple, gentle words how he had been sent to preach to the poor, to set the prisoners free, to give sight to the blind and to bring the news of God's goodness to men. At first the people listened with the deepest interest, and their hearts were touched by his kind and tender words.

But soon they began to whisper among themselves. One said, "Why should this carpenter try to teach us?" And another, "This man is no teacher! He is only the son of Joseph the carpenter! We know his brothers, and his sisters are living here." And some began to say, "Why does he not do here some of the wonderful things that they say he has done in other places? We want to see some of his marvelous cures with sick people!"

Jesus knew their thoughts, but he would not do wonders merely to be seen by men. He said to them:

"I know that you are saying, 'Let us see some wonderful work, like that on the nobleman's son in Capernaum.' I tell you in truth, that no prophet or teacher has honor among his own people.

"You remember that in the days of Elijah the prophet, when the sky was shut up for three years and six months, and no rain fell, there was a great famine in the land and a need of bread. At that time there were many widows in the land of Israel, yet Elijah was not sent to any of these, but to a widow woman in Zarephath of Zidon, a foreigner and a Gentile. And in the time of Elisha the prophet after Elijah, there were many lepers in the land of Israel, yet none of these was made clean of his leprosy, but only Naaman the Syrian."

These words, telling how God had chosen foreigners instead of Israelites for his works of wonder, made the people in the church very angry, for they did not care for the words of Jesus; they only wished to see him do some miracle or wonderful act. They would not listen to him; in their rage and fury, they leaped from their seats; they rushed upon the platform; they seized hold of Jesus and dragged him out of doors. They took him up to the top of the hill above the city, and would have thrown him down its steep side to his death. But the time for Jesus to die had not yet come. By the power of God, Jesus slipped quietly out of their hands and went away. He walked away very sadly from Nazareth, for he had longed to bring the good news of God's blessings first of all to his own people.

Approach to Jerusalem, from the railroad station on the southwest

Jewish fishermen by the Sea of Galilee

Four Fishermen Called

CHAPTER 23

THE PLACE which Jesus chose for his home, after being driven away from Nazareth, was Capernaum. This was a large city on the northwestern shore of the Sea of Galilee. Only one city beside the lake was larger—Tiberias. That was a new city, built by Herod, the ruler of Galilee, and named after the Emperor Tiberius at Rome. But Tiberias was not a Jewish city. It contained temples to idols, its people were foreigners, and very few Jews were willing to live within its walls. Then, too, Herod Antipas lived there in a palace which he had built, and Jesus did not wish to be near Herod.

But Capernaum was a Jewish city, and Jesus felt that his work was to be among the Jews. At least four of the early followers of Jesus lived in Capernaum; two pair of brothers, Simon and Andrew, the sons of Jonas; and James and John, the sons of Zebedee. These four men were partners with Zebedee in the fishing trade. They owned a number of fishing boats and had men working for them. The lake was full of fish, and many people all around it lived by fishing. The fish in the Sea of Galilee were good food, and were sent to all the nearby cities. It is said that one emperor at Rome, not long after this time, had sent to him every week a barrel full of fish from the Sea of Galilee, for his table in the palace.

The people of Capernaum had heard of Jesus, for all those who went up to the feasts in Jerusalem brought home reports of this wonderful teacher and healer of the sick. Wherever Jesus went, crowds gathered around him to listen to his words, and especially eager to see if he would do any of his wonderful works.

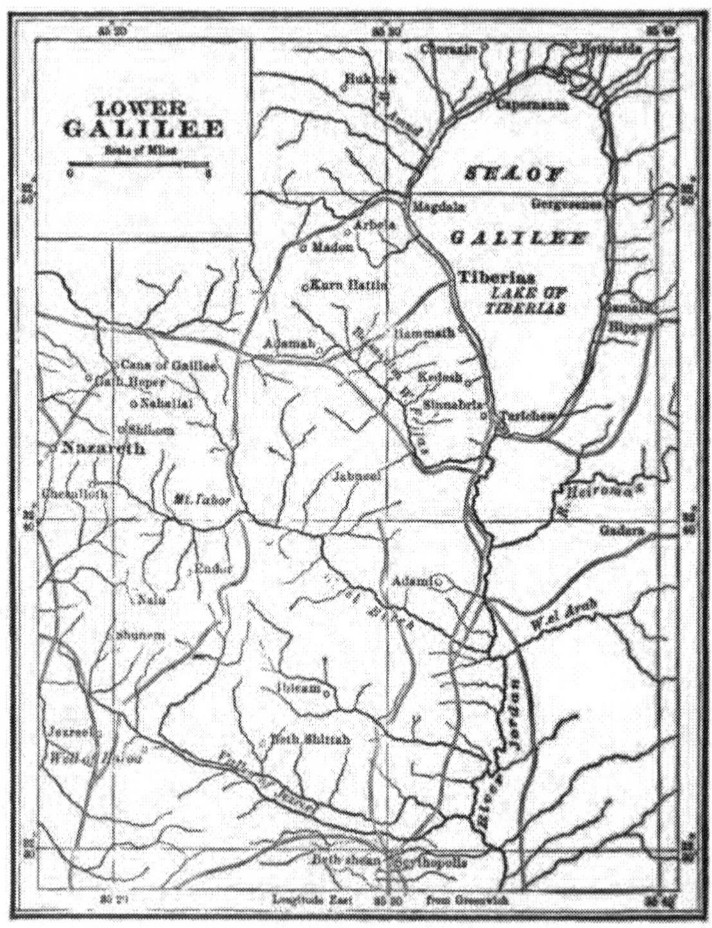

One morning while Jesus was walking on the beach, he met some of his followers. Having now come to their own home, these men had gone back to their old work, as fishermen, and their boats were lying upon the shore.

The men had been fishing in the night before, and they were now washing their nets upon the beach. Jesus spoke to one of his followers, Simon Peter, to push his boat a little way out into the water. He did so, and then Jesus sat down in the boat, while a great crowd stood on the shore, but within reach of his voice. Then from the boat as a pulpit he talked to the people on the shore. What he said at that time was not written down; but it was very much like his teachings as given in the Sermon on the Mount, which may be read in the fifth, sixth, and seventh chapters of the gospel by Matthew. There is no doubt that in his talks in many places to different crowds, Jesus often gave the same teachings over and over again.

After Jesus had ended his speaking to the people, he said to Simon, who with the other fishermen was standing beside him:

"Push out into the deep water, and let down your nets for a catch of fish."

"Master," answered Simon, "we worked all last night and caught not a single fish. However, if you tell us to try again, I will let down the nets."

They did so, and now their nets took in a great shoal of fish, so large a number that the nets began to break. Then they beckoned to their partners in the other boat to come and help them. They came, and helped to pull up the nets and to empty the fish into the boats. So many were the fish that they filled both the boats so full that they began to sink. When Simon Peter saw all this, he was struck with wonder and with fear, for he felt that this had been done by the power of God. He fell upon his knees in the boat to Jesus, saying:

"O Lord, I am full of sin, and am not worthy of all this! Leave me, O Lord!"

But Jesus said to him and to the other three men with him:

"Do not be afraid; come after me; and from this time you shall be fishers of men."

He meant that they were now to leave their nets and their boats, to stay with him; and after learning from him, they were to go out and show men the way out of sin into the Kingdom of God.

As soon, therefore, as they had brought their nets and their fishes to the land, they left them with Zebedee, the father of James and John, and with the hired men.

From that day these four men stayed with Jesus and went with him on all his journeys, listening to his words, until from hearing them often, they learned them and could repeat them to others.

Pool of Hezekiah at Jerusalem

The disciples let down their nets and took in a great shoal of fish, so large a number that the nets began to break.

Jesus in the Church, in the House, and in the Street

CHAPTER 24

THE STORY of the great catch of fish was told abroad, for many saw the boats loaded with the fish brought to the shore, and we may be sure that all who ate a breakfast of those fish spoke of the wonder. Partly as a result of this report, when the Sabbath day came, the church in Capernaum was crowded with people to see and hear this new Rabbi. "Rabbi" was the name that Jews gave to men who taught the law in their churches. Although Jesus had never taken the course of study at Jerusalem which would give him that title, he was generally called "Rabbi" by the people. The people listened with wonder to the words of Jesus, for his teaching was very different from that of the scribes who taught the law. He spoke on great things—the kingdom which God was soon to set up, and how the people were to be made ready for his coming. Then, too, he spoke with power, as Lord of all; and the listeners felt that these were the words of one who had been sent by God.

While Jesus was speaking in the church, the service was stopped by the loud screaming of a furious man who had come in. This man was suffering with a terrible evil, worse than any disease. Into his body had come in some way an evil spirit, a demon. This demon controlled the man and drove him to wild acts and words. The words which were spoken by this man's tongue were not his own, but the words of the wicked spirit within him. The spirit, using the man's voice, shrieked aloud:

From all parts of the city of Capernaum they brought those that were sick, or had evil spirits, and Jesus healed them all.

"Ha, you Jesus of Nazareth, let us alone! What business have you with us? Have you come to destroy us? I know who you are; you are God's Holy One!"

But Jesus at once said to the wicked spirit in the man, "Be still, and come out of him!"

At these words the demon threw the man down upon the floor, as if to kill him; and then went out of the man suddenly, leaving him almost dead. Soon they found that the man, whom everybody had feared before, so fierce had he been, was now perfectly well and quite free from the evil spirit.

Then surprise and wonder came upon all. They talked about it to one another, saying:

"What does all this mean? What new teaching is this? Why, this man speaks to the evil spirits with power, and they obey him and come out."

As the people left the church they told everyone whom they met of this mighty act of Jesus. These men and women told others, and soon the news of Jesus' power went through all the towns and villages in that part of the land.

After the service in the church was over, Jesus went home to dine in the house of Simon and Andrew, and with him went also the two brothers, James and John. In the house they told him that Simon's mother-in-law, the mother of his wife, was very ill, having a high fever. He came, stood by her bed, leaned over her and took her by the hand as if to raise her up. As he touched her, she felt a new power shoot through her body. Instantly the fever left her; she rose up from her bed, perfectly well, and helped to make ready the dinner and serve it.

Jesus stayed in Simon's house that afternoon. When the sun went down and the Sabbath was ended, they found a crowd of people filling the street in front of the house. From all parts of the city they had brought people that were sick, or had evil spirits, like the man whom Jesus had cured in the church. As he came out of the house he laid his hands upon these sick people, one by one; and as soon as he touched them, they rose up well. The evil spirits in some of the men tried to speak to him. But he would not allow them, and gave them command at once to come out of the men in whom they were. They dared not to disobey Jesus, came out and went away.

On that night, while everybody was sleeping, Jesus rose up long before day, while it was still dark, and went out of the city. He found a quiet place, with no houses or people near, and there for hours he prayed to his Father. In the morning he was missed, and Simon Peter, with the others, went out to look for him. They found him and said to him, "Master, come back to the city, for everybody is looking for you!"

But Jesus said, "I was sent not only to your city but to other places also. Let us go out and visit the towns that are near. It was for this purpose that I have been sent by my Father, to preach everywhere the good news of the Kingdom of God."

The Leper and the Palsied Man

CHAPTER 25

FROM THE city of Capernaum Jesus went forth and visited all the villages on the western shore of the Sea of Galilee and on the mountains near by. He took with him his disciples or followers, that they might see his works and listen to his words. Great crowds of people came to hear him during this journey; and everywhere he cured all kinds of sickness and cast out of men evil spirits that were ruling them.

At one place a man came to Jesus who was covered with a dreadful disease called leprosy and was called "a leper." No one ever touched a leper or even came near him, for they feared that a touch might cause the disease. A leper was driven out of the home, to live with other lepers in a camp outside the city. When he saw anyone coming near, he must stand at a distance, must cover his mouth with his garment, not to let his breath reach anybody, and must call out, "Unclean! Unclean!" so that no one might take his disease. Many lepers were in the land when Jesus was preaching; and lepers may still be seen in that country.

This leper who saw Jesus came as near to him as he dared. He knelt down before Jesus, touching his head to the ground, and called out to him:

"Oh, sir, if you choose to do it, you can take away my leprosy, and make my flesh pure and clean."

Jesus was not afraid to touch the leper. He went to him and placed his hand upon him. Then he said:

"I do choose; be clean!"

And at once all this man's leprosy passed way. His

skin lost its waxen, deadly whiteness, his eyes were bright, his deformed hands became perfect and his voice was no longer hollow and cracked. He was no more a leper, but was a man in perfect health.

Jesus said to him, "Do not tell anyone of your cure; but go to the priest in the temple, let him see that you are clean, and make the offering of thanksgiving to God. Let the priest give you a writing to show that you are well, and then go to your own home."

Jesus knew that if this man should tell very many of his cure, there would come such a crowd of people having diseases of all kinds, seeking to be made well, that he could have no time nor chance to preach the gospel, and his great purpose was, not to cure diseases, but to teach men the way to God. It is better to be saved from sin than to be cured of sickness.

But this man was so happy at being made well that he could not be still. Everywhere he went he told people of his wonderful cure, and roused such a desire among the people to see Jesus that Jesus could not go to the cities, for so great were the crowds that he could no longer preach. Everybody was eager to be cured of some illness or to see Jesus cure others. Jesus was driven to seek the open country, where few people lived, and even there the crowds sought him, coming from many places.

After some time, Jesus came again to Capernaum, which was now his home. As soon as the people heard of his return, they gathered in great crowds to see him, to hear him and to be cured of their diseases. He stood on the porch of a house, where every room was full of people, and a company was in front of him, crowding the court of the house to its utmost corner. In this throng were some who were ready to believe in Jesus; but there were also some men who had come from Judea

They broke open the roof and let the man down, wrapped in a blanket and lying upon a mattress, right in front of Jesus.

to see who Jesus was, what he was teaching and what he was doing. These men did not believe in Jesus, but were there to find some fault with him. They belonged to a class called "the Pharisees," who claimed to be better than others, because they carefully kept all the rules of the Jewish law; but in their hearts they were far from good, and they were bitterly opposed to Jesus.

While Jesus was speaking, four men came, carrying on a bed a man who was sick with the palsy, a disease which makes one helpless, unable to use his hands, to walk or to stand alone. They were very eager to bring this man to Jesus to be cured, but on account of the crowd they could not come into the house or even into the yard in front of it. They were bound, however, in some way to get this palsied man to Jesus. They climbed up to the roof of the house and pulled the sick man up. Then they broke open the roof, never minding the dust and litter that fell upon the heads of the people below. When they had made an opening large enough, they let the man down, wrapped in a blanket and lying upon a mattress, right in front of Jesus. All this showed their faith in Jesus. They believed that he could cure the palsied man, and were ready to take any trouble to bring him before the Saviour.

Jesus looked at the man, and said to him:

"My son, be of good cheer: your sins are forgiven!"

Some of these Pharisees, the enemies of Jesus, were sitting near, and as they heard these words they thought in their own minds, though they did not speak it aloud:

'What wicked words are these! This man speaks as though he were God! No man has the right to forgive sins; that belongs to God alone. What wickedness, for this man to pretend to have God's power!"

Jesus knew their thoughts, for he could look into their hearts. He said to them:

The leper knelt down before Jesus and called out to him: "Oh, sir, if you choose you can make my flesh pure and clean."

"Why do you think wicked things in your hearts? Which is the easier to say, 'Your sins are forgiven,' or to say, 'Rise up and walk'? But I will show you that while I am on earth as the Son of Man, God has given me the power to take away sin."

Then he turned to the palsied man lying on the couch, and said with a voice of power:

"I tell you, rise up, take up your bed, and go to your house!"

In an instant a new life came to the palsied man. He stood upon his feet in full strength, rolled up his blanket, took up the mattress upon which he had been lying, placed it upon his shoulder and walked out through the crowd, which opened to make a way for him. Through the streets the man went to his home, praising God for his cure.

By this act of healing Jesus had shown that he was the Son of God, with the right to forgive the sins of men. These Pharisees, the enemies of Jesus, could find nothing to say, but in their hearts they hated him more than before, for they saw that the people believed on Jesus. Wonder filled the minds of those who saw this cure; they praised the God of Israel and said to each other, "We have seen strange things today!"

Jesus looked at Levi-Matthew and said to him: "Come, follow me!" At once Matthew rose and went after Jesus.

How the Tax-Collector Became a Disciple

CHAPTER 26

SO GREAT were the crowds gathering from all parts of the land to see and hear Jesus, that no place could be found in the city of Capernaum large enough to hold the multitudes. The church was far too small; and there were no open places in the city where so great a company could meet. So every day Jesus went out of the city to the seaside, sometimes sitting in Peter's boat, sometimes upon the shore, while all the people stood upon the grass-covered hillside, with the blue sky above them and the blue lake before them, while Jesus spoke about the Kingdom of God and showed how every man could enter into the kingdom by turning from his sins and doing God's will.

Among these crowds of people Jesus noticed one man standing, who listened closely to every word. This man was named Levi-Matthew. He was an officer of the government, called "a publican"; and it was his work to gather the taxes which the Roman rulers had laid upon the people. Everybody was called upon to pay money to the Romans, who were the rulers of the land. The people hated the Romans, who held the land under their power, and hated also these tax-gatherers, who were often selfish and unjust men, making the people pay more than they should, robbing the poor and taking much of the money for themselves instead of paying it to the Roman treasury. Because many of these tax-gatherers or publicans were cruel and selfish, all of them were looked upon as wicked. They were called "publicans and sinners," and the people despised them.

One day Jesus was passing the office where Levi-Matthew sat at his table receiving the tax-money from the people. Jesus looked at the publican and said to him, "Come, follow me!" At once Levi-Matthew rose up, left his clerks and helpers to care for the money on the table, and went after Jesus. From that hour he was no longer a tax-collector; he became a disciple of Jesus, and followed him wherever he went, listening to his words and keeping them in his mind and memory. Many years afterward, when Jesus was no longer among men, Matthew wrote a book telling of what Jesus said and did. That book is the Gospel according to Matthew, the first book in the New Testament; and it tells what Matthew remembered of the teachings and acts of the Lord Jesus. So it was well for the people who lived after the time of Jesus, and for all the people who through the ages since have read that gospel, and for the millions all over the world who now read it, that Matthew the tax-gatherer became a disciple of Jesus. But for this man's prompt obedience to Christ's call on that day, that precious book would never have been written.

Matthew wished his fellow-publicans to meet Jesus and hear his words. He gave a supper at his house to Jesus, and invited all the publicans or tax-gatherers in that part of the country to come. Many of them came, and with their friends sat down to the supper with Jesus. The Pharisees, who were enemies of Jesus, looked scornfully at Jesus sitting at the table with all the tax-gatherers around him. They said to the disciples of Jesus:

"Why does your Teacher eat with those publicans and sinners?"

They told Jesus of these words, and he answered:

"Those who are well and strong have no need of a

doctor, but only those who are sick. I did not come to call those who think themselves good, but those who know that they are sinful and want to be saved. But let those Pharisees learn the meaning of the text where God says, 'I prefer those who show kindness and mercy, to those who offer sacrifices upon the altar.' "

This pointed to the Pharisees themselves, for while they were careful about fasting and saying their prayers and making their offerings in the Temple, they were often unjust and hard toward the poor.

Mosque El Aksa, near the ancient Temple

Jesus saw lying there upon a mat a man who had been helpless and unable to walk for almost forty years. He said to him: "Would you like to be made well?"

The Cripple at the Bath

CHAPTER 27

THE TIME came for another feast at Jerusalem, and as on the year before, Jesus went to attend it. We do not know whether his disciples were with him on this visit, for in the story as given by John in his gospel, they are not mentioned.

On one Sabbath day, while Jesus was in the city, he walked past a public bath not far from the Temple. It was a large pool or cistern, where several could bathe at once; and beside it were five porches, forming an arched-over platform. These porches, when Jesus came to the pool, were crowded with people, all suffering with disease. Some were blind, some were lame and some had legs or arms all withered and palsied.

At certain times the water in this bath used to bubble and rise up; then it would go down again and be quiet. The people believed that this bubbling up of the water was caused by an angel (whom no one could see) going down and stirring up the pool. They believed, too, that at such times when the water bubbled up, any person who was ill would be cured by taking a bath in the pool. We know that there are many springs whose water will cure diseases, and this pool may have been one of these health-giving springs.

Jesus saw lying there upon a mat beside the bath one man who had been helpless, unable to walk for almost forty years. Jesus who knew all things, knew that this man had been ill for a long time. He said to him:

"Would you like to be made well?"

This man had never seen Jesus before and did not know who he was.

"Sir," he answered, "there is nobody to put me in the bath when the water rises; but while I am trying to

Pool of Bethesda from above

crawl down and get into the water, somebody who can walk steps in ahead of me."

Jesus said:

"Rise, take up your mat, and walk!"

The crippled man had never heard words like these; but as soon as thev were spoken. he felt a new power shooting through his body. He stood up for the first time in thirty-eight years, picked up his piece of matting, rolled it up and put it upon his shoulder. Then he started to walk toward his house, carrying his burden.

You remember that it was on the Sabbath day that this took place. The Jews were exceedingly careful in keeping the Sabbath. God had said to their fathers many years before, "Remember the Sabbath day to keep it holy." But the Jews had added to this commandment many useless rules. They could not light a fire on that day, for that would be working; they could not hold a pen, for that would be carrying a load. These little rules had not been given by God, but had been made by the scribes or teachers of the law.

Some people saw this man carrying his roll of matting through the street. They said to him:

"Stop! don't you know this is the Sabbath day? You have no right to be carrying your bed."

The man did not lay down his load. He said, "A man saw me helpless by the pool, for I was nearly forty years a cripple. This man made me well; and he it was who said to me, 'Take up your mat and walk.' "

"Who was this man," said the Jews, "who told you to carry your bed on the Sabbath day?"

The man who had been cured did not know who it was that had cured him, for many were standing near, and after healing the man Jesus had walked away without being noticed. Soon after, the man went up to the Temple to give thanks to God for his cure, and there he met his healer and learned for the first time his name. Jesus said to him at that time:

"You are now free from the disease which for so many years has made you helpless. Do not sin any more against God, or something worse will come to you."

The man went away and told the Jews that it was

Jesus who had cured him. The leaders among the Jews, the priests, the scribes and the Pharisees, were very angry at Jesus, because he had made this man well on the Sabbath and because he had told the man to carry his mat on that day. The rulers tried to stir up the people against Jesus, saying that he was a Sabbath-breaker, and nobody should listen to his words.

But Jesus said to them, "My Father works on all days doing good to men; and I do only what he does."

He meant to show them that God sends his sunshine and his rain every day in the week, causing the grass and the grain and the flowers to grow as much on the Sabbath as on other days; and that it was right for him and for every man to do good works, helping men and curing their sickness, on the Sabbath day.

But his words only made the Jews all the more angry, because he had spoken of God as his Father, making himself (they said) equal with God. They would have killed him if they could, so great was their hate against him.

Jesus did not stay long in Jerusalem at this visit. Soon after the feast he went again to his home at Capernaum.

The Lord of the Sabbath

CHAPTER 28

THE QUESTION whether Jesus was a Sabbath-breaker or not, arose again soon after he came back to Galilee. On a Sabbath day Jesus was walking with his disciples through the fields of grain. Some of the disciples were hungry, and as they walked picked the heads of the wheat, rubbed them in their hands, blew away the chaff and ate the kernels of grain. The law of the Israelites allowed anyone walking by a field of grain to help himself to all that he wished to eat, but forbade him to take any to his home.

But to the Pharisees, who were very exact in their rules of keeping the Sabbath, to pluck the grain was the same as reaping it with a sickle, to carry it in the hand was the same as bearing a load, and to rub it in the hands was the same as thrashing; and to do these on the seventh day of the week was breaking the Sabbath. These were rules, not given by God, but made by the scribes; and Jesus had already taught his disciples to pay no attention to them.

The Pharisees were constantly watching Jesus and his followers, to catch them, if possible, in doing or saying something that might be thought wrong. They said to Jesus:

"Do you see that your disciples are doing what is forbidden on the Sabbath day; picking the ears of grain, carrying handfuls of them and rubbing them in their hands?"

"Have you never read," answered Jesus, "what David did when he was flying from King Saul; how he went into the house of God and took away the holy bread, laid on the table as an offering to God, which was to be eaten by the priests only; ate it himself and gave it to the men that were with him? And do you not know that the priests in the Temple do all kinds of work, killing animals for the offering, placing wood on the altar and many other things; yet they do right, for these things are necessary, and whatever is needful may be done on God's holy day. The Sabbath was made for

Jesus and His Disciples in the field of grain

the good of man and not man for the Sabbath. I tell you that One greater than the Temple is here, for the Son of Man is Lord of the Sabbath."

On another Sabbath day Jesus went into the church to worship God and to preach the word. A man was there whose hand was withered and helpless. The Pharisees watched Jesus to see if he would cure this man on the Sabbath. They hoped he would cure him, not because they cared for the poor, crippled man, but because they were eager to find something to say against Jesus.

Jesus spoke to the man with the withered hand, "Stand up and come forward." The man stood up before them all; and then Jesus, looking straight at his enemies, said:

The man with the withered hand healed by Jesus in the church

"Is it against the law on the Sabbath day to do good or to do harm; to save a life, or to try to kill a man, as you are trying to do? If one of you men owns a single sheep, and he should happen on the Sabbath day to find it fallen into a pit, would he not take hold of it and lift it out? And how much more is a man worth than a sheep? Thus it is right to do a kind and helpful act on the Sabbath."

He looked around sternly at his enemies, being sad and grieved because their hearts were so hard. They did not have a word to say; and after waiting a moment he turned to the man with the withered hand and said:

"Stretch out your hand!"

He reached out his arm, and the withered hand was at once made well and strong, as sound as the other.

Jesus went away, but the Pharisees were filled with anger against him. They talked together, seeking some way to kill Jesus; and they called upon the friends of King Herod, the ruler of Galilee, to see if they could not persuade the king to order that Jesus should be put to death.

But Jesus went on teaching and curing those that were sick, paying no attention to the plans of his enemies. He told those whom he cured, not to go out and speak to others about him, but to stay quietly at home; for the crowds coming to hear him were already great, and he did not wish them to be any greater. So many people came together from all parts of the land, and even from places outside the land of Israel, from the country of Tyre and Sidon on the north and from Edom or Idumea on the south. They thronged around Jesus, and pressed upon him; so that he spoke to his disciples to have a little boat at hand, to wait upon him, and take him out into the lake for quiet and rest.

Jesus on the Mountain

CHAPTER 29

ABOUT TWELVE miles southwest from Capernaum and six miles west of the Sea of Galilee stands a mountain which can be seen many miles away. It is now called "Kurn Hattin," which means, "The double horns of Hattin." The name is given because the mountain has two tops, one at each end, and a wide hollow between them, its form making it look somewhat like a saddle or a camel with two humps. Near this mountain, roads ran to almost every part of the land of Israel, so that from every place it could be reached.

The word went throughout the land that Jesus was coming to this mountain; and a great multitude of people gathered in the hollow place between its two crowns, all waiting to see Jesus. He came to the mountain and went up alone to one of its hill-tops. All night Jesus was there in prayer with his heavenly Father; for he had an important work to do, and before any great work Jesus prayed to God. In the morning he called forth out of the vast company of people before him twelve men, who were to be with him all the time, go with him wherever he should go, listen to his teachings, and learn them by heart, and be ready to preach his words when he should send them out. These twelve men Jesus afterward called "apostles," which means "men sent out"; but they were generally named "the twelve." They are also spoken of as "the disciples," although the word "disciples" is also used of all the followers of Jesus.

Most of the twelve men had been called before, and had been for some time with Jesus. Others were new men whom Jesus called now for the first time. Their names are arranged in pairs, two of them together. They were Simon Peter and Andrew his brother; James and John, the sons of Zebedee; Philip and his friend Bartholomew, also called Nathanael; Thomas and Matthew, who had been the tax-gatherer; James the son of Alphaeus; another Simon, who was called "the Zealot," and Judas Iscariot, the one who afterward became the traitor and sold his Lord to his enemies. About most of these men we know very little, but some of them in later years did a great work for the church of Christ. Simon Peter was always a leader among the Twelve, being a man of quick mind and ready words; and John long after that time wrote "The Gospel according to John," one of the most wonderful books in the world.

Kurn Hattin, where Jesus preached the Sermon on the Mount

In the sight of all the people Jesus called these men to stand by his side. Then he came down from the mountain-top to the hollow place between the two sum-

In the morning he called forth out of the vast company of people before him twelve men.

mits. He sat down, with his twelve chosen men around him, and beyond this a great crowd of people. To the Twelve and to the listening multitude Jesus preached that great sermon which is called "The Sermon on the Mount." Matthew wrote it down, and you can read it in his gospel, the first book of the New Testament, in the fifth, sixth and seventh chapters. How fortunate it was that Jesus called the tax-gatherer to be one of his disciples, a man who could remember and write this great sermon for all the world to read! We give here only a few parts from this Sermon on the Mount. Jesus began with words of comfort to his followers:

"Blessed are the poor in spirit; for theirs is the kingdom of heaven. Blessed are they that mourn; for they shall be comforted. Blessed are the meek; for they shall inherit the earth. Blessed are they that hunger and thirst after righteousness; for they shall be filled. Blessed are the merciful; for they shall obtain mercy. Blessed are the pure in heart; for they shall see God. Blessed are the peacemakers; for they shall be called sons of God. Blessed are they that have been persecuted for righteousness' sake; for theirs is the kingdom of heaven."

Then he spoke to his disciples of what they were to be among men:

"You are the salt of the earth; but if the salt have lost its savor, wherewith shall it be salted? It is thenceforth good for nothing, but to be cast out and trodden under foot of men."

He went on, perhaps pointing to a town not far away, built on the top of a hill and seen everywhere around:

"You are the light of the world. A city set on a hill cannot be hid. Neither do men light a lamp, and put it under a bushel, but on the stand; and it giveth light to all the house. Even so let your light shine before men, that they may see your good works and give glory to your Father who is in heaven."

He told his disciples how they should feel and act toward those who had done wrong to them:

"Ye have heard that it was said, 'You shall love your neighbor, and hate your enemy.' But I say to you, love your enemies, and pray for those who do you wrong, that you may be sons of your Father in heaven: for he makes his sun to rise on the bad as well as the good, and sends rain alike on the just and on the unjust. For if you love only those who love you, what reward do you have? Why, the tax-gatherers whom you despise do as much. And if you speak only to your friends, wherein are you better than others? For even the Gentiles do the same. You should be perfect, as your heavenly Father is perfect."

He spoke also of the aims which men should seek in their lives:

"Lay not up for yourselves treasures upon the earth, where moth and rust destroy, and where thieves break through and steal; but lay up for yourselves treasures in heaven, where neither moth nor rust destroy, and where thieves do not break through nor steal; for where your treasure is, there will your heart be also.

"No man can serve two masters: for either he will hate the one and love the other; or else he will hold to one and despise the other. You cannot serve God and Mammon, who is the god worshipped by this world. Therefore I say to you, do not be anxious for your life, what ye shall eat or what ye shall drink; nor for your body, what you shall put on. Surely, life means more than food, surely the body means more than clothes! Look at the birds flying above you; they do not sow, nor reap, nor gather into barns; and your heavenly Father feeds them. Are you not worth more than the birds?

"And why should you be anxious about your clothing? Look how the lilies of the field grow: they neither toil nor spin, and yet Solomon in all his glory was never robed like one of these! Now, if God so clothes the grass of the fields, which blooms today, and tomorrow is thrown into the fire, will he not much more clothe you, O you who trust God so little?"

"Therefore do not be anxious, saying, 'What shall we have to eat?' or 'what shall we have to drink?' or 'how can we get clothes to wear?' Your heavenly Father knows that you need all these things. Seek the kingdom of God, and do right according to his will: then all these things will be yours. Do not be anxious about tomorrow, for tomorrow will be anxious for itself. Each day's own trouble is enough to be anxious over."

Here is what Jesus said as the ending of his sermon:

"Everyone who hears these words of mine, and acts upon them, is like a wise man, who built his house upon rock. The rain fell, the floods rose, the winds blew and beat upon that house, but it did not fall, for it was founded upon rock.

"And every one that hears these words of mine, and does not act upon them, will be like a foolish man, who built his house on sand. The rain fell, the floods rose, the winds blew, and beat upon that house, and it fell, and great was its fall."

When Jesus had finished these words, the crowds were filled with wonder at his way of teaching. He spoke with the authority of a Master, unlike their own scribes. Most of the scribes when they were teaching would speak in the name of earlier teachers, and say, "Rabbi Jonathan said this," or "Rabbi Hillel said that." But Jesus spoke in his own name, saying, "I say this to you."

Jesus receives the message from the army captain: "Lord, do not trouble yourself to come to my house, for I am not worthy to have one so great under my roof; but only speak a word where you are, and my servant shall be healed."

The Good Army Captain

CHAPTER 30

AT CAPERNAUM there was an officer of the Roman army, a captain, having under him a company of one hundred men. This man was not of the Jewish people, but a Gentile, which was the name that the Jews gave to all people outside of their own race. All the world, except themselves, the Jews called Gentiles.

This army captain was a good man, and he was very friendly to the Jews, because through them he had heard of the true God, and had learned to worship him. Out of his love for the Jews he had built for them with his own money a church, and had given it to them. This may have been the very church in which Jesus taught on the Sabbath days.

The army captain had a young servant, a boy whom he loved greatly; and this boy was very sick with the palsy and near to death. The army captain had heard that Jesus could cure those who were sick; and he asked the chief men of the church, who were called its "elders," to go to Jesus and ask him to come to the captain's house, that he might lay his hands on the boy and make him well. The elders spoke to Jesus soon after he came again to Capernaum, after preaching on the mountain. They asked him to go with them to the captain's house and cure his servant, and they added:

"He is a worthy man, and it is fitting that you should help him, for though a Gentile, he loves our people, and he has built for us our church."

Then Jesus said, "I will go and cure him."

But while Jesus was on his way to the captain's

house, and with him the elders and a company of people, who hoped to see another wonderful cure, he was met by some friends of the captain, who brought this message:

"Lord, do not take the trouble to come to my house: for I am not worthy to have one so great as you are under my roof; and I sent to you, because I am not worthy to speak to you myself. But speak only a word where you are, and my servant shall be made well. For although I am myself a man under authority and rule, I have soldiers under me to carry out my will. I say to one man 'Go,' and he goes; I say to another man 'Come,' and he comes. I tell my servant, 'Do this,' and he does it. You, too, have power to command and be obeyed. Only speak the word and my servant shall be cured."

When Jesus heard this he wondered at this man's faith. He turned to the crowd that followed and said:

"In truth I say to you all, I have not found such faith as this in all Israel. And I tell you further, that many like this man, who are not Israelites, shall come from places in the east and the west, and shall sit down with Abraham, and Isaac, and Jacob in the kingdom of God. But many of those who are the children of Israel, because they have not believed, shall never enter into God's kingdom, but shall be thrust forth into the darkness outside."

And Jesus said to those who came from the captain's house:

"Go back and say to this man in my name, 'As you have believed, even so shall it be done to you.' "

They went to the captain's house, and found his servant, who had been at the point of death, now free from his palsy and brought back to perfect health.

How Jesus Stopped a Funeral

CHAPTER 31

JESUS WENT on a journey for preaching through the southern parts of Galilee, as before he had visited the villages among the mountains near the sea. He walked out of Capernaum with the twelve disciples and a crowd of followers which grew larger as he went on. They passed by Mount Tabor, and just before sunset they came to a small city at the foot of another mountain, the Hill Moreh. This place was named Nain. Outside the gate Jesus and his followers paused to allow a funeral procession to pass by. In front were women wailing aloud, flinging their arms up and down and chanting a song about the young man who had died. The body was wrapped in long strips of linen, and was lying upon a couch, carried by bearers. After it walked an old woman, the young man's mother, who was a widow, burying her only son; and with her were many of the people in the city, showing their sorrow for the widow at the loss of her son.

When Jesus saw this weeping mother, he felt a great pity for her and said to her, "Do not weep." He stepped forward and touched the couch on which the body was lying. The men who were carrying it stood still with wonder at the coming of this stranger, whose look showed power. Standing beside the dead young man, he said:

"Young man, I say unto you, Rise up!

Instantly the young man sat up and began to speak. Jesus took him by the hand and gave him to his mother. She received him into her arms, and found his cold body now warm with life, the dull eyes now bright. Her son that had died that day was alive once more.

The people who were looking on now felt that indeed a marvelous work had been done. Many of them had seen Jesus before, and knew him; and even those who had

Ruins of Nain, near which Jesus restored to life the widow's son

not seen him had heard of him, and said, "This must be that great teacher from Nazareth!" Many fell on their faces before him; and some said, "A great prophet has come among us," and others said, "Surely God has visited his people!"

The news that Jesus had raised a dead man to life

spread through all the land and even to the countries around. More and more people after this sought to see Jesus and to hear his words.

While Jesus was slowly journeying through southern Galilee, visiting the towns, teaching the people and curing the sick, two men came asking to see him. These men were followers of John the Baptist, who was still in the prison where Herod had sent him. In his prison John heard of the works that Jesus was doing and of the teaching that Jesus was giving. It may be that John was expecting Jesus to set up his kingdom at once, instead of merely going up and down the land as a teacher. Perhaps also, John, shut up in prison, had grown discouraged and doubtful. In other days he had said to all the people that Jesus was the Coming King, so high above him that he was not worthy to tie his shoestrings. But now these two men had brought from John this question to Jesus:

"John the Baptist has sent us to you to ask—are you the Coming One, the promised King of Israel? Or are we to look for another?"

Jesus did not at once answer this question. He acted for a time as though it had not been asked, and left these two men standing, while he turned to the people about him.

At the Saviour's feet were many suffering people—the sick brought upon couches by their friends, the blind crying for sight, the deaf and dumb holding out their hands toward him, the lepers with all their horrible sores, the wild people in whom were evil spirits. Jesus attended to the needs of all these sufferers. He laid his hands upon the sick, and they rose up well; he touched the eyes of the blind and the ears of the deaf, and gave them their sight and hearing; he gave each leper a new, pure, perfect body; and he cast out the evil spirits by his words. Then he went on and made his usual talk

Standing beside the dead young man, Jesus said: "Young man, I say unto you, rise up!" Instantly he sat up and began to speak.

to the crowds about the Kingdom of God, and how any man might come into it.

When at last his morning's work of healing and teaching was over, he turned to these two message-bearers from John the Baptist, and said to them:

"Go back and tell John in his prison what you have seen and heard. Here are men once blind who now can see; lame men who now can walk; leprous men who have been made clean; deaf men made to hear; men having in them evil spirits, who are now free from their power. You have heard too of dead men raised to life; and you have listened while the gospel has been preached to the poor. You go and tell John all these things that you have seen and heard. Then let John think about these things and judge whether I am not the One whom he promised should come."

That was a far better way to bring John the Baptist back to believing fully in Jesus as the promised King of Israel and the Saviour of the world than to send the answer back, "Go and tell John that I am the Saviour." For John's faith would be the stronger, because he would now have the proofs that Jesus was the promised Lord.

After these messengers from John the Baptist had left, Jesus began to talk to the people about John. Some may have thought that in sending this question to Jesus, John had showed weakness and a change of his mind. Jesus said to the people:

"What was it that you went out to the desert to see? Was it a reed swayed to and fro by the wind? No, this man John was no weak, wind-shaken reed. Did you go out to look at a man clothed in the robes of a prince, and eating delicate food? No, that skin-clad man in the desert was no such princely person. To see such people you go to the palaces of kings. Come, what *did* you go out to see? Was it a prophet, a man sent from God?

Yes, I tell you, John the Baptist was indeed a prophet, and more than a prophet. He was the King's messenger, to prepare the way for the King himself. Of a truth, I tell you all that no greater man was ever born into this world than John the Baptist. And yet he that is least in the Kingdom of God is higher even than John."

Jesus meant that those who could come into the Kingdom of God, as those who heard the gospel might come, were higher than even the greatest of those who prepare the way for the Kingdom.

The Jaffa Gate of Jerusalem

The Sinful Woman Forgiven

CHAPTER 32

WHILE JESUS was passing through southern Galilee, in one place a Pharisee named Simon invited him to his house for dinner. The Pharisees, you remember, were people who were supposed to be very religious, because they carefully followed all the rules about praying at regular hours every day, whether on the street or in their homes; fasting, or not taking food, on certain days; going to church three times every week, and doing many things to be seen by others, while they were often sharp and hard in their dealings with men. They seemed to be good, but often were not as good as they seemed. Everywhere the Pharisees were at heart enemies of Jesus. They watched him, but in no friendly spirit.

This Pharisee, Simon, wished to know Jesus and to talk with him, although he did not believe in him. But he felt that Jesus, being only a common carpenter who had turned Rabbi, or teacher, was below himself in rank; and he did not treat him with respect. When a great man came to the house, the servants took off his sandals and washed his feet; they dressed his hair and poured fragrant oil upon his head. None of these things had Simon done to Jesus. He merely invited him to his house, and without even giving him water to wash his feet, all dusty with walking, he pointed him to his place at the table.

In that land people did not sit down upon chairs at dinner. Around the table were placed couches or lounges, and on these the guests reclined, half lying and half sitting, their heads toward the table and their feet away from it. They could reach the table and help themselves to food or drink. Very little meat was eaten; and before being placed upon the table, it was always cut into small pieces, so that the guests needed no knives or forks. After each course of the meal, a servant passed around a bowl of water and a towel, and washed the hands of the guests.

While Jesus, and perhaps his disciples with him, were at the table during the dinner, people were coming in and going out freely. Soon a woman came in, looked around, saw Jesus, and went toward the couch whereon he was lying. In her hand was a jar of fragrant oil. She broke the jar, not waiting to take out the stopple, and poured the oil upon his feet. She wiped his feet with her long flowing hair; she wept over them, dropping her many tears upon his feet; and she kissed them over and over again.

All the people of that place knew who this woman was, and knew the life that she had lived. She had not been a good woman, but had been wicked, and was despised by all respectable people. Simon the Pharisee wondered that Jesus should allow such a woman to touch him. He thought within himself, though he did not say it aloud:

"This man cannot be a prophet, as they say he is; for if he were a prophet he would know what a vile creature this woman is, and he would not permit her hands to touch even his feet."

Jesus read the thoughts of the Pharisee, for he could look down into his mind. He said, "Simon, I have something to say to you."

"Well, Teacher," answered Simon, "say it."

Then Jesus said, "There was a lender of money, to whom two persons owed a debt. One owed him five

She poured fragrant oil upon his feet and wiped them with her long flowing hair. And Jesus said to Simon: "As many as her sins have been, they are forgiven, for her love is great."

hundred pieces of silver and the other owed him fifty. Neither of these two men could pay his debt; and so the money lender let them both go free. Tell me now, Simon, which of those two men will love this man the most?"

"I suppose," answered Simon, "the man who had the most forgiven."

"You are right," said Jesus. Then he turned toward the woman, and went on, still speaking to Simon. "Do you see this woman? When I came into your house, you never even gave me water for my feet; but see, she has wet my feet with her tears, and wiped them dry with her hair. You never gave me a kiss of welcome; but this woman ever since she came in has been pressing kisses upon my feet. You never anointed my head with oil; but she has poured perfume over my feet. Therefore I tell you, Simon, that many as her sins have been, they are forgiven, for her love is great; while he to whom little is forgiven loves only a little."

Then he spoke to the woman, "Your sins are forgiven."

Those at the table began to whisper to one another, "Who is this that claims the right to forgive sins?"

But he said to the woman, "Your faith has saved you; go in peace."

After this he went on visiting the villages and telling the people the good news of the Kingdom of God. With him were his twelve chosen disciples. Besides these men were some women whom Jesus had cured of different diseases. One was Mary Magdalene, from whom Jesus had cast out no less than seven evil spirits. Another was Joanna, the wife of a nobleman named Chuza, who was a high officer in the court of King Herod Antipas, the ruler of Galilee. Another was named Susanna; and with these were a number of other women. Some of these were rich, and gave freely of their money to help Jesus.

Jesus and His Enemies

CHAPTER 33

AFTER HIS journey through southern Galilee, which was the second of his preaching journeys in the land, Jesus came again to Capernaum. With him came a great multitude of people who had listened to him and longed to hear more of his words. For every one who met Jesus was drawn to him in love and desired to be with him. Nearly all who heard him loved him, but not all. Both the scribes, who were the teachers of the people in the law of Moses, and the Pharisees, who pretended to a religion which was false and not real, hated Jesus more and more and spoke evil of him to the people. They declared that a wicked spirit was in him, and that his power to work wonders came from Satan, the evil one.

One day there was brought to Jesus a man in whom was an evil spirit; and the spirit had taken away both his sight and his hearing, so that he could neither see, nor hear, nor speak. Jesus spoke to the evil spirit in the man, saying:

"Come out of this man, O wicked spirit, and never enter into him again!"

The evil spirit left the man's body, and for a moment he lay on the ground as though he were dead. But soon he rose up, entirely well and able to see, to hear and to speak. All those who saw this cure were filled with wonder, and many said, "Is not this the Son of David, whom the prophets promised should come and be our King?"

But when the Pharisees and scribes heard of this

wonder, they said, "This fellow casts out the evil spirits because the chief of all the evil spirits is in him and gives him this power."

Jesus knew their thoughts, and he said:

"Any kingdom that is divided into two sides that are fighting each other will soon fall in pieces; and any family where people are quarreling will soon come to naught. If Satan, the evil one, is casting out evil spirits, then Satan's kingdom will soon fall, for it is divided against itself. But if by the power of God I cast out the bad spirits from men, then you may be sure that God is among you."

But this report that Jesus was possessed by evil spirits went abroad among the people, and some believed it. It came to the brothers of Jesus, who at that time did not fully believe in him; and it came to Mary his mother, filling her with alarm. She feared that her Son, working without any rest, and bearing such heavy loads of care, had lost his mind. Some said that the family of Jesus should take him home and not allow him to disturb the people, for they said, "He is beside himself!"

Mary and her sons came to the house where Jesus was talking to the people and curing the sick. So great was the crowd around the door that they could not get into the house, and they sent word inside that the mother of Jesus and his brothers were out in the street and wished to speak with him. They told Jesus:

"Your mother and your brothers are outside and they wish to speak with you."

But he answered the man who told him, "Who is my mother, and who are my brothers?"

He turned to his disciples, stretched out his hands, and said:

"Here are my mother and my brothers! Whoever

will do the will of my Father in heaven, that one is my brother, and my sister and my mother!"

Jesus meant by this that dear as his mother was to him, those who were ready to follow his teachings were dearer still.

Some of the scribes and Pharisees spoke to Jesus, saying:

"Teacher, show us some sign that you have come from God."

They wished him to work some miracle, some wonder in their sight. But Jesus never would do any of his great works merely to be seen. He cured the sick and cast out evil spirits out of pity for people in trouble, but not as a show of his power. He said to these people:

"It is a wicked and unfaithful time when people seek for a sign. I will give you no sign now, but after a time you shall see a sign, though you will not believe it. It will be the sign of the prophet Jonah. For as Jonah was three days inside the great fish, so I the Son of Man will be three days under the ground, and like Jonah will come forth living.

"The people of Nineveh, to whom Jonah preached, will rise up in the day when God shall judge the world, and they shall show that they were better than the people of this time, for when Jonah preached to them, they turned from their sins and sought God. And One greater than Jonah is here, yet they will not listen to him!

"The Queen of Sheba will rise up in the day of judgment with the people of this time, and will prove them to be unfaithful. For she came from the ends of the earth to hear the wise words of Solomon; and one greater than Solomon is here, yet you will not listen to him."

The Story-teller by the Sea

CHAPTER 34

SOON AFTER his journey through southern Galilee, Jesus began to teach in a new form, that of telling stories to the people. Everybody likes to listen to a story, and sometimes a story will go to the heart when the plain truth will fail. Story-tellers have always been very abundant in the East, where Jesus lived. Even today may be found everywhere men who go from place to place telling stories, and the people flock around them and listen to their stories from morning until night.

But the stories that Jesus told were very different from those of the Eastern story-tellers. His stories were told to teach some great truth, and on that account were called "parables." A parable is a story which is true to life—that is, a story which might be true, not a fairy story—and which also has in it some teaching of the truth.

One day Jesus went out of the city of Capernaum and stood on the beach by the Sea of Galilee. A great crowd of people gathered around him, for all the opposition of the scribes and Pharisees could not keep the common people away from Jesus. The throng was so great, crowding around Jesus, that as before he stepped into a boat and told his disciples to push it out a little from the shore. Then he sat down in the boat, fronting the great multitude that filled the sloping beach. He said to the people:

"Listen! Once a sower went out to sow his seed. And as he was scattering the seed, some of it fell on the path, where the ground had been trodden hard. The

"Once a sower went out to sow his seed. Some seed fell on stony ground and some fell among briers and bushes."

seed lay there on the path until the birds lighted upon it and picked up all the kernels, so that none of them grew.

"Some of the seed fell on places where there was a thin covering of earth over stones. There the kernels grew up quickly, just because the soil was thin. But when the hot weather came, the sun scorched the tender plants, and they all withered away, because they had no moisture and no root in deep earth.

"Some other of the seeds fell among briers and bushes, and there was no room for the grain to grow up. It lived, but it did not bring forth heads of grain, because it was crowded and choked by thorn bushes all around it.

"But there were some other of the seeds that fell into ground that was soft and rich and good. There they grew up and brought forth fruit abundantly. Some kernels gave thirty times as many as were sown, some sixty times and some a hundred times."

Jesus did not tell the people what the teaching of the parable was. He only said, "Whoever has ears, let him hear what I have spoken." He meant that they should not only listen but think and find out for themselves the meaning.

When Jesus was alone with his disciples, they said to him:

"Why do you speak to the people in parables? What do you mean to teach in this story about the man sowing seed?"

Jesus said to them:

"To you who have followed me it is given to know the deep things of the Kingdom of God, because you seek to find them out. But to many these truths are spoken in parables, for they hear the story, but do not try to find out what it means. They have eyes, but they do not see, and ears, but they do not hear. For they do not wish to understand with the heart and turn to God to have their sins forgiven. But blessed are your eyes, for they see, and your ears, for they hear. Listen now to the meaning of the parable of the sower.

"The sower is the one who speaks the word of God, and the seed is the word which he speaks.

"The seed on the roadside, the trodden path, means those who hear, but do not take the truth into their hearts. Then the Evil Spirit comes and, like the birds, snatches away the truth, so that they forget it.

"The seeds on the rocky soil are those who hear the word and seem to take it gladly into their hearts; but they have no root in themselves: just as soon as they meet with any discouragement or trouble, or find enemies to the truth, they are turned away and their goodness does not last.

"That which is sown among the thorns and briers are those who listen to the word, but the worries of life, and the desire for money, and the pleasures of the world, crowd the word in their hearts, and the gospel does them but little good.

"But the seed sown on the good ground are those who listen to the gospel and understand it; who take the word into honest and good hearts and keep it and bring forth fruit in their lives."

More Stories Told by the Sea

CHAPTER 35

HERE IS another parable story that Jesus told to the people as he sat in the boat and the people stood on the shore. This is the parable of "The Wheat and the Weeds."

"There was a man who sowed good wheat in his field; but while people were asleep, an enemy came and scattered the seed of weeds over all the ground. Then the enemy went away, leaving his seed to grow up. When the sprouts of grain began to form into heads of wheat, the men saw that everywhere in the field the weeds were among them, for weeds always grow faster than good seed.

"So the servants of the farmer came to him and said:

"'Did you not, sir, sow good seed in your field? How comes it that it is full of weeds?'

"He said to them, 'Some enemy of mine has done this.'

"'Shall we go,' said the servants, 'and pull up the weeds that are growing with the wheat?'

"'No,' answered the farmer, 'for while you are pulling the weeds, you will root up the wheat with them. Let them both grow together until the harvest; and in the time of the harvest, I will say to the reapers, "When you have cut down all the crop, then take out the weeds and put them into bundles to be burned; but gather the wheat into my barn."'"

Jesus gave to the people another parable about "The Growing Grain." He said, "The kingdom of God is as if a man should throw seed upon the ground.

[illegible] seed will [illegible] bears fruit [illegible] grain, and [illegible] heads of grain [illegible] reaps, because the [illegible]

[illegible] Seed." "The

[illegible]

[illegible] is like a grain of mustard seed which a man [illegible] sowed in his field. This is the smallest of all seeds; but it grows up to become a [illegible] like a tree, putting out great branches, and the birds light upon them and rest under their shadow."

He gave one more parable, "The Leaven, or Yeast." He said, "The kingdom of God is like the leaven or yeast that a woman uses when she makes bread. She mixes

While people were asleep, an enemy came and scattered the seed of weeds over all the ground

up a very little yeast in a large mass of dough, and leaves it to rise. Presently all the dough is changed by the yeast, and made into good bread. So it is with the truth to those who take it into their hearts."

After Jesus told these five parables, "The Sower," "The Wheat and the Weeds," "The Growing Grain," "The Mustard Seed," and "The Leaven," he sent the crowd away and went into a house with his disciples. When they were alone they said to him, "Tell us what is the meaning of the parable of "The Wheat and the Weeds."

Jesus answered them, "He who sows the good seed is the Son of Man, whom God has sent into the earth. The field is the world. The good wheat are those who hear his word and are the children of God. The weeds are the children of the wicked one. The enemy that sowed them is the devil, Satan. The harvest is the end of the world and the reapers are the angels of God. Just as the weeds are gathered from among the good grain and burned in the fire, so shall it be at the end of the world. The Son of Man will send his angels, and they will gather out of his kingdom all that do evil and cause harm, and shall throw them into the furnace of fire; there men will weep and wail and gnash their teeth. But in that day, the children of God, the true wheat, shall shine like the sun in the kingdom of their heavenly Father."

Then to his disciples, not to the crowd, Jesus gave three more parables. The first was "The Hid Treasure." He said, "The kingdom of heaven is like a heap of money which a man found while he was working in a field. He hid it again, and told no one about it; but went home, sold all that he had and gladly bought that field, that the treasure might be his own."

The next parable was that of "The Pearl." "There was a man who went into many places to find pearls, which he bought to sell to others. In one place he found a pearl of great price, far more precious than any that he had seen before. He went and sold everything that he had, and with the money bought that pearl."

The last of these parables was "The Drag Net." "Once more," said Jesus, "the kingdom of heaven is like a large net that was cast into the sea and took in fishes of every kind, large and small, good and bad. When the net was full they drew it to the shore. There they sat down and took the fishes out, one by one. They looked them over and put the good fish, those that were fit to be eaten, into baskets, but those that were useless they threw away. So will it be at the end of the world. The angels will come and will take out the people that are wicked from among the good, and shall fling them into the furnace of fire; there men will weep and gnash their teeth."

After Jesus had finished telling these parables to his disciples, he said to them, "Have you understood all these?"

They said to him, "Yes, we have."

And he said to them, "Every teacher who has been made a learner in the kingdom of God is like a man who brings out of his store some things that are new and some that are old."

Jesus looked around, saw the dashing waves and said just these words: "Peace, be still!"

Sailing Across the Sea

CHAPTER 36

AFTER THE day of teaching in parables, when the evening came on, as the crowds were still pressing upon Jesus and giving him no time to rest, he said to his disciples:

"Let us sail across the lake to the other side." So they made ready the boat and took Jesus on board. Some of the people were so eager to be with Jesus that they also went into other boats and sailed with him. Jesus was very tired after his day of teaching and he lay down in the rear end of the boat, resting his head upon one of the cushions. In the steady motion of the oars and the gentle rippling of the waves, Jesus soon fell asleep, while the boat moved onward over the lake. Soon the night came and the disciples rowed on in the darkness.

On the Sea of Galilee, storms often arise very suddenly. The water may be perfectly calm for a time and then in a few minutes lashed into fury by the wind. So it came to pass while Jesus was sleeping. A great wind arose, the waves rolled high and dashed into the boat; but Jesus slept on peacefully.

At least four of the twelve disciples, and we know not how many more, were fishermen. They knew how dangerous these sudden storms might be; and as they saw the boat filling with water and beginning to sink, they were frightened. Coming to Jesus, they awoke him, crying out, "Master, Master, we are lost! Help us or we shall drown!"

The storm, with all the noise of creaking sails and

roaring winds and dashing waves, had not awaked Jesus, but the cries of his frightened disciples aroused him from his sleep. He looked around, saw the dashing waves and said just these words:

"Peace, be still!"

At once the wind ceased, the waves smoothed down and there was perfect calm upon the sea. Then Jesus spoke to his disciples, saying:

"Why are you so fearful? Have you so little faith in me?"

They might have known that whether their Master was awake or asleep, they were safe if he was with them. They wondered at this new proof of Jesus' power, and said to each other:

"Who can this be that can speak to the winds and the waves and they obey his words!"

They were sailing from Capernaum in a direction southeast, and after rowing about seven miles, they came to the eastern shore of the lake, where was a village called Gerasa. This region was called "the country of the Gadarenes," from a large city, Gadara, not far away. It was a part of Decapolis, a name given to all the country on the east of the Sea of Galilee. The word Decapolis means "The Ten Cities," and because in that land were ten large Roman cities, the whole country was called "The Country of Ten Cities."

It must have been very early in the morning when Jesus and his disciples brought their boats to the shore at Gerasa. Just as they were landing, a man came running down the hill to meet them, and from his wild acts they saw that he was one of those wretched people who were under the power of evil spirits. This man wore no clothes; he would not live in any house, but stayed in the caves in the hillside, which were used as burial places. They had tried to bind him with ropes and chains, but when the evil power was on him, he would break all his bonds and even snap his chains apart. He stayed all the time among the tombs, crying, moaning and gashing himself with sharp stones.

This wild man ran toward Jesus and fell at his feet. As soon as Jesus saw the state he was in, he spoke to the evil spirit within the man:

"Come out of this man, you vile spirit!"

The spirit answered Jesus, crying out, "Jesus, son of the Most High God, what business have you with us? In the name of God, I call upon you not to make us suffer!"

Jesus saw that this man's state was far worse than even most of those who were ruled by evil spirits. He said to the spirit, "What is your name?"

"My name is Legion," answered the evil spirit; meaning that in the man was not only one, but many of the evil spirits, a whole army of them, for the word "legion" means an army.

The demons, or evil spirits, begged Jesus not to send them far away. On the top of the hill was a herd of many hogs feeding. The Jewish people were not allowed to keep hogs nor to eat their flesh, so this drove of hogs must have belonged to foreign people, whom the Jews called Gentiles.

The evil spirits asked Jesus if when they left the man, they might go into these hogs; and Jesus allowed them. Then the demons or evil spirits went out of the man, leaving him lying upon the ground, naked but well. They went into the drove of hogs, and the hogs instantly became wild and could not be controlled. They rushed in a great mass down the steep side of the hill and into the water. There they were all drowned, about two thousand in number. The men who kept the hogs ran to the town near by, and told all the people what had happened; how the demons at the command of this stranger had left the man, had gone into the drove of hogs and had caused them to drown in the waters. The people of the city came out to see for themselves what had taken place. They saw the man in whom had been the fierce evil spirits, now sitting at the feet of Jesus, clothed and in his right mind, calm and peaceful.

These Gadarene people evidently knew nothing of Jesus and the many good works that he had done.

The evil spirits went out of the man into the hogs, causing them to rush down the hill into the water

They were filled with dread of his power, and scarcely looking at the man whom Jesus had helped so wonderfully, thought only of the hogs which they had lost. They begged Jesus to go away from their land and not to come to their town. Think what blessings Jesus might have brought to them, in curing their sick, giving sight to the blind, and hearing to the deaf, besides the good news of his teaching! But with no knowledge of these good gifts, they asked Jesus to leave them.

And Jesus took them at their word. Sadly he turned away, went down to the beach and stepped into the boat.

The man who had been set free from the evil spirits begged most earnestly to be allowed to go with Jesus. He may have feared that the people of the city would be angry with him because the demons in him had killed their hogs; or he may have thought that the evil spirits might come back to him if he was left alone, without his mighty helper near. He knew that he would be safe if he were with his Lord, and he asked again and again that he might go away with Jesus, wherever he might go.

But Jesus would not grant his prayer. He said to the man:

"Go home to your own people, and tell them what great things the Lord has done for you, and how he has taken pity on you."

The man went through all the country of Decapolis and told everybody whom he met what great things Jesus had done for him. When they heard this, they all wondered, and no doubt many wished that they had welcomed Jesus instead of sending him away.

Joppa

The woman came forward trembling with fear and told Jesus how she had touched his clothing and been made well. Jesus said to her: "Daughter, your faith has made you well."

The Sick Woman Made Well and the Dead Girl Brought to Life

CHAPTER 37

A GREAT CROWD of people were on the shore at Capernaum, looking earnestly over the sea. On the evening before they had seen Jesus with his disciples in their boats pushing off from the beach and sailing out into the lake; and now they were watching for their return. Close by the water was standing one man, whose face showed that he was in great trouble, as he gazed anxiously in every direction over the sea.

This man was named Jairus. He was the chief elder over the church in the town, which they called the synagogue. At home his little daughter twelve years old was lying very ill and likely to die at any moment. Jairus knew that if Jesus should come ashore in time, before his daughter would die, he could save her life; so with hope and fear mingled, he stood on the shore watching for Jesus to come, but fearing that he might come too late.

At last he could see the large boat rising in sight and drawing nearer, with other smaller boats around it. Before Jesus could step ashore, Jairus fell down upon his face before him and cried out:

"O Master, come to my house just as soon as you can! My little daughter is lying at the point of death; I pray you, come and lay your hands upon her so that she may live and be made well."

Jesus went with him, and all the crowd followed, pressing closely upon him; some showing pity and hope for Jairus in his trouble, but more of them wishing to see

Jesus do one of his wonderful works. In the edge of the crowd was standing a poor woman, wasted by sickness and as pale as death. She had a running sore, which for twelve years had drained away her blood. She was very eager to go to Jesus, for she believed that he could cure her sore, although many doctors had tried in vain to help her. She had spent all her money upon the doctors, one after another, but no one of them had done her any good, and she was all the time growing worse. Jesus was in the middle of this great crowd, and this woman was very weak, but by making a strong effort she was able to get near enough to Jesus, not to speak to him, but to reach her hand between those who were walking nearest to him and to touch his clothes.

Suddenly a great hope arose in her heart. She said to herself, "I really believe that if I can just touch the Master's clothes I will be made well!"

She reached out with trembling hand and touched the outer robe of Jesus. In an instant she felt a strange power come into her body and she knew that the sore was cured. She was well and strong!

At that moment Jesus stopped in his walk, while Jairus was trying to hurry him onward. He stood still, looked all around, and said, "Who touched my clothes?"

His disciples were beside him, and Peter answered:

"Why, Master, the crowd is all around, pressing close upon you, and yet you say, 'Who touched me?' while people are touching you all the time."

But Jesus said, "I am sure that somebody touched me, because I felt that power had gone out from me."

As he stood still and looked all around to see who had done this, the woman came forward out of the crowd and fell down at his feet, trembling with fear, afraid that she had offended him. She told of what she had suffered, how she had touched his clothing and had been made well. Jesus said to her:

"Daughter, your faith has made you well; go in peace and be free from your sickness."

But while Jesus was delaying for these few moments, Jairus was standing by his side in growing alarm, for to him and his dying child every minute was precious. Just then some one from his own house came up to him through the crowd and said:

"Your daughter is dead; what is the use of asking the Teacher to come any further? Not even he can help her now."

These people had not heard how Jesus some weeks before had raised to life the widow's son at Nain, for that village was at least twenty-five miles from Capernaum.

But Jesus spoke encouragingly to the sorrowing father. "Have no fear; only believe, and she shall yet be well."

They went to the house of Jairus, and the crowd would have followed him inside, but Jesus forbade them. He allowed none to go with him into the house, except the father and three of his disciples, Peter, James and John.

The house was full of people, weeping and wailing, playing on flutes and making a great noise, as the manner was then and is even now in that land. Men and women are paid to come to the house where one is lying dead, and to scream and cry aloud, so that all in the town may know of the death and of the sorrow of the family.

Jesus said to the people in the house, "Why do you make such a noise? The little girl is not dead, but only sleeping."

Jesus meant by these words that we need not be filled with sorrow when our friends die; for death is only a sleep until the time when God shall awaken them.

Jesus went into the room where the daughter of Jairus was lying dead on the bed, and taking her hand into his own said: "Little girl. I say to you, rise up!"

But this they did not understand; and they would not be comforted, for they knew that the child was dead.

Jesus ordered all these hired mourners to leave the house. He went into the room where the dead child was lying on the bed, taking with him only her father and mother, with his three chosen disciples. Standing beside the dead body, he took its little hand into his own and said:

"Little girl, I say to you, rise up!"

And instantly the girl stood up, looked around and began to walk. How happy were that father and mother as they clasped in their arms their little girl, no longer dead, but living and well. All were filled with wonder. They would have told everybody about this mighty work, but Jesus said to them:

"Give the child something to eat, but do not talk about her being brought back to life. Tell no one of it."

Jesus healing the sick

Sight to the Blind and Voice to the Dumb

CHAPTER 38

AS JESUS was coming out of the house where he had raised to life the young girl, two blind men met him; for the news of his return to Capernaum had gone abroad, and these two men, eager to obtain their sight, at once set out to find Jesus. They followed Jesus on the street, crying out aloud:

"Have mercy on us, O Son of David!"

You know that Jesus came from the family of which David had been the head long before. All the people looked for him, as sprung from David, to take David's throne, and like David, become king over all the land. The people who believed that Jesus was to be king often called him "Son of David."

These two blind men followed Jesus, crying to him, until he went into the house where he was staying, which may have been the house where Simon Peter lived. The blind men came into the house after Jesus. He said to them:

"Do you believe that I can do this which you desire?"

They answered him, "Yes, Lord, we believe that you can."

Then Jesus placed his hands upon their eyes, first on one man and then on the other. As he touched their eyes, he said to them, "As you believe, let it be done to you."

At once their eyes were opened and they could see. Jesus spoke to them very strongly, and gave them special orders, saying, "See that nobody knows of this."

He did not wish always to have crowds around seeking for miracles of healing, for he felt that he had a greater work to do in preaching to the souls of men than in curing their bodies. But these men went away and told all whom they met what a wonderful thing Jesus had done for them. It was not strange that they should speak of it, even though he had forbidden them, for all who had known them before as blind men saw the great change in their looks, now that they could see, and asked them how it had come to pass; so that it was not easy to avoid telling people about it. But wherever it was told, people who had any disease, or were blind, or deaf and dumb, or lame, were filled with desire to find Jesus and be made well.

Soon after these two men left Jesus, cured of their blindness, another man was brought to Jesus. This was a dumb man, in whom lived an evil spirit. Jesus always cast out the evil spirits, without waiting to be asked, whenever he found them ruling over men. He spoke to this evil spirit, and it left the man. Then all at once the man began to speak, for it was the evil spirit in him that had made him dumb. All the people wondered, and said to one another:

"Such power as this has never before been seen in the land of Israel!"

But the scribes and Pharisees, who were enemies of Jesus, said again, as they had said before:

"This man casts out the evil spirits, because Satan, the prince of the evil spirits, helps him."

Twelve Preachers Sent Out

CHAPTER 39

JESUS HAD now preached in nearly all parts of Galilee, except in the middle portion, the region around Nazareth, the home of his younger days. You remember that when he had tried to speak in Nazareth, soon after coming from Judea, the people refused to listen to him, thinking that one who had been only a workingman and not a Rabbi or scribe could not teach them anything.

But Jesus loved those people in Nazareth, for many of the men had been with him boys at school; and his own sisters lived there with their children, boys and girls, who were his nephews and nieces. He longed to see them all, and made up his mind to go again to Nazareth, and see if its people would this time listen to him. On his earlier visit he had been alone, and the men of Nazareth in their anger had tried to kill him by throwing him down a very steep hill; but now Jesus had with him his twelve disciples and many more who followed him from place to place. On this visit the men of Nazareth did not venture to do him harm, because of his many friends around him.

As before, Jesus went to the village church on the Sabbath day and preached. Again the people listened to him with wonder at his words; but again they said:

"Is not this the carpenter who used to make plows and hoes and tables for us? How can he teach us?"

He could only do a few of his great works, because the people would not believe in him. He did, indeed, lay his hands upon a few that were sick, and made them well;

but he could only wonder at the hardness of heart in those among whom he had lived so many years.

Leaving Nazareth with a sad heart, he went around the villages in middle Galilee, teaching in the churches and curing sickness of all kinds. As he saw how poor the people were, how little they knew of the truth, and how greatly they longed for it, he felt a great pity for them. They seemed to Jesus like sheep that were lost and wandering, not having any shepherd. He said to his disciples:

"Peace be to this house"

"The harvest truly is rich, but the workers in it are very few. Pray very earnestly to the Lord of the harvest that he may send out workers to gather in his harvest."

Jesus knew that the time of his work in Galilee was nearly ended. There were other parts of the land of Israel where he had not yet preached, and he wished to visit them. He knew, too, what none but himself knew, that in a year he would be taken away from the earth, and his disciples would be left alone to carry on his work and preach to all the people the news of God's kingdom. He made up his mind to send out his twelve disciples, whom he named "the apostles," and to let them begin their work by preaching in the villages of Galilee which he had not found time to visit.

So he called together his twelve disciples, and divided them into pairs, sending two men together, that they might help each other. He poured upon them some of his own power to cure diseases and to cast out evil spirits from men. He gave them commands about their work, to whom they should go and how they should act. He said:

"Do not go to any city of the Gentiles, the foreigners; and keep away from the villages of the Samaritan people. Your work just now is to be among the lost sheep of the house of Israel. Go to the Jews throughout the land, and tell them that the kingdom of God has come, and that they may enter it. Cure the sick, raise the dead to life, cleanse the lepers, cast out the evil spirits from men. Give freely, without being paid; for you have received the gift of God freely.

"Do not take with you any money of gold or silver or copper in your girdle; nor a bag to carry food for the road; nor two shirts, nor a pair of shoes; but go wearing only sandals on your feet. For God's workman deserves his food, and it will be given to him.

"When you come to a village, ask for some good man, go to his house, and stay there while you are in that village. Do not go visiting from one house to another. When you come to a house say, 'Peace be to this house.' If the people dwelling in that house are worthy of your peace, then peace shall be given to them; if they are not worthy, your peace shall come back to you. And if in any place the people will not hear you nor give you welcome, then as you go out of that house or that city, take off your sandals and shake the dust of that place from them as a sign. I say to you in truth that in the day of judgment it shall be worse for the cities that have refused you than for Sodom and Gomorrah, the cities upon which God rained down fire.

"You are sent forth like sheep among wolves; so be wise like serpents, yet harmless like doves. But you must watch against evil men, for they will seize you and hand you over to courts to be judged; you will be beaten in their court-rooms; you will be brought before governors and kings, because you are my followers. Now, when they bring you up for trial, do not be anxious about what you shall speak or how you shall say it; for what to speak shall be given you when you need it. For it is not you that speak, but the spirit of your Father in heaven that speaks in you."

"Whoever gives to one of these little ones even a cup of cold water because he is my disciple, he will not lose his reward"

Many more words Jesus spoke to his twelve disciples: and at the end of his charge he said this:

"Whoever receives you and listens to you, it is the same as though he received me, your teacher; and whoever receives me, receives my Father who sent me. He that receives a prophet because he is a prophet shall receive a prophet's reward. He who receives a good man because he is a good man shall receive a good man's reward. And whoever gives to one of these little ones even a cup of cold water because he is a disciple of mine, I tell you truly, he will not lose his reward.'

After giving his commands to the twelve disciples, Jesus sent them out to preach, while he himself went to other places telling the people the good news of the Kingdom of God.

The great mosque at Damascus

A Dance; and How It Was Paid For

CHAPTER 40

DURING NEARLY all the year of Jesus' teaching and preaching in Galilee, John the Baptist was in Herod's prison at a lonely place called Machærus, on the east of the river Jordan, near the Dead Sea. You remember that John was put into prison because King Herod's queen, Herodias, became angry against him, when John said to Herod that it was not right for him to take away his brother's wife and have her as his own. Herodias hated John and tried many times to have him killed, but Herod held John in high respect and would not suffer him to be slain.

But at last the chance came for Herodias to carry out her purpose. On King Herod's birthday, he held at Machærus, which was not only a prison but a palace, a great feast to his lords, the captains of his army, and the chief men of his kingdom. At this feast the daughter of Herodias, a young girl, came in and danced before the company. Herod and the guests with him were so delighted with the girl's dancing that the king made her a very foolish promise. He said to her:

"You may ask for anything that you please, and I will give it to you." He went further and even swore with an oath to her, "I will give you whatever you choose, even to half of my kingdom."

The girl went to her mother and said to her, "What shall I ask?"

And Herodias hissed out the words, "You ask for the head of John the Baptist."

The girl went in haste to the king, and said, "I want you to give me here on a platter the head of John the Baptist."

The king was greatly displeased and very angry. He knew that his wife Herodias had led the girl to make this choice, and he would have liked to break his promise. But because he had given his word and was ashamed to call it back before all the nobles at his feast, he gave

The daughter of Herodias dancing before Herod

orders, very unwillingly, to his guards to have her will carried out. They went into the prison, and with a sharp sword cut off the head of John the Baptist, the best and noblest man in all his kingdom. The head was laid on a platter and given to the young girl, who carried it to her mother. So the man whom Jesus called "a prophet and more than a prophet" was slain to satisfy the whim of a dancing girl and her wicked mother!

The few followers who had still clung to John the Baptist, and visited him in his prison, took up his headless body and buried it. Then they went to Jesus and told him all the sad story of John's death.

But Herod was not yet done with John the Baptist. Soon he began to hear wonderful stories of the new prophet, Jesus the Nazarene, who had risen up in John's place. He heard that amazing powers were shown by Jesus, that the sick were cured, the lepers were made clean, the blind were made to see, and, most wonderful of all, the dead were raised to life.

People were saying to each other, "Who is this great Prophet that is working all these wonders?"

Some said, "This is the old prophet Elijah, who has come to earth again."

Others said, "If he is not Elijah, it may be Jeremiah or some other prophet of the old times."

But Herod was filled with a terrible fear, for his conscience troubled him on account of his wicked deeds. He said:

"I know who this is. It is John the Baptist, whose head I had cut off. He has come to life again. It is on his account that all these wonderful things are taking place!"

Thus the bloody head of John the Baptist, like a terrible ghost, rose before the sight of Herod the king!

After he had blessed the food and broken it, Jesus gave a portion to each of his disciples, who went among the people and fed them. As the loaves and fishes were broken they grew in their hands until every one had enough to eat.

The Boy with His Five Loaves

CHAPTER 41

THE NEWS that King Herod had slain the holy prophet John the Baptist sent a thrill of horror to all who heard it. It came to the twelve disciples, who were just completing their work of preaching in the villages of Galilee. They feared that Herod might seize them and put them in prison; but they were more alarmed for their Master. Having slain John who had made Jesus known to the people, they feared that Herod might now try to kill Jesus himself.

They all hastened to Capernaum, where they found Jesus, and gave him the report of the places which they had visited, the work which they had done in healing and helping people and the message which they had given everywhere about the Kingdom of God. The disciples found the crowds around Jesus greater than ever before; for not only had the preaching of these disciples aroused an interest in Jesus and led many to leave their homes and seek him, but the Passover, the greatest of all Jewish feasts, was to be held soon, and the city of Capernaum was thronged with people who were on their way to Jerusalem; for as you know, this feast was held only in that city, and from every part of the land people went up to Jerusalem to attend it.

So many were the people coming and going and those who were looking for Jesus and seeking his power to cure their diseases, that Jesus and his disciples could scarcely find a chance to eat. The crowds were constantly pressing upon them. He said to his disciples:

"Come, let us take the boat and go across the lake to

some quiet place, away from the crowds, and there rest for a time."

They went into the boat and started to row over the lake. But the people saw them going and many tried to follow them. Those who had boats sailed in them after the course in which they saw the boat with Jesus and his disciples. And the others, a great multitude, walked and ran around the head of the lake, waded across the river Jordan where it enters the Sea of Galilee, still keeping Jesus' boat in sight, and were at the beach to meet Jesus when he landed near the town of Bethsaida, which was on the northeastern shore. Here Jesus was safe, for Bethsaida was outside the rule of King Herod and in the land governed by Herod's brother Philip.

When Jesus stepped out of his boat on the shore near Bethsaida, there he found a great throng of people, more than five thousand men, besides some women and children. When Jesus saw how eager they were and how glad to meet him, his heart of love and pity went out toward them. He cured some sick people that they had brought and he spoke to them about the kingdom of God.

The day began to draw to its close and the sun was almost sinking below the hills of Galilee, when the disciples said to Jesus:

"It is getting late and will soon be night. These crowds of people came so suddenly that they have brought with them nothing to eat. Send them away, so that they may go to the city of Bethsaida and the villages around and buy food and find places to stay through the night. We are here, you see, in a desert place, where there is neither food nor lodging for them."

But Jesus said to his disciples, "There is no need for them to go away; do you give them something to eat."

They said to him, "Shall we go into the town and

buy thirty dollars' worth of bread, so that each one of them may have a little?"

Jesus turned to Philip, one of his disciples, and asked him, "Philip, where shall we find bread that all these people may eat?"

Jesus said this to try Philip's faith, for he himself knew already what he would do. Philip looked over the crowd gathered upon the level ground, and he answered, "Thirty dollars' worth of bread would not be enough to give to each one even a little piece."

Jesus said to his disciples, "How many loaves have you? Go and see."

Just then another of the disciples, Andrew, the brother of Simon Peter, came up to Jesus and said, "There is a boy here who has five loaves of barley bread and two little fishes; but what use would they be among so many people?"

Jesus said, "Bring them to me."

So they led to Jesus this boy with his lunch basket, in which his mother had placed five large flat biscuits of barley and two small salted fishes.

Jesus said to his disciples, "Go out among the people and tell them to arrange themselves into companies, with fifty or a hundred in each company, and to sit down upon the grass."

The disciples did as Jesus ordered, and soon all the crowd was divided up into groups of fifty or a hundred people, all seated on the ground. On the green grass, arranged in rows and squares with their clothes of different colors, they looked like beds of flowers.

Then, in the sight of all the people, Jesus took the five loaves and the two fishes. He waved his hand for silence, and while all were still, looked up to heaven, gave thanks to God for his gift of food, and blessed it. He broke the loaves which were like large flat crackers or biscuit, and gave to each of his disciples a piece and also a piece of dried fish. The disciples went among the people breaking off pieces of the loaves and fishes and handing them out. As they were broken, the loaves and fishes grew in their hands, until every one in the company had enough to eat.

Then Jesus said, "Go and gather up the pieces of food that are left, so that nothing may be wasted."

Each of the twelve disciples carried a basket among the people, and took from them all that was left. When they came back to Jesus, all the twelve baskets were filled with the pieces left over of the loaves and fishes. There had been in the beginning only five loaves and two fishes. Of these, five thousand men, besides women and children, had eaten as much as they wanted. And now came back twelve baskets full of bits left over—much more at the end after all had eaten than at the beginning.

When the people saw that here was one who could give them food, all that they wanted, they said to each other, "This is the man that we want for our king! He can give us bread to eat without our working for it. Let us break away from the rule of the Romans and make Jesus our king!"

Jesus knew their thoughts and what they were saying to each other, for he knew all things. He knew, too, that he *was* a king, but not such a king as they wished. His kingdom was to be in the hearts of those who loved him, not a kingdom won by armies and by swords. Jesus found that his disciples were pleased to find the people so eager at once to crown Jesus as their King, for that would mean high rank and offices for themselves.

Jesus, therefore, began by sending away his disciples. He compelled them, much against their will, to get into the boat, and to row over the lake toward Capernaum. After sending away his disciples, he sent away the multitudes, who were also unwilling to go, for they could not understand why Jesus should refuse to be made king.

When all were gone away and quiet was around him and the night had come on, Jesus went to the top of a mountain near by, and spent some hours in prayer to his heavenly Father. He needed prayer, for he saw in this attempt to make him king another effort of Satan to bring Jesus under his power, by giving him a worldly kingdom, instead of a heavenly.

A distant view of "The Horns of Hattin," in the hollow of which Christ sat while he preached "The Sermon on the Mount" to the multitude gathered about him

As Jesus drew near, Peter cried out, "Lord, if it is really you, command me to come to you on the water."

How the Sea Became a Floor

CHAPTER 42

ON THE night after the multitude was fed with the five loaves, while Jesus was praying alone on the mountain, his disciples were rowing over the lake toward Capernaum. It was very dark; and soon after midnight a terrible storm arose, as storms often come very suddenly upon the Sea of Galilee. From his mountain top, through all the darkness and miles away, Jesus could see them struggling with the waves, and in great danger of losing their lives, for he could see all things.

While the disciples were pulling hard with their oars, suddenly they saw someone walking upon the waves and drawing near their boat. They were more alarmed, when they saw this form walking over the waves as though the waters were a solid floor, than they had been at the storm threatening to swallow them up, for they thought that surely this was a spirit from the world of the dead, coming to give warning that death was awaiting them. They cried out in their terror; but soon heard a voice speaking to them above the roaring of the wind and the dashing of the waves; a voice which they knew well. It was the voice of Jesus, saying:

"Be of good cheer! it is I; do not be afraid!"

Then they knew that it was no spirit or ghost from the grave, but their own Lord and Saviour coming to help them. What a load of fear was lifted from them when they heard that voice!

But one of the disciples, one who was always putting himself in the front, thought that if Jesus could walk on the water, he would like to do the same. You would know that this one was Simon Peter, a good man, but very quick in his impulses. He cried out, as Jesus drew near, "Lord, if it is really you, command me to come to you on the water."

And the Lord said, "Come." Then Peter leaped overboard from the boat and began to walk on the water toward Jesus. But after a few steps on the sea, he saw how heavy the storm was, and was afraid; and at that moment he began to sink. He shouted out, "Lord, save me!"

Jesus reached out his hand and caught him and kept him from sinking, saying to him:

"How little you trust me! Why did you doubt my word?"

When Jesus, holding Peter's hand, came with him into the boat, the wind stopped, and the sea became calm. They found that they were close to the land. Then all the men in the boat fell down at the feet of Jesus and said, "Truly you are the Son of God!"

Soon the daylight came, and they saw that their boat was beside a plain, reaching into the lake, a few miles south of Capernaum, called the land of Gennesaret. They went ashore and drew up their boat on the beach. The people of that place knew Jesus, for many of them had heard him in Capernaum. They were glad to have him come to their land; and sent word through all the plain that Jesus, the great teacher and healer, had landed on their shore. From all the country around they brought on their beds those that were sick, and laid them before Jesus, begging him to cure them. Many came near his side, and asked him if they might only touch the border of the mantle which he wore; and all who touched it were made perfectly well, so strong was their faith in Jesus.

The Bread of Life

CHAPTER 43

ON THE morning after the day when Jesus had fed the five thousand people with the five loaves, the crowd came together once more, hoping again to see Jesus; and some of them expecting to have the miracle or wonder-work repeated. On the evening before, they had seen the twelve disciples go out upon the lake in their boat, and had noticed that Jesus did not sail with them. They thought that Jesus must still be there, and looked all around for him, not knowing that in the night he had walked upon the sea to help his disciples in the storm. Failing to find Jesus, they thought that he must have gone back to his home in Capernaum. They found some other boats upon the shore, and in these they crossed the lake to Capernaum.

They found Jesus at the church in Capernaum, and said to him, "Rabbi, when did you come here?"

"I tell you the truth," answered Jesus, "it is not on account of the signs of power which you saw that you are looking for me, but because you ate of the bread which I gave you, and had your fill. You should work, not for the food which does not last, but for that which endures to everlasting life; that bread the Son of Man will give you, for upon him the Father has set his seal of power."

Jesus wished them to understand that the truth which he could give them was more to the soul than food was to the body, for it would give the life of God, which never passes away.

"In what way," they asked him, "can we do the work that God would have us do?"

"The work that God would have you do," answered Jesus, "is to believe in him whom God has sent to you as his message-bearer."

"Well, then," they said to Jesus, "show us the sign that will prove that you have come from God, then we will believe in you. What is the work that you are doing? Our fathers under Moses in the desert ate the manna that Moses gave them. You remember that it is written, 'He gave them bread from heaven to eat.'"

You see, the people wanted Jesus to show his power again by repeating the miracle with the loaves, and giving them more bread in the same way.

"In truth I tell you," replied Jesus, "it was not Moses who gave your fathers the bread from heaven; it was my Father, the Lord God. And my Father does give you now the real bread from heaven. For God's bread is that which comes down from heaven and gives life to the world."

"Master," they said, "give us that bread always!"

"I am the life-giving bread," answered Jesus. "He who comes to me shall never be hungry, and he who believes in me shall never be thirsty. But, as I told you, you have seen me, and yet you do not believe in me. All those whom the Father gives me will come to me; and no one who comes to me will I ever turn away. For I have come down from heaven not to carry out my own will, but the will of Him who sent me; and his will is this—that I should not lose even one of all those whom He has given me, but shall raise them up to life at the last great day. For it is the will of my Father that every one who sees the Son, and believes in him, should have everlasting life; and I myself will raise him up at the last day."

The Jews who heard Jesus began to find fault with him for saying, "I am the bread which came down from heaven."

"Is not this Jesus, the son of Joseph? We know his father and mother. How can he say, 'I came down from heaven?'"

They could not understand his words, and they were angry with him because he would not again work the miracle of giving them bread. Also they now found that Jesus was not willing to be a king such as they wanted, one that would sit on a throne and live in a palace; would raise an army to drive away the Romans and make the Jews a ruling people upon the earth. It was, as we have seen, the time of the Passover, and one reason for the great crowds around Jesus was that all were expecting him to lead the people to Jerusalem and take his place as the king of Israel. But this year Jesus did not go, as he usually did, to the feast in Jerusalem, for he had other plans for himself and his disciples.

When the crowd following Jesus found that he would not be a king according to their desires, that he would not do wonders for them to look upon, and that his words were such as they could not understand, nearly all of them turned against Jesus. They went away, leaving the twelve disciples alone with him.

Jesus said to the Twelve, "Do you, too, wish to leave me?"

Simon Peter answered for them all, "Lord, to whom shall we go if we leave you? You have the words that will give us everlasting life. And we believe and are certain that you are the Holy One of God."

These men did not understand all the words of Jesus, but they had learned to love him and to believe that he was the promised King. They were ready to stay with him until death.

"Did I not choose you to be the Twelve?" said Jesus, "and yet, even among you there is one who is doing the devil's work."

They did not know of whom he was speaking; but he meant Judas, the son of Simon Iscariot; the one of the twelve disciples who a year afterward was to give up his Master to death. At that time Judas himself did not know this. Jesus, who could read the hearts of men, saw in Judas the signs all unknown to himself that he would do this dreadful deed.

A view of the village of Nain, and rising in the background is Mount Tabor

Jesus in a Strange Country

CHAPTER 44

WITH HIS sermon on "The Bread of Life," given in the church at Capernaum, Jesus finished his work among the people of Galilee. He had lived in that land for more than a year; he had traveled through every part of it; he had spoken in most of its villages and cities, and had sent out his disciples to preach in many other places. Everybody in Galilee had either heard Jesus or had heard about him. If they did not believe in him and his gospel, it was because they would not.

There was another and important work which now lay before Jesus. That was the training of his twelve disciples. These men, the apostles, as they were called later, had been with him for nearly a year. They had listened to his preaching and had heard his sermons many times, over and over again; for in different places Jesus gave the same talks to the people; but those talks and parables the Twelve heard in each place, as Jesus wished those men to hear his words until they knew them by heart and could give them as his message to others who had not heard Jesus himself.

One reason why we have in the four gospels, by Matthew, Mark, Luke and John, so many of the teachings and parables of Jesus, is that the disciples heard them so many times, learned them, could tell them to others; and thus at least thirty years after Jesus passed away from earth, his words were remembered and could be written down.

But besides the public teachings of Jesus, such as

the Sermon on the Mount and the parables. there were other great truths of the gospel that could not be given to the people, for they were not ready for them and could not understand them. We can see how the common people were puzzled by his words about "the bread of life." Jesus saw that it was needful for him to take the twelve disciples apart by themselves, that he might teach them some of the deeper truths of his gospel. In Galilee he could not be alone with these men; for wherever he might go there would always be many sick people coming to be cured and others leading men held in the power of evil spirits begging Jesus to cast them out. Then, too, in every place were the Pharisees and scribes, bringing their questions, asking for miracles, and trying to stir up the people against Jesus. Wherever Jesus was, a crowd was always around him, and he could find no time to teach his disciples some truths needful for them to know.

He made up his mind to go away from Galilee to some quiet place where no one would know of his coming. On the northwest of Galilee was a narrow land, on the other side of the Lebanon mountains, beside the great Mediterranean Sea. It was called Phœnicia, from the people who lived there, the Phœnicians; and also called "the land of Tyre and Sidon," from its two leading cities. The people who lived in that country were not Jews, and few of them even spoke the Jewish language. Jesus thought that this would be a quiet place where he could talk alone with his disciples.

Jesus and the Twelve quietly left Capernaum, and walked over the mountains to this land of Tyre and Sidon. There they found a house and went into it, intending for a time to live there. Jesus wished nobody to know of his coming; but he could not be hidden. A woman of that country heard of him, and at once went

The woman threw herself at Jesus' feet and cried aloud: "Have mercy on me, O Lord, son of David!"

In the Land of the Ten Cities

CHAPTER 45

JESUS SOON found that if he wished to be alone with his disciples, he must leave the land of Tyre and Sidon; for after he had cured the woman's child of her evil spirit, the people were coming to him for other mighty works. He made up his mind to go farther away, and taking his disciples, he went to Sidon, north of Tyre, and then not through Galilee, but around it, to the river Jordan, north of the Sea of Galilee. He crossed the Jordan, and on the eastern side of the Sea of Galilee came to a country called Decapolis, or "the land of the Ten Cities," from ten large places in that region. While they were on this journey, few people saw them, and as they walked together he talked to his disciples and taught them many things.

The place to which Jesus came was not far from the town where some months before he had cast out from a poor man a whole army of evil spirits and had sent them into the drove of hogs. At that time, you remember, the people had come to Jesus and had begged him to go away from them, for they had seen his power, but knew nothing of his goodness. But after that miracle, the man who had been cured went all through this land of the Ten Cities, telling the people everywhere of the good work Jesus had done to him and how much they had lost in sending him away.

On this second visit of Jesus to this land, the people were ready and eager for his coming. They gathered around Jesus with great joy, and came from near and from far to see him. He went up into a mountain and sat down with his disciples, hoping to be alone. But the people came to him in great crowds, bringing with them those that were lame, and ill with different diseases. They laid these suffering people at his feet, and asked him to cure them. He made them all well. They all wondered, as they saw the dumb talking, the cripples made

View of Tyre

sound, the lame walking about and the blind seeing; and they all praised the God of Israel.

At this time they led to Jesus a man who was very deaf, and who stammered so that people could scarcely understand his words. They asked Jesus to place his hand on this man and cure him. But Jesus would not do this in public, with a crowd of people looking on. He led him away out of the throng to a place where they could be by themselves. He put his fingers into the man's ears, and then, moistening one finger upon his own tongue, with it touched the man's tongue. Looking up to heaven with a sigh, he said, "Be opened." The man's ears and his tongue were at once set free; he could hear and could speak plainly. Jesus forbade the man and his friends to tell anyone about the cure; but contrary to his command they made it known everywhere. All who saw this man were astonished; and they said of Jesus, "He has done everything well! He makes even the deaf to hear and the dumb to speak!"

The crowd clung to Jesus and followed him for three days. By that time whatever food the people had brought with them had been eaten and yet they stayed with Jesus, never thinking of their needs. Jesus called his disciples together and said to them:

"My heart is touched on account of all these people; for they have now been with me three days and they have nothing to eat. Some of them have come from distant places, and I cannot bear to send them away hungry for fear that they may break down by the way."

"Where can we," the disciples asked him, "in a lonely place like this, with no towns near, find bread for such a crowd as this?"

"How many loaves have you?" asked Jesus.

"We have in all seven loaves," they answered, "and with them a few small fishes."

Jesus told all the crowds to sit down upon the ground; and when they had done so, he held up the loaves and the fishes, and gave thanks to his heavenly Father for them. Then he broke the loaves into pieces, also the dried fish, and gave them to the disciples. The disciples distributed them among the people; and everyone had all that he wanted to eat.

After the meal, the disciples went around with large baskets, and picked up of the food left over seven baskets full. At this time the people who were fed by Jesus were four thousand men, besides women and children. When all were satisfied, Jesus told them to go back to their homes; then with his disciples, he went into the boat and sailed across the Sea of Galilee.

Sidon

Again on the Sea of Galilee

CHAPTER 46

FROM THE land of the Ten Cities, Jesus and his disciples sailed straight across the Sea of Galilee, and on its southwestern shore they came to a city called Magadan or Magdala. One of the women who went with Jesus on his journeys in Galilee, Mary Magdalene, that is, Mary of Magdala, was from this city. Jesus came to this place for rest and for quiet talking with his disciples; but as soon as he landed he was met by some Pharisees and others who did not believe in him. They said to him:

"Teacher, show us some sign from heaven that you are a prophet or one whom God has sent."

They wished Jesus to do some miracle or wonderful work, not that they might believe in him, but only that they might see what he could do. Everywhere the Pharisees, who looked upon themselves as leaders, were opposed to Jesus and stirred up the ignorant people against him.

We have already seen that Jesus never gave any cures or wonderful works merely to be looked upon. He would help those who were in need or in trouble; but he would not merely satisfy an idle desire to see a miracle. He answered these Pharisees as he had answered others:

"I will give you a sign from heaven. In the evening, at sunset you say, 'It will be fine weather, for the sky is as red as fire.' But in the morning, if the sky is red, you say, 'It will be a stormy day, for the sky is red as fire, and threatening.' You learn to read the signs in the sky, yet you do not know how to read the signs of the times. If you would look, you might see whether I come from God or not. It is a wicked and a disobedient people who continually ask for signs. No sign shall be given to this people, except the sign of the prophet Jonah."

He did not even tell them how Jonah was to be a sign or token to them. Perhaps a few months later, when these people heard that Jesus had been slain and buried; then after three days had risen again to life, just as Jonah had come forth alive after being buried for three days in the great fish, they would then understand how Jonah had been as a sign of Jesus.

Jesus saw at once that this was no place to find quiet and a chance to teach his disciples, so he went into the boat again, with his disciples, and sailed away up the lake. They left in such haste that the disciples did not think, while they were ashore, to buy some bread, and they had with them in the boat only one loaf for Jesus and twelve men.

While they were rowing over the sea, Jesus said to them:

"Take care and be on your guard against the leaven of the Pharisees and the leaven of Herod."

They thought that he was speaking to them about their having failed to bring more bread, and they began talking among themselves. Jesus noticed this, and he said:

"Why are you talking to one another about your being short of bread? How little trust you have in me! Do you not remember the five loaves with which I fed the five thousand, and the twelve baskets full of pieces that you picked up afterward? Have you forgotten about the seven loaves among the four thousand, and the seven baskets full that you picked up? How is it that you do not see that I was not speaking to you about bread? No, be on your guard against the leaven of the Pharisees and the leaven of Herod."

In warning his disciples against the leaven of the Pharisees, Jesus meant their pride and pretense of religion and exactness in obeying rules, while failing to serve God with the heart. By the leaven of Herod, he meant the spirit of living for the world, of guilty pleasure, without a thought of doing God's will.

They came to Bethsaida; and as soon as the people saw Jesus they brought to him a blind man and begged him to touch him, hoping to see Jesus give him his sight. But Jesus would not let them look on the curing of the man. He took him away from the crowd, and outside the town, to a lonely place. There, after spitting upon the man's eyes, he laid his hands upon him, and asked him:

"Can you see anything?"

The man looked up, and said, "Yes, I can see a little, but not very clearly. I see men moving about, but they look like trees."

Then Jesus placed his hands on the man's eyes. He looked around, and now could see everything distinctly.

Jesus said to him, "Now go directly to your home; and do not go into the town, where men will see you and ask how you received your sight."

Jesus and his disciples did not stop in Bethsaida; for he felt that he must find some quiet, lonely place, where he could teach his disciples the great truths of which they knew nothing; truths, too, which it would be hard for them to believe and to understand. So from Bethsaida he went on, following a road beside the river Jordan to the foot of Mount Hermon, far in the north.

The Great Confession

CHAPTER 47

FROM BETHSAIDA by the Sea of Galilee Jesus led his twelve disciples northward, to the very end of the land of Israel, at the foot of Mount Hermon. Here, at one of the great springs from which the river Jordan flows, was the city of Cæsarea-Philippi, or "Philip's Cæsarea," so called because it was in the land ruled by Herod Philip, the brother of Herod Antipas, who was ruling in Galilee. Jesus did not go into the city of Cæsarea-Philippi, but into one of the villages near the city, for he wished not to have a crowd around him, but to be alone with his disciples.

The time had now come for the disciples to know more about Jesus, who he was, the work that he was to do and what he was soon to suffer. His plan of teaching them was not to tell them, but to lead them on by questions so that they might learn the truth by finding it out themselves. One day, after he had been alone praying to his Father, he asked his disciples:

"Tell me, who do the people say that I am?"

"Some say that you are John the Baptist, raised up from the dead," answered the disciples; "others say that you are Elijah the prophet come to earth again; and still others say that you are the prophet Jeremiah or some other one of the old prophets."

"But you, who do you say that I am?" asked Jesus.

At once Simon Peter answered, for he was the one among the Twelve always ready to speak:

"But you, who do you say that I am?" asked Jesus of Simon Peter.

"You are the Messiah, the Christ, the Son of the living God!"

You know that the Jews everywhere were looking for a king to rule over them, set them free from the Roman power and make of them a great conquering nation. This king, in their own language, they called "the Messiah," which means, "the Anointed One," for in Israel a new king was chosen by having oil poured upon his head. The word "Messiah," in the Greek language, which was spoken everywhere, was "Christ," also meaning "The Anointed One." Peter, in speaking those words, "Thou art the Messiah, the Christ," meant to say that Jesus was the King of Israel, for whom all the people were looking.

"You are a blessed man, Simon, son of Jonah," answered Jesus, "for no human being has made this known to you, but my Father who is in heaven. Yes, and I say to you, 'Your name is Peter—a Rock—and on this rock I will build my church; and all the powers of the underworld shall not succeed against it.' Also, Simon Peter, I will give to you the keys of the kingdom of heaven. Whatever you forbid on earth shall be forbidden in heaven, and whatever you allow on earth shall be allowed in heaven."

Because Simon Peter was the first to make this confession of Jesus as the Messiah-Christ, the King, he was given special honor among the followers of the Lord. You remember that more than a year before, when Jesus met Simon for the first time, beside the river Jordan, he gave him the new name Peter, which means "a rock."

Then Jesus told the disciples that they were not to speak to any of the people of what Peter had said, that Jesus was the Christ, the King, for the time had not yet come to make it public. But now, since they knew that he was to be a king and rule over Israel, he began for the first time to speak of certain other things, which they found very hard to understand.

"Very soon," said Jesus, "we are going up to Jerusalem; and there I must endure great suffering from the rulers of the people, the chief priests and teachers of the law. I must be slain and buried; and on the third day I shall rise again."

The disciples could not understand how if he was to reign as King of Israel, it could be possible for him to suffer these things and to die. Peter took Jesus aside, where he could speak with him alone.

"Master," said Peter, "you must not speak of such things. God will not allow these things to come to you. You are not going to be put to death in Jerusalem; you are going to Jerusalem to sit on the throne of David, and reign over the land!"

But Jesus turned his back upon Peter, and looking upon his disciples, said:

'Get away from me, Satan! You would turn me away from doing God's will! For you look at things, not as God looks at them, but as man does!"

Jesus saw that in Peter's mind was the view of the kingdom that Satan had shown him in his great temptation on the mountain, not as a kingdom of God, but as a kingdom such as men were expecting, a kingdom like those of the world.

Then Jesus called to his disciples, and to the people that were around them, and said:

"If any man has the will to come after me and be my disciple, let him give up his own will, and take up his cross and follow me. For whoever wants to save his life will lose it, and whoever for my sake loses his life shall find it. What good will it do to a man to gain the whole world if in gaining he loses his own life? What will a man give that is worth as much as his life? For the Son of Man is coming in the glory of his Father with his angels; and then he will give to every man what his acts deserve. And I tell you truly, there are some standing here who will not die until they have seen the Son of Man coming to reign in his kingdom."

Nazareth

The three disciples beheld with wonder the change which had come over their Lord. His face shone with a glory so great they could not bear to look upon him, and beside him they saw standing the prophets, Moses and Elijah.

The Vision on the Mountain

CHAPTER 48

AT ONE time while Jesus was staying in one of the villages at the foot of Mount Hermon, in the far north of the land, he took with him three of his disciples, Peter, James and John, and went up the mountain to pray. It was in the afternoon, when they walked up the mountain, and when night came on he was still in prayer. The three disciples were tired from climbing the mountain and fell asleep for a little time. When they awoke they were filled with wonder at the change which had come over their Lord.

Although it was night, they saw the face of Jesus shining as brightly as the sun at noon, with a dazzling glory so great that they could not bear to look upon him. His clothes too were shining white and glittering. Not only his face, but his hands, his feet and even his body beamed through his garments with brightness.

They saw standing beside Jesus in his splendor two men who had lived long before on the earth and were now living no more. How the disciples knew them we are not told. Perhaps the knowledge flashed upon their minds, given them by God; or it may have been that as they listened to these two men, they learned from their words who they were. One was the great prophet Moses, who led the Israelites out of Egypt and died on Mount Nebo; the other was the prophet Elijah, who spoke bold words to the wicked King Ahab and was taken up to heaven in a chariot of fire. Both these men had passed from earth many hundred years before.

As the three disciples looked and listened, they could

hear what these two prophets of the old times were saying. They were talking to Jesus about his death which was to take place at Jerusalem. So these two great men of the past knew already what Jesus had tried to tell his disciples, and what they were so slow to believe, that he was soon to die!

Peter was always eager to speak, and he spoke now, though he scarcely understood what his own words meant.

Mount Hermon—the Mount of the Transfiguration

"Master," he said, "this is a good place for us to stay in. If you are willing, I will make here three tents; one for you, one for Moses and one for Elijah."

He thought that the two prophets, Moses and Elijah, had come back to stay upon the earth; and that if tents were made for them, they would live upon that mountain.

While Peter was speaking a bright and glorious cloud came over them all, over Jesus, over the two prophets and over the three disciples, who were filled with fear as they found the cloud around them. And a greater fear came upon them as they heard the voice of God out of the cloud saying:

"This is my Son, the Beloved, in whom I delight. Listen to him!"

And as they heard these words, knowing that God had spoken them, they fell down upon their faces in great terror. Jesus came to them and touched them gently, saying:

"Rise up, and do not be afraid."

Then they looked up. The bright cloud had passed away, the two prophets were no longer to be seen, and Jesus was standing alone over them, some of the glory still remaining upon his face.

As they were walking down the mountain, Jesus said to his three disciples, Peter, James and John:

"Tell no one what you have seen this night, until the Son of Man has risen from the dead."

So, much as they wished to tell their fellow-disciples of this wonderful sight, they obeyed their Master, and said not a word about it while Jesus was still with them.

They said to Jesus, "How is it that the teachers of the law say that the prophet Elijah must come before the Messiah-King appears?"

"Elijah does come," answered Jesus, "and he prepares the way for the coming of the King. And I tell you that Elijah has already come, but the people have not known him. They would not listen to him, and have done to him as they pleased. And just as it was with him, so will it be with the Son of Man. He shall also suffer at the hands of men."

Then the disciples understood that Jesus was speaking to them of John the Baptist, who like Elijah had lived in the wilderness, wore a mantle of skin, and fed on desert-food, and who, like Elijah, gave God's message to the people, preparing the way for the coming of Jesus Christ.

As Jesus and his three disciples came down to the village at the foot of Mt. Hermon, a man eagerly besought him to cast an evil spirit out of his son.

The Boy with the Dumb Spirit

CHAPTER 49

WHEN JESUS and his three disciples came to the village at the foot of the mountain, they found a great crowd gathered around the other nine disciples, and some of the Jewish teachers of the law, the scribes, talking with them very earnestly. Some of the glory of the last night still lingered upon the face of Jesus, and as the people looked upon him, they were filled with wonder and bowed down before him.

Out of the crowd came a man running, whose face showed that he was in great trouble. He knelt before Jesus and cried out:

"Teacher, I brought to you my son, in whom is an evil spirit, which has made him dumb. I pray you have mercy on him, and cure him, for he is my only child. Often the spirit seizes him and dashes him down. It makes him foam at the mouth and grind his teeth. He is wasting away, and I fear will die unless help comes to him. I brought him here, hoping to find you. But you were away, and I spoke to these men, your disciples. They tried to cast out the evil spirit, but they could not. Now that you have come, will you not help me?"

"O you people who will not believe, and who turn away from God!" said Jesus, "how long must I be with you? How long must I have patience with you? Bring your boy to me."

They brought the boy to Jesus; but no sooner did the boy see him, than the wicked spirit threw him into a spasm. He fell on the ground, his body twitching and tearing; and rolled about, foaming at the mouth.

"How long has he been like this?" asked Jesus of the boy's father.

"Ever since he was a little child," the man answered, "and it has many times thrown him into fire and into water, almost killing him. If you can do anything, do take pity on us both and help us."

"'If I can!'" said Jesus, taking up the man's word. "Do you not know that all things can be done for the one who believes?"

"I do believe," cried out the father of the boy. "O Master, help my lack of faith!"

Jesus saw that a crowd was rapidly gathering around, and he spoke to the evil spirit.

"Deaf and dumb spirit," he said, "I command you at once come out of this boy, and never again trouble him!"

With a loud cry, the evil spirit threw the boy into a violent spasm of pain and then left him. The boy lay on the ground, looking like a corpse. In fact, many who were standing near, as they saw him, said, "The boy is surely dead!"

But Jesus took his hand, lifting him from the ground. The boy stood up and walked away well, free from the evil spirit and able to speak.

When Jesus was alone with his disciples in the house, they asked him, "Why was it that we could not drive out the evil spirit from the boy?"

"It was because you have so little faith. I tell you that if your faith were only the size of a grain of mustard-seed, you could say to this mountain, 'Move from this place to that,' and move it would; for nothing would be impossible to you."

But he added, "An evil spirit of this kind is harder to drive away than most. Only by special prayer can it be cast out."

Soon after this Jesus left that place at the foot of the mountain, and led his disciples toward the south. They saw that he was now going in the direction of Jerusalem, and were quite sure that there he would set up his throne and kingdom. But Jesus knew what they were thinking of, and he said to them,

"Listen carefully to my words. The Son of Man is to be given into the hands of his enemies. They shall kill him, and three days after he has been killed, he shall rise again to life."

But the disciples could not understand these words, for they would not believe that he was to die, and they were afraid to ask him what these sayings meant.

The Jordan near Dan

The Last Visit to Capernaum

CHAPTER 50

WHILE JESUS was passing through Galilee for the last time, he wished not to do in that land any more wonderful works or to give any further teachings in public. He desired not to have crowds around him, but to be alone with his disciples, for there were many things to be told them before he should be taken away from them.

As they were on their way to Capernaum, which had been his home during the year before, he saw that his disciples as they walked were having some dispute or quarrel. He well knew what they were saying to each other, for he knew all things; but at the time he said nothing.

He came to Capernaum, for the first time followed by no crowd, but with his twelve disciples only. In the evening, as they sat together in the house, he said to them:

"What was it that you were talking about today as we were walking on the road?"

The disciples looked at each other, a little ashamed, and at first did not speak. Finally, one of them said:

"We were asking each other who of us should hold the first place in your kingdom."

Although Jesus had more than once told these men that he must suffer and die, they did not believe it. They saw that he was on his way toward Jerusalem, and like all the people who believed in him, they thought that when he came to that city, he would take his kingdom and rule; and each of his disciples wanted a place for himself next the throne.

"The first place!" answered Jesus. "If any of you has the will to be first in the kingdom of heaven, that one shall be the last of all and shall serve all the others!"

A little child was playing near him, for the children were never afraid of Jesus and loved to be with him. Jesus reached out his hand, took the child in his arms and held it close to him. Then he said to his disciples:

"I tell you, unless you change your spirit and become like little children, you will not enter into the kingdom of heaven at all! Whoever of you will become humble and gentle, like this little child, not seeking great things for himself, that is the one who shall be the greatest in the kingdom of heaven. And any one who helps even a little child to be one of my followers is helping me. But if anyone puts a snare or stumbling-block in the way of one of these little ones, to keep him from following me, it would be better for that man to have a great millstone hung on his neck, and to be thrown into the deep sea! Woe to the world on account of snares and hindrances, keeping men away from God and from salvation! There must be these snares and hindrances, that cannot be

Whoever will become like this little child, shall be the greatest in the Kingdom of Heaven

helped; but woe to the man who puts them in the way!

"If your hand or your foot becomes a snare to you, keeping you from God, you must cut it off and throw it away. It is better for you to enter into life a cripple, and with only one hand, than with two hands or two feet, to go away to everlasting death. And if your eye would lead you to forsake God, pluck it out and throw it away. It is better for you to be saved having only one eye, than to be lost having two eyes.

"I tell you, never despise or think lightly of one of these little ones; for I say to you, their angels always see the face of my Father who is in heaven."

Then John, one of the disciples, said:

"Teacher, we saw a man who is not one of your followers using your name to cast out evil spirits; and we told him not to use your name, since he is not with us."

"Do not forbid him," said Jesus, "there is no man who will do a mighty work in my name, and be able also to speak against me. Whoever is not against us is for us. Why, if any one will give you even a cup of water to drink, because you belong to Christ, I tell you truly, that man shall not fail of having a reward."

At that time Jesus told his disciples how to treat those who had done them any wrong. He said:

"If your brother does wrong, go to him and speak to him about it when you are alone with him. If he listens to you, then you have won your brother. But if he will not listen, take with you one or two others, and talk with him again, that there may be at least two witnesses in every case. If he will not listen to these men, speak to the church; and if he refuses to listen to the church, then have nothing more to do with him, but treat him as a stranger, as the people treat those who collect the taxes for the Romans.

"I tell you, my disciples, that whatever you forbid on earth shall be forbidden by those in heaven; and whatever you allow on earth shall be allowed by those in heaven. I tell you another thing: if two of you shall agree on earth upon anything that they ask in prayer, it shall be done for them by my Father who is in heaven. For where two or three have come together in my name, I am there among them."

Then Peter came up to Jesus and asked him a question. It was this:

"Master, how often should I forgive my brother when he has done me wrong? Shall it be as many as seven times?"

"Seven times?" said Jesus. "No, I say, seventy times seven! For the kingdom of heaven may be compared to a king who wished to have his servants pay him the debts which they owed him. When he had begun to make up their accounts, one servant was brought before him who owed him more than a million dollars. He could not pay his debt, and his master ordered that he should be sold, and his wife and children with him, and everything that he had, toward the payment of his debt. The servant fell down upon his face before him, and said, 'Only have patience with me, my lord, and I will pay it all.' His master knew that he could never pay so great a debt; he felt a pity for him, and let him go free, forgiving him all that he owed.

"But as he was going away, that servant met one of his fellow-servants who owed him a small debt, only about fifteen dollars. He took him by the throat, and said, 'Pay me what you owe me!' The man threw himself on the ground and begged for mercy, crying out, 'Have patience with me, wait a little while, and I will pay all that I owe you.' But he refused to have mercy;

he took him into the court and had him put into prison until he should pay the debt.

"When the other servants saw him sending this man to prison, they felt troubled and told the king what he had done. At this the king became very angry. He sent for that cruel servant and said to him, 'You wicked servant! When you asked me for mercy, I gave to you all your great debt and let you go free! Should not you, also, have shown the same kindness to your fellow-servant that I showed to you?' Then his master, being very angry, handed him over to the jailor, to be kept in a dungeon until he should pay the whole of his debt. So also will my Father in heaven do to you, unless you forgive your brother with all your heart."

While Jesus was at this time in Capernaum, the officer who collected from the Jews the tax for the Temple came to Peter and said:

"Does not your Master pay the Temple tax?"

"Yes," answered Peter.

But when he went into the house, before he could speak, Jesus said to him,

"Tell me, Simon, from whom do the kings of this world take taxes? From their sons, or from foreigners?"

"From foreigners," answered Peter.

"Then their own people are free from being taxed, are they not? We are the sons of God, and we should be free from the tax for the house of God. However, in order not to displease them, do you go to the sea, throw in a hook and take the first fish that comes up; open its mouth, and you will find in it a piece of silver money. Take that and give it to the tax collectors for you and me."

Good-bye to Galilee

CHAPTER 51

WHILE JESUS was still in Capernaum, the fall of the year came on, and with it the time drew near for the Jewish Feast of Tents, or Feast of Tabernacles. In the Bible, the word "tabernacles" always means "tents." This feast was called "the Feast of the Tents" because every year the people who went up to Jerusalem to attend it lived for a week in little tents or huts made of green branches; to keep in mind the forty years, long before, when, after coming out of Egypt, the Israelites lived in the desert in tents, moving from place to place.

The younger brothers of Jesus, the sons of Joseph and Mary, heard that Jesus was in Capernaum; and they came to see him. At this time these brothers of Jesus did not believe in him as their King and Saviour; although afterward they were among his followers. These men said to Jesus:

"Why do you not go to Judea and Jerusalem and let your disciples see there what you can do? No one who wishes to be known stays in a place apart from the people. Since you can do these great works, you should show yourself to the world."

"My time," said Jesus, "has not come yet; but your time is always here. The world is not against you, but it is against me, because I speak against its evil deeds. Go yourselves up to the feast; I am not going as yet up to this feast, because my time has not yet come."

Jesus did not wish to have as his companions at

the feast men who did not believe in him, even though they were his brothers. So, while his brothers went on to Jerusalem, he stayed a little longer in Galilee. Before he left the city of Capernaum he gave one last call and warning to its people and those in the cities near by. He spoke to those who lived in Chorazin, a town only a few miles from Capernaum; and those in Bethsaida,

Christ's call to the sick and weary: "Come unto me, all ye who labor and are heavy laden, and I will give you rest."

five miles away, at the head of the lake. He said to these cities:

"Woe unto you, Chorazin! and woe to you, Bethsaida! If the mighty works that were done in you had been done in the cities of Tyre and Sidon, long before this time they would have turned from sin to God, weeping in rough garments, with ashes on their heads! I tell you that when God comes to judge the lands, it will be harder for Chorazin and Bethsaida than for Tyre and Sidon. And you, O Capernaum, shall you be lifted up to heaven? No, you will sink down to death. For if the great works that were done in you had been done in Sodom, that city would have lasted until today. But I say to you, it will be easier for Sodom in God's day of judgment than for you, O Capernaum!"

At the same time Jesus spoke these words also:

"I thank thee, O Father, Lord of heaven and earth, for hiding these things from the wise and the learned, and for making them known to those who are child-like in spirit. Yes, Father, I praise thee that this has been the way that thou hast chosen.

"All power has been given to me by the Father; and no one can fully know the Son except the Father; and no one fully knows the Father except the Son, and he to whom the Son will make him known.

"Come unto me, all ye who labor and are heavy-laden with your troubles; and I will give you rest. Take upon you the yoke that I bear, and learn from me how to live; for I am gentle and lowly-minded, and you shall find rest for your souls. For my yoke is easy and my load is light."

With these words Jesus left Capernaum and Galilee for the last time.

But one of the ten men when he found that he was a leper no longer, stopped and praised God with a loud voice, and ran to Jesus' feet, giving him thanks for his cure.

Passing Through Samaria

CHAPTER 52

AFTER MOST of those who were going up to Jerusalem for the Feast of Tents had left Capernaum, Jesus began his journey with his disciples. All who saw him going toward Jerusalem, and even his disciples, thought that now he was surely on his way to take his throne and rule the people as king of Israel.

Just as they were starting, a man who was one of the teachers of the law came to Jesus and said:

"Master, I will follow you wherever you may go." He thought that by following Jesus he might have some high place in his kingdom. But Jesus saw that this man was following him only for gain. He said to him:

"You will gain nothing by following me. The foxes have holes, and the wild birds have their nests; but the Son of Man has not a place where he can lay his head."

To another man, Jesus said, "Follow me!" The man answered, "First let me go and bury my father."

Jesus said to this man, "Let those who are dead bury their dead; but do you go and spread everywhere the news of the kingdom of God."

Jesus meant by this that such matters as the burial of the dead could be cared for by others, even though they did not have a knowledge of the truth which gives life; but Jesus wanted this man to go at once and preach his gospel.

There was another man who said to Jesus, "I will follow you; but let me first go and say 'good-bye' to my friends at my home."

"Whoever looks back," answered Jesus, "after he has put his hand to the plough is of no use for the kingdom of God."

For his work Jesus wanted men who were single-hearted, giving up all, that they might follow and serve him.

On this journey to Jerusalem Jesus did not take the road down the Jordan valley, the way usually followed. He made up his mind this time to go through Samaria, perhaps because he did not wish to have a crowd of people with him, and few of the Jews went to Jerusalem by way of Samaria.

As he drew near a Samaritan village, he sent some of his disciples to find in it a lodging place. But the Samaritan people would not allow Jesus and his disciples to come into their village, because they saw that they were Jews on their way to Jerusalem. The Samaritans and the Jews hated each other and would not show kindness to one another.

James and John, two of the disciples, were exceedingly angry at these people, who would shut out their Master. They said to him:

"Lord, shall we call down fire from heaven, as the prophet Elijah did, and burn up that wicked village?"

But Jesus said to them, "Your spirit is not right. I did not come to destroy the lives of men, but to save them. Let us go to some other village."

While he was still on the border of Galilee and Samaria, as he was going into a village, he met ten men who had the terrible disease of leprosy. They stood at a distance, for lepers were not allowed to come near people; and they cried aloud, saying:

"Jesus, Master, have mercy on us!"

"Go," answered Jesus, "and show yourselves to the priests."

In the Temple was a room where a man went who had any disease like leprosy, with a breaking out upon his skin. At this room he was kept for a time; and if it was found that his disease was not leprosy, after certain offerings and washings, he was allowed to go home and be among men. These men started for their Temple; those who were Jews for the Temple in Jerusalem, any that were Samaritans for their Temple on Mount Gerizim, near the city of Shechem. As they went, and by going showed their faith in Jesus, they found all at once that their leprosy was gone and they were entirely well.

Nine of these ten men, after they were cured, went on their way toward the Temple. But one of them, when he found that he was a leper no longer, stopped, with a loud voice praised God; and ran to Jesus' feet and fell on his face before him, giving him thanks for his cure. This man was a Samaritan.

"Were there not ten men cured?" said Jesus. "But where are the nine? Was there only one to turn back and give thanks to God, and that one a stranger?"

And Jesus said to this grateful Samaritan, "Rise up, and go your way; your faith has made you well."

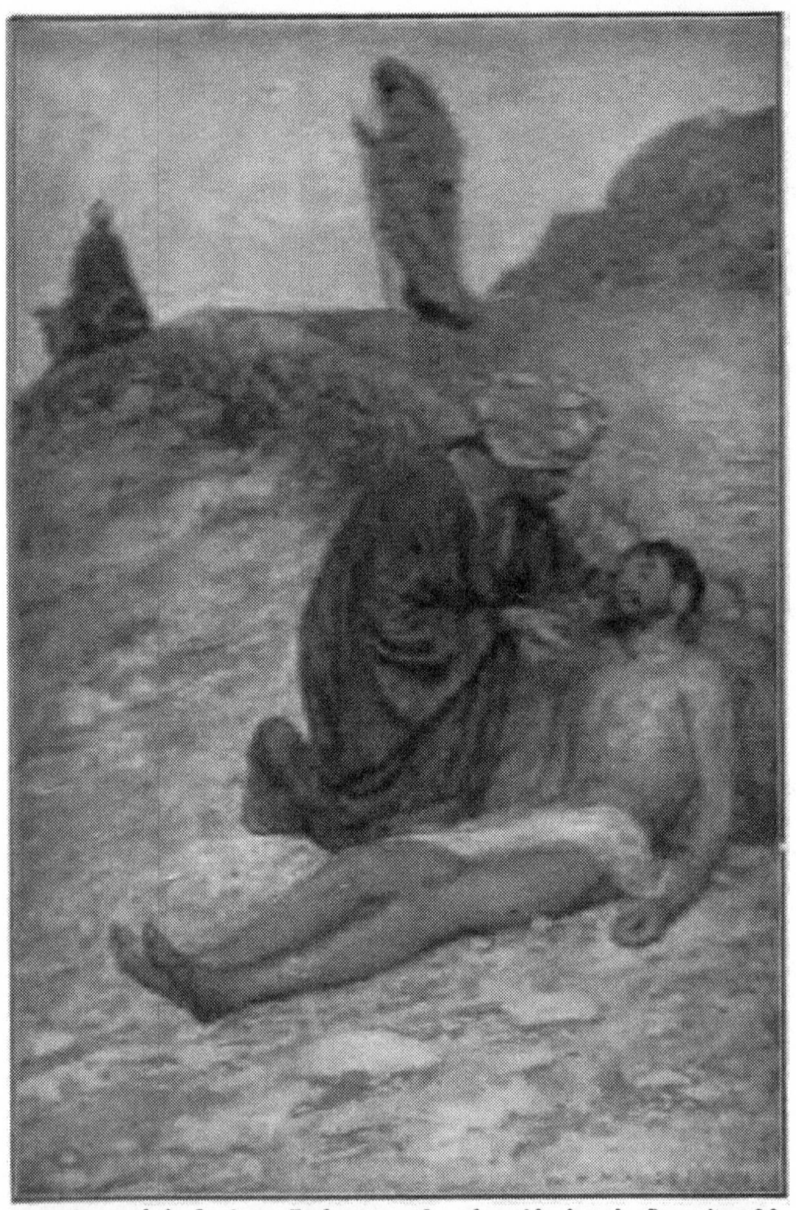

The priest and the Levite walked past on the other side, but the Samaritan felt a pity for the poor man lying in the road and came down and poured oil on his wounds and bandaged them.

The Scribe's Question; and Mary's Choice

CHAPTER 53

WHILE JESUS was on his way to Jerusalem one of the teachers of the law—whom the Jews called "scribes"—came to him with a question. These Jewish scribes were everywhere enemies of Jesus, and were continually asking him questions, not that they might learn, but that in some way they might give him trouble.

This scribe said to Jesus, "Teacher, what shall I do that I may have the life everlasting?"

"What is said in God's law?" answered Jesus. "What do you read there?"

He answered, "You must love the Lord your God with all your heart, with all your soul, with all your strength, and with all your mind; and you must love your neighbor as yourself."

"That is a right answer," said Jesus; "do that and you shall live."

But the scribe, wishing to make an excuse for himself, and thinking to puzzle Jesus, said, "But who is my neighbor?"

Then Jesus told to this man the parable or story of "The Good Samaritan."

"There was once a man," said Jesus, "who was going down by a lonely road from Jerusalem to Jericho. The robbers who hide among the mountains in that region rushed at this man, stripped him of everything, and beat him near to death; then ran away and left him almost dead on the roadside. It happened that a priest was going down the same road. He saw the man lying there, but instead of coming to help him, walked past him on the other side of the road. Then a Levite, one of those who help the priests in the services of the Temple, came to that place; and he too went by on the other side, carefully keeping away from the suffering man.

"But soon after, a Samaritan, one of those people whom all the Jews hate and despise, came down the same road. This man, when he found the poor man lying in the road, got off from the ass on which he was riding and stood over the man. He felt a pity for the sufferer and put bandages on his wounds, after pouring into them a little oil and wine. Then he lifted up the man and carefully placed him on his own ass, and walking by his side, brought him to an inn and cared for him all that night. On the next morning he took out from his purse two pieces of silver, handed them to the inn-keeper and said to him, "Look after this man until he is well; and if you spend more than this, I will repay it to you when I come this way again."

"Now," asked Jesus, "which one of these three men, the priest, the Levite and the Samaritan, do you think showed himself a true neighbor to the poor fellow who fell among the robbers?"

The scribe answered, "The one who showed kindness to him."

Jesus said to him, "Then go and do as this man did." He meant to show the scribe that "our neighbor" is the one who most needs our help, whoever he may be.

When Jesus drew near to Jerusalem, he did not at once enter the city and find a lodging place within its walls, for he knew well that it was filled with his enemies; and that the priests and rulers would try to seize him

"Martha, Martha," replied the Lord, "you are anxious and troubled about a great many things."

and put him to death. He expected after some months to die at Jerusalem, as he had so many times told his disciples—although they could not believe it—but the time for his death had not yet come. For a home while attending the Feast of Tents, he went to a village about two miles from Jerusalem, on the east of the Mount of Olives. This village was called Bethany, and in it was living a family all of whom were strong friends of Jesus: Martha, her sister Mary and their younger brother Lazarus. With this family he stayed while he was visiting Jerusalem.

Martha was the older sister and the head of the house. She gave Jesus a hearty welcome and made herself busy in attending to his needs. But Mary, her younger sister, left everything and seated herself at the feet of the Lord, eager to listen to his words. Martha, somewhat worried by her many cares, especially in making ready a dinner for Jesus, was not pleased at her sister's conduct. She came to Jesus and said:

"Lord, do you think it right for my sister to leave all the work to me? Tell her to help me."

"Martha, Martha," replied the Lord, "you are anxious and trouble yourself about a great many things. Only one thing is really needful. Mary has chosen the best dish, and she will not be dragged away from it."

Jesus meant to say that Martha need not prepare a dinner with many dishes, for he needed only a simple meal; and that Mary had chosen well instead of food the words that he was speaking, which were really a feast to her soul.

At one time Jesus was praying in a certain place. It may have been on the Mount of Olives, between Bethany and Jerusalem, for Jesus went there often to pray. When his prayer was over, the disciples came to him and said:

"Master, John the Baptist taught his disciples how to pray. Will you not also give us a prayer that we may use?"

Jesus said to them, "I will give you this prayer. When you pray, say, 'Our Father, who art in heaven; Hallowed be thy name. Thy Kingdom come. Thy will be done in earth, as it is in heaven. Give us day by day our daily bread. And forgive us our debts, as we forgive our debtors. And lead us not into temptation, but deliver us from evil. For thine is the kingdom, and the power, and the glory, for ever and forever. Amen.'"

Jesus also gave to his disciples a parable or story about earnestness in prayer. He said:

"Suppose that one of you who has a friend should go to his house in the middle of the night, and should knock at his door loud enough to wake him from his sleep, and should say to him, 'Friend, please do get up and let me have three loaves of bread! A friend of mine has suddenly come to my house and I have nothing for him to eat;' and suppose the other should answer him from inside the door, 'Don't bother me; the door is locked and I am in bed with my children. I can't get up and give you anything!' I tell you, though he will not get up and give you anything merely because you are a friend of his, if you keep on knocking long enough, he will at last rise and give you whatever you want, because you persevere in seeking after it.

"So, I say to you: ask, and the gitt shall be yours; seek, and you shall find; knock, and the door will be opened to you. For every one who asks, receives; he that seeks, finds; and to him that knocks, the door shall be opened.

"Is there a father among you, who if his son asks for bread, will give him a stone? If he is asked for a fish, will he give his son a snake? Or, if asked for an egg, will he give him a scorpion? If you then, even not as good as you should be, are willing to give good things to your children, how much more will your Father in heaven give this Holy Spirit to his children that ask him?"

This massive ancient wall is known as the Wailing Place. Here the Jews of Jerusalem come to mourn over the splendor of Israel that is no more

Jesus at the Feast of Tents

CHAPTER 54

AT THE TIME when Jesus came to Jerusalem, the Feast of Tents was half over. Many had been looking for him, for all through the land he was talked about. At the Feast the people were saying, "Where is he? Has he come up to the Feast?"

Some said, "He is a good man." Others said, "No, he cannot be a good man, for he is leading the people away from the law of Moses." But no one spoke freely about him, for fear of the rulers and the people of Jerusalem whose minds had been set against Jesus by the priests and the scribes or teachers of the law.

From his home in Bethany at Martha's house, Jesus came quietly into the Temple and began teaching the people who gathered there during the Feast, going out at evening to Bethany. All who heard him wondered at his words, and every day the crowds around him grew. People said to each other, "How did this man get all his knowledge? He has never studied in the college of the scribes."

"My teaching," said Jesus in answer, "is not my own; but it comes from Him who sent me. Any one who chooses to do God's will, will know whether I speak in God's name, or whether I am talking in my own name. Did not Moses give you the law? Yet none of you honestly tries to keep the law. If you did try to keep the law, you would not try to kill me!"

The crowd replied to Jesus, "You are crazy! Who is trying to kill you?"

But Jesus knew that he was speaking the truth, for he knew what was in the minds of the rulers and of many in Jerusalem. He said to the crowd:

"I will be with you only a little longer, and then I am going to him who sent me. You will look for me, but you will not find me, and where I am going, you cannot come."

"If any man thirst, let him come unto me and drink"

"Where is this man going," said the Jews, "that we cannot find him? Is he going among our people in foreign lands, to teach the foreigners? What does he mean by words like these?"

Jesus meant that after they should kill him and he should rise from the tomb and live again, he was going back to his home in heaven, a place to which they could never come.

The last and greatest day of the Feast of Tents came. On that day they brought water into the Temple and poured it out, amid great rejoicing; calling to mind how God had given water from the rock to the Israelites in the desert.

In the midst of the pouring out of the water,

Jesus cried with a very loud voice, so that all heard him:

"If any one is thirsty," he said, "let him come to me and drink! He who believes in me, out of him shall flow rivers of living water!"

Some of the people, when they heard this, said, "This must be really the Prophet who is to come!"

Others said, "This is the Christ, the King of Israel!"

But there were those who said, "No, this cannot be Christ the King, for this man comes from Galilee, and the Bible says that Christ is to come from the line of King David and from David's town of Bethlehem."

These people knew that Jesus came to them from Galilee, but they did not know that he had been born in Bethlehem and belonged to the royal line of David. They were divided over Jesus: some thought that he was their promised king, while others wanted to seize him as a teacher of falsehood. The rulers sent out officers to make him their prisoner, but somehow no man dared to lay hands upon him.

When the officers came back to the chief priests and leading men, they were asked, "Why did you not bring this man with you?"

The officers answered, "No man ever spoke as this man speaks!"

"What! has this man led you astray, too?" said the rulers. "Have any of the leading men, or the Pharisees, believed in him? As for this crowd who know nothing of the law, they are of no account!"

Nicodemus, that one of the rulers who a year before had come by night to talk with Jesus, said to them:

"Surely our law does not allow any man to be treated as guilty before hearing what he has to say and finding out what he has done!"

"Are you too from Galilee, like all the followers of this man?" they answered him. "Search, and you will find that no prophet ever comes from Galilee."

In the evening all the people went to their homes, and Jesus went over the Mount of Olives to his friends at Bethany.

View of Bethany

Jesus and the Sinful Woman

CHAPTER 55

AFTER THE Feast of Tents Jesus stayed near Jerusalem, making his home in Bethany, for nearly two months, until another feast came, the Feast of the Dedication of the Temple. About two hundred years before that time, the Temple had been held by enemies, who had stopped the services, had set up images in the building and had done many things to make it vile. At last the enemies were driven away; and then the Jews made the Temple clean again, destroyed the images and began once more the regular service. After this, every year they kept the day of the reopening of the Temple as "The Feast of the Dedication." At this feast the Temple was lighted up every night very brightly, and on that account the feast was also called "The Feast of Lights."

During the days of his stay, Jesus went often to the Temple and sat down in a room called "The Court of the Women," because on one side of it was a gallery where the women worshipped, looking down on the services at the altar. It was also called "The Treasury" on account of the gift-boxes on its walls, where people dropped in their money for the poor and for the support of the Temple. In this court, which was very large, and open to the sky, without a roof, the Jewish teachers held their classes for the study of the law; and many came to Jesus to listen to his words.

One morning the teaching of Jesus was interrupted by a noise in the court. Some of the scribes and Pharisees, who were enemies of Jesus, planned to get

Jesus replied to the accusers of the sinful woman: "Let the one among you who has never done wrong throw the first stone at her."

him into trouble with the Roman rulers. They came, dragging in a poor woman who had done a wicked deed; and bringing her forward directly in front of Jesus.

"Teacher," they said, "this woman was caught in a wicked act. Now, Moses in the law commands that any person committing that crime shall be stoned to death; but what do you say should be done with her?"

Jesus very well knew that they had brought this question to him hoping, whatever he said, to make trouble for him. If he should say, "Let her go free," they would declare that Jesus was a breaker of the law and cared nothing for crimes. If, on the other hand, he said, "Let her be punished," they could say to the Roman rulers, "This man is acting as a judge and claims to be the King of Israel;" and this might cause the Romans to put him to death. So, whatever Jesus might say, they could find some reason to accuse him.

But Jesus seemed to pay no attention to their words. He stooped down, and began to write with his finger on the floor. But as they kept on asking him the same question, finally he rose up, looked his enemies full in the face, and said:

"Let the one among you who has never done wrong throw the first stone at her."

Then he stooped down again and continued writing with his finger. They stood silent for some time and then began quietly to go away, the oldest men first and the younger men later. After a while, Jesus looked up and saw the woman standing alone before him. He rose up and said:

"Woman, where are those men? Does no man say that you are guilty?"

She answered him, "No man, Lord."

Jesus said to her, "Neither do I call you guilty. Go away, and never sin again."

Then Jesus went on with his teaching, which had been stopped by the bringing in of the woman by his enemies. He said:

"I am the light of the whole world. He who follows me and obeys my words will not walk in darkness, but shall have the light of life."

"I am the light of the whole world. He who follows me and obeys my words will not walk in darkness, but shall have the light of life"

Many other things Jesus said to the people at that time; and some of those who heard him began to believe that he was a teacher come from God. To those who believed, he said:

"If you stand faithful to my words, you are truly my followers; and you shall understand the truth, and the truth shall make you free."

"What do you mean by those words, 'You shall be made free'? said the people. "We are sprung from Abraham, and have never been slaves. How can we be made free?"

"In very truth, I tell you," answered Jesus, "every one who sins is a slave. Now the slave does not stay in the home always, but the son stays, for it is his home, and he has a right to be there. So, if the Son of the heavenly Father sets you free from sin, you will be free indeed."

As Jesus went on speaking, the people who listened became very angry. At last he said:

"Your great father Abraham longed to see the day when I should come to the earth; and he saw it coming, and it made him glad."

"Why," the Jews said, "you are not fifty years old, and do you say that Abraham saw you?"

"I tell you truly," answered Jesus, "before Abraham was born, I was living!"

At this, they picked up stones to throw at him; but Jesus hid himself from them and left the Temple.

The so-called tower of David in Jerusalem

The Blind Man at the Pool of Siloam

CHAPTER I

On a Sabbath morning, which was not Sunday, but Saturday, the seventh day of rest and worship-going—Jesus and his disciples were on their way to the service in the Temple, when they passed a blind man. They had seen this man before and knew that he had been blind all his life. He had come into the world without eyesight, to the great sorrow of his father and mother; and he lived upon the little gifts that people gave him as they were on their way to the Temple.

The Jews believed that every disease was caused by some act of sin; that if a man became ill, it was because he had done some wicked deed and was being punished for it; and if a child was born blind, or dumb, or crippled, it must have been because either his father or mother had sinned against God's law. Some of the scribes, who were the teachers of the law, said that each soul lived many times on the earth; that when a man died, his soul went into a body that was born at that moment; and if the new-born baby was blind, or diseased, it was because it had done wrong in some life before that one. None of these things are believed now since Christ has taught men, but they were held by nearly all people while Jesus was on the earth.

As the disciples were passing by this blind man, one of them said to Jesus:

"Teacher, whose sin was it that caused this man to

be born blind? Was it the fault of his parents? Or was it his own fault?"

"It was through no fault of his, nor of his father or mother that this man was born blind," answered Jesus. "It was that God might show a wonderful work in him. While daylight lasts, we must be doing God's work; the night will soon come when we can work no longer. As long as I am in the world I am the light of the world, and give light to men."

As he said this, he spat on the ground and mixed the spittle with dust, making it into mud, and smeared it on the man's eyes. He said to the blind man:

"Now, go down to the pool of Siloam and wash."

The Pool of Siloam at the present time

The pool of Siloam was a large tank or reservoir on the southeast of the city, where the valley of the brook Kedron and the valley of Hinnom meet. To go to that place the blind man with two great blotches of mud on his face must walk across the city of Jerusalem, passing all the crowds on their way to worship. He went down to the pool of Siloam, climbed down its steps to the water and washed the mud from his face. In a moment his white, sightless eyes flashed with a new light. He looked up, and for the first time in all his life he could see!

As he went to his father's house, everybody who saw him noticed how differently he looked. All had known him as a blind man, groping his way to the place where he used to sit as a beggar. The people asked each other:

"Is this the same blind man that begged in the street?"

Some said, "Yes, this is the same man."

But others said, "No, this cannot be the man; but he is one who looks somewhat like him."

He said, "I am the same man."

"Then how did you get your sight?" they asked.

"The man whom they call Jesus," he answered, "made some mud and put it on my eyes, and said, 'Go to Siloam and wash your eyes.' So I went and washed them; and my sight came to me."

"Where is this man who cured you?" they asked.

"I do not know," he answered.

They took the man who had been blind to the Pharisees, who were the leaders of the people. We have seen that the Pharisees were always enemies to Jesus. So the Pharisees asked him to tell again how he had gained his sight; and he told them:

"The man named Jesus smeared some mud on my eyes, and I washed them, and now I can see."

Some of the Pharisees said, "This man Jesus cannot be from God, because he does not keep the Sabbath."

The scribes had made a rule that mixing up mud on the Sabbath day was working; that carrying it from one place to another was bearing a load; and that to give any treatment to a sick man on the Sabbath, unless it was necessary to save his life, was Sabbath breaking. So to their eyes, Jesus in curing the blind man had broken the Sabbath rules in more than one way.

But some others said, "How can a bad man do such wonderful works? Is not this work of cure a sign that God is with him?"

So there were two parties among them in their opinion about Jesus. They asked the blind man again:

"What do you say of this man who has opened your eyes?"

"I say that he is a prophet from God," answered the man.

Many of the Jews, however, would not believe that this man had been born blind and had gained his sight, until they sent for his father and mother.

"Is this your son," they asked, "the son you say was born blind? How is it that now he can see?"

"This is our son," his parents answered, "and he was born blind; of that we are sure. But how it is that he can see now, we do not know, nor do we know who opened his eyes. Ask him—he is old enough—he can speak for himself."

His parents spoke in this way because they were afraid of the Jews, for the rulers had agreed that any one who said that Jesus was the Christ should be turned out of the church. That was why they had said, "He is old enough; ask him." So the Pharisees again sent for the man who had been blind, and said to him:

"Give God all the praise for your sight; we know that this Jesus is a bad man."

"I know nothing about his being a bad man; one thing I do know, that once I was blind, and now I can see."

"What did he do to you?" they asked. "How did he open your eyes?"

"I have told you all about it already," he replied, "and it seems you do not listen. Why do you want to hear it again? Do you intend to be his disciples?"

Then they were in a rage at him, and said, "You may be his disciple, but we are disciples of Moses, and we obey his laws. We know that God spoke to Moses, but we do not know where this fellow comes from!"

"Well, this is very strange!" answered the man. "You do not know where he comes from; and yet he has opened my eyes. We know that God does not listen to bad men; but if any man is God-fearing, and does God's will, that man God will hear. Since the world began, no one ever heard before of a man that could open the eyes of one born blind. If this Jesus were not of God, he could do nothing."

"Are you trying to teach us?" they answered. "You, who were born a sinner?"

Then they turned him out of the church; they forbade him to sit in the meetings or to go into the Temple; and after that none of them would so much as speak to him. Jesus heard that he had been put out of the church; he sought him out, and when he had found him, he asked:

"Do you believe in the Son of Man?"

"Tell me who he is," said the man, "and I will believe in him."

"You have seen him," answered Jesus, "and it is he who is now speaking to you."

The man said, "I do believe, Lord," and he fell on his face before him.

And Jesus said, "I came into the world to put men to this test, in order that those who cannot see, and know they are blind as this man was, might be made to see; and that those who think they can see should remain blind."

Some of the Pharisees who heard this knew that it was a rebuke to them, because they failed to see in Jesus one sent from God. They said:

"Then are we blind, too!"

"If you were really blind," said Jesus, "you would have no sin to answer for; but as it is, you say, 'We can see' and so your sin remains against you."

Again the Jews were divided over the words of Jesus. Some said, "He is crazy! Why listen to him?"

But others said, "These are not the words of a crazy man. Can a man who is crazy open the eyes of a blind man?"

The modern village of Siloam

The Good Shepherd

[illegible]

[illegible] because you do not belong to my flock. My sheep listen to my voice. I know them, and they follow me: and I give to them the life everlasting; and they shall not be lost, and no one will ever snatch them out of my hands. My Father who has given them to me is stronger than all: and no one can snatch anything out of my Father's hand."

Then Jesus gave the parable or story of "The Good Shepherd." He said:

"I tell you in truth, whoever does not go into the sheepfold through the door, but climbs up somewhere else, that man is a thief and a robber. But the man who goes through the door is a shepherd of the sheep. The watchman opens the door for him; and the sheep listen to his voice. He calls his own sheep by their names, for he knows each one of them, and leads them out. When he has brought all his sheep outside, he walks in front of them; and his sheep follow him, for they know his voice. When a stranger speaks to them, they will not follow him, but will run away from him, for they do not know a stranger's voice."

Jesus spoke to them this parable, but they did not understand its meaning. So he explained it to them.

Eastern sheepfold

"In truth I tell you," he said, "I am the Door for the sheep. All who ever came before me and not in my name, were thieves and robbers, but the sheep would not listen to them. I am the Door, whoever enters by me will be safe; and he shall go in and out and find pasture. The thief comes only to kill and to destroy. I have come that they may have life and have it to the full.

"I am not only the Door, but also the Good Shepherd. The Good Shepherd lays down his own life for his sheep. The hired man, who is not a shepherd and does not own the sheep, when he sees a wolf coming, runs away and leaves the sheep. Then the wolf tears them and scatters the flock. The hired man does this, just because he is only a hired man, and does not care about the sheep.

"I am the Good Shepherd; I know my sheep, and

my sheep know me—just as the Father knows me, and I know the Father—and I lay down my life for the sheep.

"I have other sheep, too, which do not belong to this fold; these also I must lead, and they will listen to my voice; and so it will be one flock and one Shepherd.

The Good Shepherd

"On this account my Father loves me because I lay down my life, to take it up again. No one took it from me, but I lay it down of myself. I have power to lay it down, and I have power to take it up again. This is the command which my Father has given me. I and my Father are one."

Suddenly, as he spoke these words, the Jews began again to pick up stones to throw at him. Jesus said to them:

"I have done many good works of God. For which of these works would you now stone me?"

The Jews answered, "It is not for any good work that we would stone you, but for those dreadful words, words that would make you, a mere man, to be God!"

Jesus answered, "Is it not written in your law, 'I said, you are gods'? If the law calls those 'gods' to whom God spoke his word—and God's book must speak the truth—then why is it such a terrible thing for one whom God has set apart and sent into the world as his messenger, to say of himself 'I am God's Son'? If I am not doing the work of my Father, do not believe me; but if I am doing it, even though you will not believe me, believe what my work shows. Then you will learn and understand that the Father is in me and I am in the Father."

Once again they tried to seize him, but he escaped from their hands and went away from Jerusalem.

Jerusalem from the north

Sending Out the Seventy

CHAPTER 58

AFTER LEAVING Jerusalem, at the time of the Feast of the Dedication, Jesus went across the Jordan, and followed the river upward to the place twelve or thirteen miles below the Sea of Galilee; the place where he had been baptized by John, and where soon after his baptism he found his earliest followers. This place was called by two names, "Bethabara," which means, "the town of the ford," that is where one could wade across the river; and "Bethany beyond Jordan," to keep it distinct from the other Bethany near Jerusalem, where Martha and Mary lived.

The twelve disciples were with Jesus at Bethabara, and some who came with him from Jerusalem and Judea. Also when the news went abroad in Galilee that Jesus was at this place, many more hastened to meet him; so that soon a large number of his followers gathered around him. Jesus was now near the border of the land on the east of the Jordan, known as Perea. This word means "beyond," and the land was so named because it was "beyond the Jordan" from Judea.

Jesus had never visited this land, although he had preached in every other part of the country; in Judea on the south; in Galilee on the north; in Decapolis on the northeast; and even in Samaria, where the people were not Jews but Samaritans. He made up his mind now to go through Perea preaching, as he had preached in all the other parts of the land. But in Perea, his time must be short, because now only three months remained before the Feast of the Passover, and at that time he must be in Jerusalem. In order to make the people of Perea ready for his coming, and to bring together as many as possible to hear him, he chose the places in that land to be visited. Then he called seventy men from among his followers, and sent them by two and two to these cities and the villages around them, to preach to the people and tell them that Jesus was soon to come among them.

To these seventy preachers, Jesus gave the same commands that he had given to the Twelve some months before, when he sent them out to preach in Galilee. He said:

"Do not take with you a purse of money, or a bag for food, or an extra pair of sandals. Do not stop to give greetings to any who meet you on the road. Wherever you go into a house, first say, 'May peace be to this house!' Then if one is there who is in the spirit of peace, your peace will rest upon him; otherwise it will come back to you. Stay at that same house while you are in that city, and eat and drink whatever they offer you, for the workman has a right to his wages. Do not move around from one house to another. Whatever town you visit, if the people give you welcome, eat what is given you; cure those that are sick; and be sure to say to the people everywhere, 'The kingdom of God is coming very soon.'

"But whatever town you visit, if the people will not receive you nor listen to your message, go out into the streets of that place and cry aloud, 'The very dust of your city that clings to our feet we wipe off as a sign against you; but be sure of this, that the kingdom of God is coming to you soon.' I tell you that in God's day when he will judge men, the punishment of Sodom will be easier to bear than the punishment of that town!"

The seventy men went out from Bethabara, going in pairs, two men together, making thirty-five pairs. They visited all the cities and villages in the country of Perea to which Jesus had sent them, the places which he was expecting to visit later; gave to the people the message of Jesus, that the kingdom of God was soon to appear, and thus aroused the people everywhere to an interest in the coming of Jesus. Their errand was finished in a few weeks, for thirty-five pairs of men could soon visit many places; and when they came again to Bethabara, they found Jesus still there.

They told Jesus what places they had visited and how they had wrought many cures in his name and 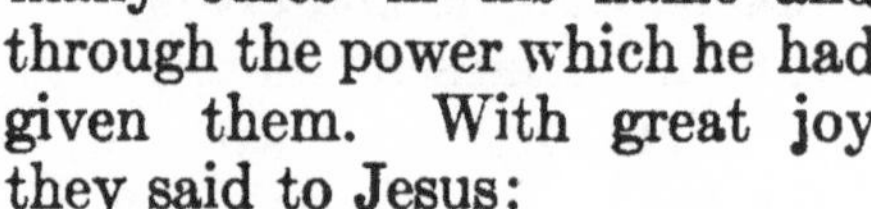 through the power which he had given them. With great joy they said to Jesus:

A scorpion

"Master, even the evil spirits obey us when we use your name!"

And Jesus answered them, "Yes, I have seen Satan, the chief of the evil spirits, fall from heaven like a flash of lightning from the sky. Remember, I have given you the power to tread on serpents and scorpions, and to trample under your feet all the power of the enemy; nothing shall in any way do you any harm. Only, do not rejoice merely because the evil spirits submit to you; but rejoice more because your names are written in heaven as the children of God."

While Jesus was at Bethabara, many people came to see him and to hear his words. As this was one of the places where John the Baptist had preached three years before, they compared Jesus with John, and many of them said:

"John the Baptist never gave any wonderful works as signs that God had sent him; but he spoke about this man; and all that he ever said of this man was the truth."

And while Jesus was at Bethabara many people believed in him and became his followers.

Lazarus Called Out of His Tomb

CHAPTER 59

WHILE JESUS was still at Bethabara, and expecting soon to begin his journey through Perea, news came to him which led him for a time to change his plans.

At Bethany, near Jerusalem, as you remember, were living his dear friends, Martha and Mary and Lazarus. The two sisters sent to Jesus at Bethabara the word:

"Lord, your friend Lazarus is very ill."

They did not ask Jesus to come and cure Lazarus, but they hoped that he might come, although it would call for a journey sixty miles from Bethabara to Bethany. But Jesus did not at once go to the sick man. He said:

"This sickness is not to end in his death; the end of it will be to give glory to God and to the Son of God."

Jesus loved Martha and Mary and Lazarus. Yet, when he heard that Lazarus was very ill, he stayed two days longer at Bethabara. Then, after that, he said to his disciples, "Let us go again to Judea."

At this the disciples were greatly surprised. They said to him, "Why, Master, only a little while ago the men of Judea were trying to stone you. Is it safe for you to go there again?"

"Are there not twelve hours in the day?" answered Jesus. "If a man walks about through the day, he does not stumble, because he can have the light of the sun; but if he walks at night, he does stumble, because he has no light."

With a loud voice, Jesus called: "Lazarus! Come out!" And out from the tomb came the man who had been dead.

Then he added, "Our friend Lazarus has fallen asleep; I am going to wake him."

"If he has fallen asleep, Master," said the disciples, "he will get well."

They thought that Jesus was speaking of taking rest in sleep, which would show that a fever was passing away; but Jesus meant that Lazarus was in the sleep of death. Then he told them in plain words:

"Lazarus is dead; and on your account I am glad

Bethany, where Martha, Mary and Lazarus lived

that I was not there; for now you will learn to believe in me more fully. Come, now, let us go to him."

At this, Thomas, one of his twelve disciples, who was also called "Didymus," a word meaning "The Twin," said to his fellow disciples:

"Let us go too; and if he dies, we will die with him."

So from Bethabara they went again to Bethany, two miles from Jerusalem; a journey of about sixty miles. When Jesus came to Bethany, he found that Lazarus had been already four days in the tomb. In the house with Martha and Mary were a number of their friends who had come to show their sympathy with the sisters by weeping with them over their brother's death.

Someone went into the room and told Martha that Jesus was coming, and was near the village. She rose up quietly and hastened to meet Jesus, while Mary sat still in the room. When Martha saw Jesus, she said to him mournfully:

"Lord, if you had been here, my brother would not have died. And even now, I know that whatever you ask of God, he will give it to you."

"Your brother shall rise to life again," said Jesus.

"I know that he will rise again," said Martha, "when all the dead shall be raised up, at the last day."

"I, myself," said Jesus, "am the one who raises the dead to life. He who believes in me shall live again, even if he dies; and he who lives believing in me shall never die. Do you believe that?"

"Yes, Lord," she said, "I do believe that you are the Christ, the Son of God, who was promised to come into the world."

After saying this, Martha went again to the house, leaving Jesus still outside the village. She whispered to her sister Mary:

"The Master is here, and he has asked for you."

On hearing this, Mary rose in haste and went to the place where Jesus was. The friends who were with her, seeing her go out of the house, thought that she was going to the tomb, to weep there, and they followed her, to weep with her. It was the custom in that land, and still is the custom, for those who had lost a friend, to meet at his grave, day after day, and there to mourn for him.

But Mary did not go to her brother's tomb. She went to Jesus, who was still at the place where Martha had met him; and threw herself at his feet, saying, as her sister had said before:

"O Master! if only you had been here, my brother would not have died!"

When Jesus saw her wailing, and saw the friends with her wailing, he too was troubled and greatly distressed.

"Where have you laid him," he asked.

"Come and see, Master," they answered.

Jesus now began to weep, in feeling for the two sisters.

"How he must have loved him!" said the Jews to each other. But some of them said:

"Could not this man, who gave sight to a blind man, have kept this man from dying?"

Again groaning, but quietly, Jesus came to the tomb. Like many of the graves in that land, it was a cave in the rocky hillside, and a large stone covered its mouth.

"Move away the stone," commanded Jesus.

"Master," said Martha, "remember that he has been dead four days, and by this time there may be a strong smell from the body."

"Did I not tell you," said Jesus, "that if you will only believe in me you will see the glory of God?"

They moved the stone away from the door of the cave, and Jesus, lifting his eyes upward, said:

"Father, I thank thee for listening to my prayer. I knew that thou always hearest me; but I spoke on account of those around me, that they might believe that thou hast sent me."

Then with a loud voice, Jesus called:

"Lazarus! Come out!"

Out from the tomb came the man who had been dead. He could scarcely walk, for his hands and feet were wrapped with bandages; his face, too, had been covered with a cloth tied over it.

"Set him free," said Jesus, "and let him go!"

They took away the cloth from his face, and unwrapped the bandages from his body; and Lazarus stood up living and well, in the presence of all the people! How happy were Martha and Mary, as they placed their arms around him, and felt his flesh, warm with the life-blood once more flowing through his veins!

As the Jews who had come to visit Martha and Mary saw this wonderful work, calling back to life a man who had been in his tomb four days, many of them believed in Jesus. These told the story to others, and the number of believers grew larger and larger.

Some of those who had seen or had heard of the raising of Lazarus to life went to Jerusalem and told the Pharisees, the enemies of Jesus, what had taken place. These men told the chief priests, and the priests and Pharisees called together the high council to talk of these things and to decide what should be done with Jesus.

This high council was a board or company of leading men, which, next to the Roman governor, ruled over the Jews. It was made up of seventy-two men, some of them priests and some of them scribes or teachers of the law. They met in a room set apart for their use in the Temple; and they formed the highest court in the land to deal with any who were accused of having broken the laws.

When this council came together and heard of what Jesus had done and of the people who, in greater number than ever, were beginning to believe in Jesus, they said to each other, "What shall we do, now that this Jesus has done another work, more wonderful even than any of his works in the past? If we leave him alone, all the people will believe in him, and will seek to make him their King. Then the Romans will come, and will destroy our Temple, and will no longer let us live as a nation."

But one of these men in the council was the high priest, whose name was Caiaphas. He said to them:

"You are entirely mistaken. You do not understand that whether Jesus is or is not a prophet coming from God, it is better that one man should die, instead of having all the people destroyed. Let us all agree that Jesus shall be killed, and that the people of Israel shall be saved from death."

These words of Caiaphas the high priest meant more than he knew when he spoke them. He was himself, being the high priest, speaking a prophecy, that Jesus was to die for the people; for that was what Jesus was soon to do. He was to die for the sins of the people; not only for the Jewish people but for all the people of the world. By his death, Jesus was to bring together into one body all the children of God scattered throughout all the lands.

At that meeting of the council, the rulers decided that Jesus must be killed. Not all of them agreed in this, for Nicodemus, who long before had come at night to talk with Jesus, and a rich member of the council, named Joseph—of whom we shall hear later—and a few others, were friendly to Jesus. But his enemies were so many and so fierce that these few friends of Jesus did not venture to speak for him. So the vote was taken that Jesus was to be put to death.

Jesus, knowing all things, knew their plans; and he knew that when the time came he should die. But that time had not yet come, for he had promised to preach his gospel in Perea, across the Jordan. He went, therefore, to a town on the edge of the wilderness, called Ephraim, and there for a few weeks he stayed with his disciples.

The great Feast of the Passover was drawing near, and many people were coming up to Jerusalem to prepare themselves for the Feast. They were looking out for Jesus, and said to each other as they walked in the courts of the Temple:

"What do you think? Do you think that Jesus will come to the Feast?"

The chief priests and the leading Pharisees had given orders that if any one found out where Jesus was, they were to be told, so that they might send men to arrest him.

The Via Dolorosa, or Sorrowful Way, over which, it is said, Christ walked carrying his cross

Jesus Preaching in Perea

CHAPTER 60

JESUS DID not stay long in the village of Ephraim. He went down the mountains to the river Jordan, crossed it, and began preaching in the land of Perea, going to the places where his seventy messengers had given the news of his coming.

Everywhere the people thronged in great crowds to see him and to hear him. The rich and the poor met in the crowd, the rulers and the common people, the Pharisees who were his enemies, and the publicans or tax-collectors who had been leading lives full of sin. There was a great desire among the people to listen to the Teacher and Prophet from Galilee, of whom they had heard so much, and whom they had not seen before. Many went to see him because they believed that he was the long-looked-for Christ, who was at last on his way to Jerusalem to sit on his throne and rule all the lands. So great were the crowds to see and hear Jesus that it is said that the thousands trod on each other around him.

While he was speaking in one place to a great multitude of people, a voice was heard from the throng.

"Teacher," cried out a man, "tell my brother to divide with me the property which belongs to our family."

This man supposed that Jesus, being the King of Israel, would rule in all matters of difference between the people. But Jesus answered him:

"Man, who made me a judge or a settler of disputes over your affairs?"

Then he added, "Take care to avoid the love of

money; for no matter how rich one may be, his true life does not depend on what he owns."

And he gave to them the parable or story of "The Poor Rich Man." He said:

"There was once a rich man whose farm gave him very large crops. He began to ask himself, 'What am I

Home of a rich man in Palestine

to do? I have no room to store the grain and fruits that have grown on my land. This is what I will do. I will pull down my old barns and build larger ones in place of them. There I shall store all the fruits from my orchards and the grain from my fields. And then I will say to myself, "Now you have plenty of good things stored up to last for many years; take your ease, eat, drink and have a good time."' But God said to him 'Fool! this very night your life is taken away; and who will have all that you have stored up?' So is it with everyone who lays up money for himself, instead of gaining the riches of God."

And Jesus said again to his disciples some of the things that he had already taught them in his great "Sermon on the Mount"; for he often repeated the same teachings, over and over, until the disciples knew them by heart, so that after he should be taken from

"Look at the lilies, and see how they grow"

them, they in turn could tell them to others. At this time he said:

"Therefore I tell you, do not be anxious about your life here on the earth, what you can get to eat, nor what you can get to wear. Life is something more than food and the body is more than its clothes. Look at the crows flying through the air! They neither sow nor reap; they have no storehouse nor barns; and yet God gives them food. How much more are you worth to

God than are the birds? And however anxious you may be, can you add one minute to your life? And if you cannot do even this, why be anxious about other matters?

"Look at the lilies, and see how they grow. They neither spin nor weave; and yet, I tell you, even King Solomon in all his splendor was not dressed like one of these. Now, if God so beautifully clothes the grass in the field, which blooms today, and tomorrow will be thrown into the fire, how much more will he clothe you, O men, who trust God so little?

"So do not worry about food and drink and clothes; these are the things for which the nations of the world who know not God are seeking after, and you should not wish to be like them. Besides, your Father in heaven knows that you have need of these common things. Only seek the kingdom of God, and your heavenly Father will see to it that you have these things. Do not be afraid, my little flock, for your Father has been pleased to give you a place in his kingdom."

At this time some people brought to Jesus the news that Pilate, the Roman governor, had killed in the Temple some men from Galilee, while they were worshipping at the altar, so that their blood was poured out with the blood of their offerings. This act of the governor had terribly shocked the people.

"Do you suppose," said Jesus, "that because those Galileans suffered these things, that they were worse sinners than the rest of those living in Galilee? I tell you, no; unless you turn from your sins and seek God, you will all perish as they did.

"Then, too, think of those eighteen men in Siloam, just outside of Jerusalem; those men on whom the tower fell and killed them all; do you suppose that they had been worse than all the other people living in Jerusalem?

No, I tell you; unless you turn to God, you will all perish as they did."

Then Jesus gave to the people the parable of "The Fruitless Fig Tree." He said:

"A man who had a fig tree growing in his garden came at the time when figs were ripe, looking for fruit, but found on it not a single fig. So he said to the gardener, 'Here I have come for three years looking for fruit on this tree, without finding any. Cut it down! Why should it take up room and rob the soil?' But the gardener answered him, 'O please, sir, leave it one year more. I will dig around it and enrich the soil; then it may bear fruit next year. If it does not, then let it be cut down.' "

Beneath an olive tree is a delightful place to rest, for all about it usually grow flowers of many kinds

"O Jerusalem, Jerusalem! How often would I have gathered your children around me, as a fowl gathers her brood under her wings!"

In the Church and at the Feast

CHAPTER 61

WHILE JESUS was in Perea, on the Sabbath days he went into the churches and spoke there; and in every place the church was crowded with those who were eager to hear him. On one Sabbath day he saw in the church a woman who for eighteen years had been bent double and could not possibly stand up straight. When Jesus saw her, he called her to him.

"Woman," he said, "you are set free from your weakness."

He placed his hands upon her, and instantly power came to her. She stood up erect, and with a loud voice praised God for her cure. But the president of the board in the church was greatly displeased that Jesus had done this on the Sabbath. He said to the people:

"There are six days in the week for work; come on one of these to be cured, and not on the holy Sabbath."

"O you false-hearted men, making a pretense of serving God!" said the Lord Jesus. "Does not each one of you on the Sabbath day unloose his ox or his ass from its manger, and lead it out to drink? And this woman, a daughter of Abraham our father, whom the evil one has held bound for all these eighteen years, should she not be set free on the Sabbath?"

As he said this all those who were opposed to him felt ashamed of themselves; while the people rejoiced to see all his wonderful doings. As Jesus went through the towns and villages, all the time on his way toward Jerusalem, he repeated many of the parables and teachings that he had given in other parts of the land, such as

"The Narrow Door," "The Mustard Seed," "The Yeast in the Dough," and others.

The land of Perea, where he was now teaching, belonged to the Kingdom of Herod. Some Pharisees, who were enemies of Jesus, came to him and said:

"You had better get away from this land, for King Herod means to kill you."

This they said, not to save the life of Jesus, but to make him leave their land. But Jesus answered them:

"You may go and tell that fox that I am casting out the evil spirits and curing diseases today and tomorrow, and on the third day I shall finish my work. But I must go on my way today, tomorrow and the day after tomorrow, for it would never do for a prophet to meet his end except in Jerusalem. O Jerusalem, Jerusalem! killing the prophets and stoning those whom God has sent to you! How often would I have gathered your children around me, as a fowl gathers her brood under her wings! But you would not come! Truly, your house is left to you to be destroyed. Never, I tell you, shall you see me again until the day comes when you will say, 'Blessed be He who comes in the name of the Lord.' "

In one place he was invited by one of the rulers who was a Pharisee to come to his house for dinner. There were at the table other Pharisees and people not friendly to Jesus, and they watched him closely. He saw in the room a man who was swollen with the dropsy; and Jesus asked the teachers of the law and the Pharisees:

"Is it according to the law to cure a sick man on the Sabbath, or is it not?"

They said nothing. Then Jesus laid his hands on the man and cured him, and sent him away. Afterward he said:

"Is there any one of you who, finding on the Sabbath day that his ass or his ox has fallen into a pit, will not at once pull him out without waiting for a working day?"

They could not answer him this question. He noticed that those who had been invited to the dinner picked out for themselves the best places, near the head of the table; and he gave them this advice.

"When you are invited to a marriage feast, do not take one of the best places. It may be that some person of higher rank than you has been invited; and then the one who gives the feast comes to you and says, 'Here, make room for this man!' Then you must get up ashamed and take a place down at the foot of the table. No, when you come to the feast, go to the lowest place, then when the giver of the feast sees you, he will say, 'My friend, come up higher,' and you will be honored in the presence of all your fellow-guests. For every one who lifts up himself shall be humbled; and the one who humbles himself shall be lifted up."

Jesus said also to the ruler who had invited him, "When you give a dinner or a supper, do not ask your friends, or your brothers, or those who are your relatives, or your rich neighbors, for they may invite you in turn, and thus you will be repaid. No, when you give a dinner, invite the poor, the cripples, those who have lost an arm, and the blind. Then God will give you his blessing; for these people cannot repay you; and you will receive your reward when God raises up the good from their graves to everlasting life."

One of those at the table heard these words of Jesus; and he spoke out, "Happy will he be who shall sit down at that feast in the kingdom of God!"

Jesus answered him by giving the parable of "The Supper and the Excuses." He said:

"There was once a man who was giving a great

supper, to which he had invited many of his friends. At the hour for the supper, he sent out his servant to say to the guests who had been invited, 'Come at once, for everything is now ready!' But all of them with one mind began to decline his invitation. The first man said to the servant:

"'I have bought some land, and I must go and look at it. Please to excuse me.'

"The second said, 'I have bought five pair of oxen, and I am going to give them a trial. Please to have me excused.'

"Another said, 'I cannot come, because I have just married a wife.'

"The servant went home and told his master all these answers. Then the master of the house was very angry. He said to his servant:

"'Go out quickly into the streets and alleys of the town, and bring in here the poor, the cripples, the blind and the lame.'

"Soon the servant came back, saying, 'Your orders have been carried out, sir; but there is still room for more.'

"'Go out into the country,' said the master of the house, 'to the roads and the hedges, and make the people come in, to fill up my house; for I tell you that not one of those that were invited shall taste of my supper.'"

On Counting the Cost

CHAPTER 62

AT THIS TIME while Jesus was in Perea, preaching in the towns, greater crowds than ever before were following him, claiming to believe in him as the son of David and the King of Israel. Most of these people saw that he was going toward Jerusalem, and the report went abroad among them that when he reached that city he would take the throne that had been King David's; and not only would be king of that land but lead the Jewish people to conquer all the lands. Very many of the crowd following Jesus had no thought of what it meant to be his disciples. They were expecting great things—riches and honor and power—but knew nothing of the sufferings that Jesus must endure and that his followers must face in the days soon to come.

Jesus was not willing to have such careless and thoughtless followers as these. He spoke to them words that seemed harsh and forbidding, but were meant to make them think of what they must meet if they would be among those who believed in him. Turning to the multitudes that were flocking around him, he called out to them:

"If anyone comes to me, and does not hate his father, and mother, and wife, and children, and brothers and sisters, yes, and his own life besides, he cannot be a disciple of mine. Whoever does not carry his own cross and walk in my steps cannot be a disciple of mine!"

Jesus did not mean quite all these words he seemed to speak. He did not wish sons and daughters really to hate their fathers and mothers, nor parents to hate their own children; but he did mean that no one should say, 'My father and mother do not consent to my following Jesus, and therefore I cannot be his disciple.' Nor did

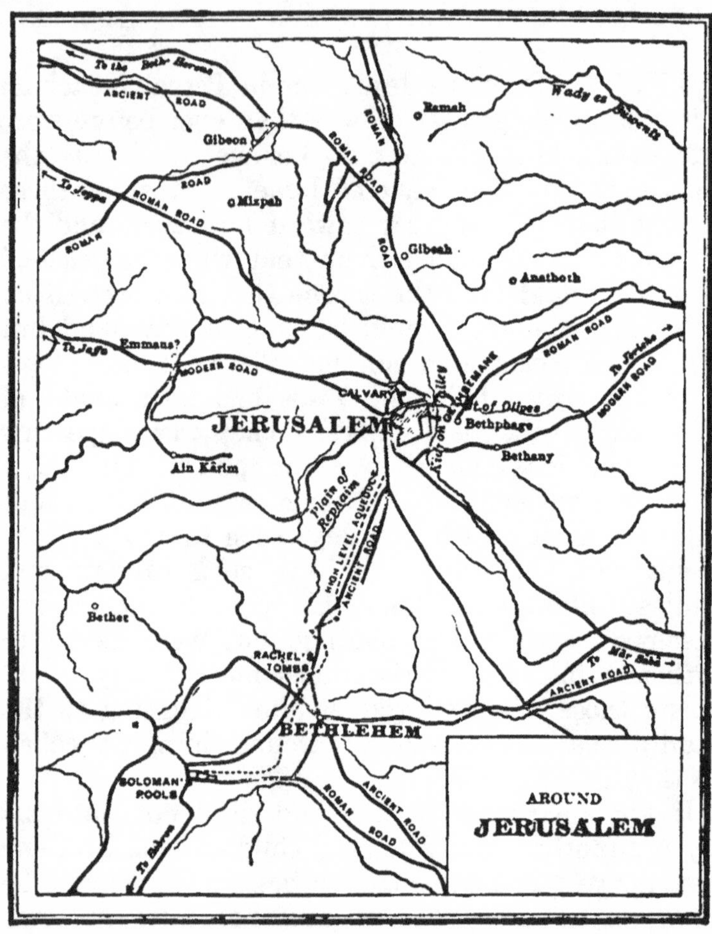

AROUND JERUSALEM

he wish that parents should say, 'I have children to care for, and I must not believe in Jesus, and become his disciple.' He wished those who were following him without thought, to ask themselves whether they were willing to lose all for Christ's sake, and to serve him, no matter who were opposed to him or what they might suffer in his service.

"Who of you," said Jesus, "when he wants to build a tower, does not first sit down and count the cost, and see whether he has enough money to finish it? If he can only lay the foundation, and then must leave the work unfinished, everybody who sees the half-completed wall will laugh at him and say, 'This fellow began to build, but he could not finish!'

"Or what king sets out to go to war with another king, and does not first sit down to consider whether with ten thousand soldiers he can fight the king who comes against him with twenty thousand? If he does not dare to meet his enemy, then while his army is still a great way off, he sends an officer to ask for terms of peace. So will it be with every one of you who will not give up all that he has; he cannot be a disciple of mine."

What Jesus meant was this, "Think whether you will hold out to the end, if you would be among my followers. And think, too, whether you will dare to meet the hate and opposition that you must overcome in becoming my disciples." He went on with such words as these:

"Every true disciple of mine is like salt; and salt is good as long as it has its own salty taste. But if it loses its saltiness and becomes tasteless, is there any way to make it good salt again? It is of no use either for the land, nor even for the manure heap, but people throw it away as useless. So will it be with everyone who loses the salt of my life in himself. Now, do not let these words of mine go into one ear and out from the other. Listen, and think of what I have said!"

Seeking the Lost

CHAPTER 63

THE PHARISEES were very careful to keep all the rules of the Jewish law, and were supposed to be very religious, because they prayed often in public places and went regularly to church. But Jesus saw that their religion was only pretended and not real, and would have nothing to do with them, except rebuke them for their sins. The scribes, who were the teachers of the law in the churches, expected Jesus to give them special honor. But both Pharisees and scribes were very angry when they found that Jesus paid them no attention, and was friendly with the

"But one was out on the hills away . . .
Away on the mountains wild and bare"

tax-collectors whom all the Jews despised and hated. Jesus even allowed some to come near him who were outcasts, people who did not go to church and did not try to keep the rules of the Jews.

The Pharisees and the scribes said in great scorn of Jesus, "This man welcomes sinners, and even sits down at the table to eat with them!"

Searching for the lost silver-piece

Jesus heard of their words, and answered them in the parable of "The Lost Sheep." He said:

"If one of you has a hundred sheep, and loses one of them, does he not leave the ninety and nine sheep in the sheepfold out in the fields, and go after the lost one until he finds it. When he has found it, he puts it on his shoulders with great joy and carries it home. And when he comes to his house, he calls together his neighbors and his friends, saying to them, 'Come and be glad with me; for I have found my sheep which was lost.'

"So I tell you, there is more joy in heaven over one outcast sinner who turns away from his sin to God, than over ninety-nine religious men who are good already and do not need to turn from sin."

A lady has written this parable in verses that have been set to music and sung many times. These are her verses:

The Ninety and Nine

There were ninety and nine that safely lay
  In the shelter of the fold.
But one was out on the hills away,
  Far off from the gates of gold—
Away on the mountains wild and bare,
Away from the tender Shepherd's care.

"Lord, thou hast here thy ninety and nine;
  Are they not enough for thee?"
But the Shepherd made answer, "'Tis of mine
  Has wandered away from me;
And although the road be rough and steep
I go to the desert to find my sheep."

But none of the ransomed ever knew
  How deep were the waters crossed;
Nor how dark was the night that the Lord passed through
  Ere he found his sheep that was lost.
Out in the desert he heard its cry,
Sick and helpless, and ready to die.

"Lord, whence are those blood drops all the way
  That mark out the mountain's track?"
"They were shed for one who had gone astray
  Ere the Shepherd could bring him back."
"Lord, whence are thy hands so rent and torn?"
"They are pierced tonight by many a thorn."

But all through the mountains, thunder-riven,
  And up from the rocky steep,
There arose a cry to the gate of heaven:
  "Rejoice! I have found my sheep!"
And the angels echoed around the throne,
"Rejoice! for the Lord brings back his own!"

Mrs. Elizabeth C. Clephane.

Jesus also gave to the people another parable, "The Lost Silver-piece." He said:

"Or, if there is a woman who has ten silver coins, and loses one of them, what will she do? She will light her lamp, and sweep her house, and search carefully for her money, until she finds it. And when she finds it, she goes out and calls together her women-friends and neighbors, and says, 'Come and rejoice with me, for I have found the silver-piece which I had lost.'

"Even so, I tell you there is rejoicing among the angels of God over one sinner that turns to God."

It might be asked—why did the woman need to light a lamp when searching for her lost coin? In that land, the houses of the plain people have either no windows, or one window for the whole house, which is merely a hole in the wall. The rooms are dark, even at mid-day, and to look on the floor thoroughly, and especially in the corners, a lamp must be lighted and carried close to the floor.

Silver Denarius of Tiberius. (Penny, Matt. 18: 28, etc., 16 cents.)

The Parable of the Lost Son Found

CHAPTER 64

YOU REMEMBER that the enemies of Jesus, the Pharisees and scribes, said of him, "He gives welcome to bad men, and eats at the table with them!" Jesus in answer gave a parable or story to show how God welcomes a sinner who turns from his sin and seeks his heavenly Father. This is one of the most beautiful among all the parables of Jesus. It is called "The Prodigal Son." The word "prodigal" means one who spends his money, throwing it away in a careless manner; and this story is of a young man who spent all the money that his father gave him. Here is the parable:

"There was once a man," said Jesus, "who had two sons. The older son stayed at home and helped his father in the care of his farm, but the younger son was restless and wanted to go away. The young man said to his father:

" 'Father, give me now the share of what you own which will come to me after you die.'

"So the father divided all that he had, his land, his vineyards, his olive orchards, his fig trees, his houses, his flocks of sheep and goats, and his money, into three equal parts. Two of these parts he kept for the older son; and the third part he gave to the younger son; for in that land it was the rule for the older son, as the head of the family, to receive twice as much as a younger son.

"After a few days, the young man sold out his share of the property for ready money, and then went away to a land far off, where he could live as he pleased. There he began to lead a foolish and wild life, feasting and drinking wine with worthless men and women. It did not take him many months to spend all his money and to be in great want. None of these people who had helped him in his pleasures were now ready to help him in his need. And what added to his trouble was that just then food became very scarce in that country and there was not bread enough for all the people.

"There in the open field among the grunting hogs sat this young man"

"This young man was in want of everything. His clothes became rags, his shoes were worn out, and what was worse, he could get nothing to eat and was starving for the want of food. Never before had he done any work, but now, driven by hunger he went everywhere looking for something to do which would give him a mouthful of bread. At last he found a man who was willing to hire him. This man sent him out into his field to take care of his pigs and feed them. This was a work felt to be disgraceful, for no Jew wou'd eat pig's meat or in any way touch the vile animals. But even this work the poor young man was compelled to do rather than starve to death. In the field he was so hungry that he was ready to snatch up some of the bean-pods on which the pigs were feeding; and no one in that country cared for him or would even give him something to eat.

The father fell on his son's neck

"So there in the open field among the grunting hogs sat this young man, ragged, famished and almost ready to die. Suddenly the thought came to him of his father's house, where once he had enjoyed plenty and lived at ease, waited upon by servants. He now saw how foolish, how ungrateful to a kind father, and how wicked he had been. It seemed to him as if he had been living in a dream, had now for the first time awaked and had come to his senses. He said to himself:

"'Why, even the hired men on my father's farm have more food than they can eat; and here I am almost dead with hunger! I will get up and will go to my father; and I will say to him, "Father, I have sinned against God in heaven and against you. I don't deserve any more to be called your son; only make me one of your servants working for wages."'

"So the poor young man left the field and the pigs, and went back to his father's house. There in the door sat his father waiting and watching for his wandering son. While the son was still a long distance away, the father saw him and knew him, barefoot and ragged as he was. He felt pity for his son, whose looks showed his utter misery, and ran to him, fell upon his neck, placed his arms around him and kissed him.

"'Father,' said the young man, 'I have sinned against God in heaven and against you. I don't deserve any more to be called your son—' But the father did not wait to hear him any further. He called out to the servants:

"'Be quick, bring some new clothes, the very best in the house, and put them on him; bring a ring to place around his wrist and sandals for his feet; go pick out the fattest calf in the stall, and kill it for a feast! Let us all eat and have a happy time together. For this son of mine was dead and has come to life again; he was lost and is found!'

"So they began to make merry. Now the older son was out in the field; and as he came near the house, he heard the sounds of music and dancing. Wondering what was the cause of such gladness, he called to him one of the servants and asked what all this meant.

" 'Your brother has come home,' answered the servant, 'and your father has killed the fattest of the calves, and is having a feast, because he has h m back safe and sound.'

"This made the older son very angry. He would not go in to the supper, but stayed outside. His father came out and begged him to come in and give a welcome to his brother.

"But he refused, saying, 'Think of all the years that I have been serving you! Never have I once disobeyed you; and yet you have never given me even a little kid out of the flock of goats, for me to have a merrymaking with my friends. But as soon as this son of yours comes home, who has wasted your money with vile people, you kill the fatted calf and for him make a great feast.'

" 'My son,' said the father, 'you and I are always together, and everything that I have is yours. We could not help being glad and rejoicing; for your brother here was dead, and is alive again; he was lost and is found.' "

You can see that in this elder brother of the story was the spirit of the Pharisees and the scribes, who were displeased because Jesus was willing to welcome those who had been sinful, when they came to him, sorry for their sins.

The Parable of the Dishonest Steward

CHAPTER 65

AT THIS TIME Jesus gave to his disciples the parable of "The Dishonest Steward." A steward is a man who takes care of any business or lands or houses belonging to another man who employs him. Jesus said:

"There was a rich man who had a steward who took charge of all his business. Some one told the rich man that his steward was cheating him and making a wrong use of his money. So the master sent for the steward and said:

" 'What is this that I hear about you? Hand in your accounts, for you shall not be my steward any longer.'

"The steward was at first greatly troubled at this; and he did not know how he could live if his office as steward was taken away.

" 'What shall I do,' he said to himself, 'now that my master is taking away from me my place as steward? I am not strong enough to dig in the ground as a farmer, and I am ashamed to beg in the streets. Oh, I know what I can do, so that when my office as steward is taken away the people will invite me to their homes to live with them.'

"One by one the steward called to him the men that were owing his master.

" 'How much do you owe my master?' he asked of the first.

" 'A hundred barrels of oil,' answered the man.

" 'Here, take your bill,' said the steward, 'and instead of a hundred barrels, make it fifty barrels.' "

This, you see, was making a present to the man of fifty barrels of oil; but not from the steward himself; instead, stealing it from his master, to give to the man who owed him.

"Then to the next man he said, 'And how much do you owe?'

The dishonest steward

"'A hundred bushels of wheat,' answered the man.

"'Here is your bill,' said the steward; 'make it eighty.'

"And so he treated all those who were owing to his master, giving to each one a part of his debt; so that they would be friendly to him and give him help when he should need it.

"When his master heard of all this, he praised the steward, not for doing rightly, but for looking ahead and taking care for the time to come."

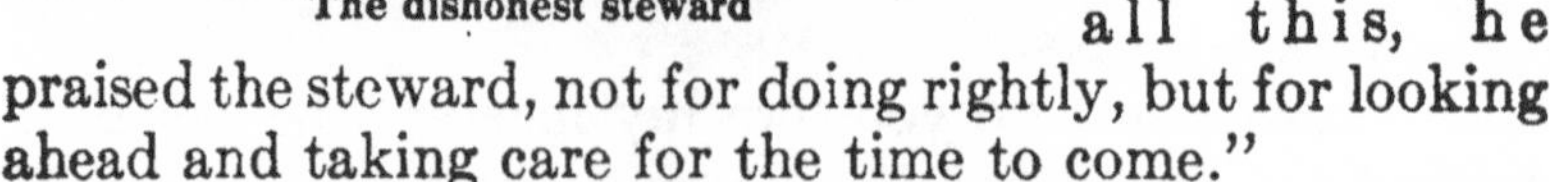

And Jesus said, "The people of this world often are wiser in looking ahead, and planning for the days to come, than are those who have the light of God. And I say to you: use the money of this world to make friends with it, not on earth, but in heaven; so that when you leave the earth, they may welcome you to homes in heaven that never pass away. He who is faithful with a small trust is also faithful with a large trust; and he who is not honest but tries to cheat in little things, will be dishonest and try to cheat in great things. So if you cannot be trusted with the money of this world, who will trust you with the riches of God? And if you are not faithful with what belongs to another, how can you expect to have anything forever as your own?

"No servant can serve two masters at the same time; for either he will hate one master and love the other; or else he will stand by one master and despise the other. You cannot serve God and at the same time live for money."

All these things were spoken in the hearing of the Pharisees, who were fond of money and grasping. They listened, with contempt and scorn in their hearts.

Jesus knew what was in their minds, and he said to these Pharisees:

"You are the men who make people believe that you are good, but God sees and knows what is in your hearts. What is lofty in the sight of men is vile in the sight of God."

A Parable for the Lovers of Money

CHAPTER 66

JESUS KNEW that the Pharisees, for all their church-going and their carefulness in keeping the rules of their law, were in their hearts lovers of money, and were living for the things of this world and not for God. He gave to them a parable about a rich man who suddenly became poor, and a poor man who became rich. It is called "The Parable of the Rich Man and Lazarus."

"There was a rich man," said Jesus, "who dressed in purple robes, like a king, and lived in a splendid great house, with many servants to wait upon him, and feasted every day upon the finest food. Outside the door of the rich man's house was laid every morning a poor beggar named Lazarus, who was covered with sores and was glad to eat the crumbs and broken pieces from the rich man's table. The dogs of the street used to come and lick his sores.

"After a time, the poor man died, and his soul was taken by the angels to be in heaven with Abraham, the father of God's people; because in all his poverty he had lived for God, trying always to do God's will. The rich man died, too, and was buried. But no angels came to carry him to the land where Abraham was living in happiness. His soul went to the place of woe and sorrow and suffering; not because he had been rich, but because in his riches he had never thought of God.

"The rich man, being in torment, looked up, and far away saw Abraham, with Lazarus in his arms.

"'O Father Abraham,' he called out, 'take pity on me, and send Lazarus to dip the tip of his finger in water and cool my tongue, for I am burning in this flame!'

"'My son,' answered Abraham, 'remember that when you were alive on the earth you had all your enjoyment, while Lazarus in his life had poverty and pain. Now Lazarus has comfort for all his trouble and you are in misery. Besides all that, between us in

Lazarus before the rich man's door

heaven and you in the dwelling place of the wicked, there is a great valley, a gulf which no one can cross, either to go from us to you or to come from you to us.'

"'If that be so,' said the once-rich man, now so poor, 'and Lazarus cannot come to me, I beg of you, Father Abraham, to send Lazarus to my father's house; for I have five brothers; let him speak to them in time, so that they may not come to this place of terrible suffering.'

" 'They have the writings of Moses and the words of all the prophets,' said Abraham; 'let them listen to these.'

" 'But, Father Abraham,' he said, 'if some one from the dead should go to them, they would turn from sin to God.'

" 'If they will not listen to Moses and the prophets,' said Abraham, 'they will not believe, even if some one should rise from the dead.' "

As the twelve disciples of Jesus heard this parable, they said, "Lord, make our faith stronger!"

"If you had faith like a grain of mustard seed," said Jesus, "you could say to this mulberry tree, 'Be uprooted and planted in the sea,' and it would obey you.

"Which one of you, if he had a servant plowing in the field or tending sheep, when he comes in from the field will say to him, 'Come at once and take your place at the table for your supper'? No, he will say to his servant, 'Get my supper ready; then make yourself ready to wait on me while I am eating and drinking; and after that you may have your supper.'

"Does a master thank his servant for doing what he has been told? Well, it is the same with you; when you have done all that you have been told, say, 'We are only servants; we have done no more than we ought to have done.' "

Two Parables Upon Prayer

CHAPTER 67

JESUS TOLD his disciples a parable to show that they should always keep on praying and never be discouraged. This parable is named "The Parable of the Unjust Judge."

"In a certain city," he said, "there was a judge who in his rule did not try to do right, but was often unjust and wicked; for he had no fear of God and no care for what men said about him. And in that city there was a widow who came many times to this judge, crying over and over again, 'Do for me what is right against the man who has done me wrong!'

"For some time the judge paid no attention to her, for right and wrong were both the same to him. But after a while the judge said to himself:

" 'Although I have no fear of God and no care for man, yet as this widow is so troublesome to me, and gives me no rest, I will do what she asks, for I am tired of her coming and of her calling out for her right every day.'

"Listen," said the Lord Jesus, "to what this unjust judge says. And if a man who does not care for right or wrong will at last answer a prayer, how much more will your heavenly Father listen to his own children when they call upon him day and night, even though he seems to make them wait long for the answer to their prayers? I tell you that God will do right by them and answer their prayers, and that very soon! Yet when the Son of Man comes, will he find on earth those who are looking for him and who believe in him?"

[illegible] some people who were [illegible] and looked down upon others. [illegible] "The Pharisee and the Tax-gatherer."

"Two men," said Jesus, "went up to the Temple to pray. [illegible] men was a Pharisee, and the other was a tax-gatherer. The Pharisee stood up and began praying to himself [illegible] God in words like these:

"Two men went up to the Temple to pray: one was a Pharisee and the other a tax-gatherer"

"'O God, I thank thee that I am not like other men—thieves, wrongdoers, and wicked—or even like this tax-gatherer. Twice in every week I eat no food to show that I am worshipping God; I give to God's house one-tenth of all that I get.'

"But the tax-gatherer stood far away, and would not raise his eyes toward heaven. He beat his breast, saying: "'O God, have mercy on me and forgive my sins!'"

"I tell you," said Jesus, "this tax-gatherer went to his house with his sins forgiven, instead of the Pharisee. For every one who uplifts himself will be brought low; and every one who humbles himself will be lifted up."

The Little Children; and the Rich Young Man

CHAPTER 68

WHILE JESUS was still passing through the land of Perea, on his way to Jerusalem, at one place the fathers and mothers brought their babies to him, asking him to place his hands on their heads and speak upon them a blessing. When the disciples saw them doing this, they were not pleased.

"Take these babies away!" they said. "The Lord is too busy with greater things to attend to them!"

But Jesus heard them, and he was displeased, not with the parents and their children, but with his disciples.

"Let the little ones come to me," he said, "and do not stop them; for the kingdom of God comes only to those who are child-like. I tell you, whoever will not give himself up to the kingdom of God as a little child shall never come into the kingdom."

Then he took the little ones up into his arms, laid his hands upon them and gave them his blessing. After that he went away from that place.

Soon afterward a young man who was one of the leaders in the church of his town came running, and bowed low before Jesus. "Good Teacher," said the young man, "tell me what to do if I am to be saved and have life everlasting."

"Why do you call me 'good'?" answered Jesus. "There is only one who is really good; that is God. To be saved, you have only to do God's will. You know what his commandments are; keep them."

Jesus and the rich young man. "Sell everything that you have, and give all the money to the poor."

"Why, what commands do you mean?" asked the young man. He supposed that Jesus, like many of the scribes, who were the teachers of God's law, had given some special rules of his own.

Jesus said to him, "I mean the ten commandments of God, such as, 'Thou shalt not steal; thou shalt not

Jesus laid his hands upon the little ones and gave them his blessing

kill; thou shalt not say what is false; honor thy father and thy mother,' and so on."

The young man said, "Teacher, all these I have kept ever since I was a child. What more do I need?"

As Jesus looked at this young man, so eager in his wish to please God, he loved him, and felt a special longing to have him among his disciples.

"If you really wish to be perfect," he said to the young man, "you do need one thing more. Sell everything that you have and give all the money to the poor and you will have your treasure in heaven, and come, follow me and be one of my disciples."

When the young man heard these words, he felt greatly disappointed, and turned away unwilling to do what Jesus asked, for he was very rich, and he loved his money. After he had left them, Jesus turned to his disciples:

"How hard it is," said Jesus, "for a rich man to come into the kingdom of God!"

As the disciples heard this, they were greatly surprised, for all the Jews thought that to have riches was a sign of God's special favor. As they stood silent, not knowing how to answer these words, Jesus said again:

"Children, how hard it is for those who trust in their riches to enter into the kingdom of God! It is easier for a camel to go through the eye of a needle, than for a rich man to get into the kingdom of God!"

They were amazed at this, and said, "Then who can be saved?"

"What is impossible with men," answered Jesus, "is possible with God."

"But we," said Simon Peter, "have left everything, and have followed you. What shall we have in the kingdom for all this?"

Peter thought, as did all the crowds who were going up to Jerusalem with Jesus, that there he would set up his kingdom and give rich rewards to his disciples.

"In truth I say to you," answered Jesus, "that you who have followed me, in the new kingdom when the Son of Man shall sit upon his throne, you twelve men, my disciples, shall sit upon twelve thrones, ruling over the twelve tribes of Israel. And every one who has left home, or wife, or children, or parents, or brothers, or sisters on my account, and for the sake of God's king-

"Let the little ones come to me," said Jesus, "for the kingdom of God comes only to those who are childlike."

dom, shall receive in this life a hundred times as much as he has lost, and in the world to come, life everlasting. But many that are first in this world shall be last in the kingdom; and some that are the lowest here will be the highest there."

The Bay of Acre and the modern town Haifa

The Workers in the Vineyard

CHAPTER 69

JESUS EXPLAINED by a parable what he meant in saying, "Many that are first shall be last, and some that are lowest here will be the highest in God's kingdom." This parable was "The Workers in the Vineyard."

"There was a man," said Jesus, "who owned a vineyard. He needed men to work in his vineyard; and one day, early in the morning, went out to hire them. Some men met him and agreed to work for him at fifteen cents for each day's work; so he sent them out to his vineyard. At about nine o'clock he was walking through the market place, and seeing some other men standing around, waiting for work, he said to them:

" 'You go to work in my vineyard, and whatever is fair, I will pay you.'

"He went out again at noon; he found men wanting work and sent them also into his vineyard, saying to them, 'Whatever are fair wages, I will pay you.' Again at three o'clock, he found other men and sent them, too, making them the same promise. He went into the market place at five o'clock, almost at the end of the day, and found some men standing there. 'Why do you stand here doing nothing?' he said to these men. They answered him:

" 'We would be glad to work; but nobody is ready to hire us.'

" 'You go into my vineyard, too,' he said, 'and I will pay you whatever is right.'

"When the evening came, the master of the vineyard said to his foreman, 'Now call the workers together and pay them their wages. Begin with those who came to work last, then pay those who went into the vineyard at three o'clock, and so on, ending with those who went to work earliest.'

"So those came up first who had been hired last, and had worked only one hour; and to each of them was paid fifteen cents, the wages of a full day's work. When the first came, they supposed that they would be paid more, because they had worked longer; but each was paid his fifteen cents, as had been agreed upon. These men complained to the master of the vineyard.

" 'Those men who came in last, when the day was almost ended,' they said, 'have been made equal to us, who have borne the hard work and the heat of the day. That is not fair!'

" 'My friend,' said the master to one of these men, 'I am not cheating you. Did you not agree with me to work for fifteen cents a day? Take up your wages and go. I choose to give to this last man the same as to you. Haven't I the right do so as I please with what belongs to me? Are you jealous because I am generous?'

"So," said Jesus, "there are last who will be first; and there are first who will be last."

This parable shows how God gives his rewards differently from men. Men pay only for work that is done; but God gives his pay to those who are *willing* to work for him, whether they are able to work or not; for while men look at the deed, God looks at the heart.

Every day Jesus was drawing nearer to Jerusalem, and his twelve disciples with all the multitude of those who were following him, fully expected that in Jerusalem Jesus would reign as the King of Israel. He had told them before, and more than once, that he was going up to Jerusalem to die there; but their minds were so fixed upon thrones and kingdoms and worldly power that they could not understand his words.

Now Jesus called together his twelve disciples, apart from the crowd.

"Listen!" he said, "We are going up to Jerusalem, and there everything that is written in the books of the prophets about the Son of Man shall come to pass. He will be given up to his enemies, the chief priests and the scribes, the teachers of the law; and they shall sentence him to be put to death, and shall hand him over to the Romans to be mocked and beaten and nailed to a cross to die; and on the third day after, he will rise from the dead."

But the disciples did not understand what these words meant. They were just as certain as they had been before, that he was going up to Jerusalem to take the throne and rule, and they even talked among themselves about the chief offices in his kingdom and who should have them.

When they were drawing near to Jerusalem, but still in the land of Perea, a woman came to Jesus with her two sons. This woman was named Salome; and she was the wife of Zebedee, and the mother of James and John, two of the leading disciples of Jesus. She bowed low even to the ground before Jesus, and begged him to grant her a favor.

"What is it that you want?" said Jesus to her.

"I want you to promise me," said Salome, "that in your kingdom these two sons of mine shall sit, one on your right hand and the other on your left."

"You do not know what you are asking," answered Jesus. "Can you drink of the cup that I am to drink? Can you receive the same baptism that is coming to me?"

"Yes," the two men said, "we can!"

"You shall indeed drink my cup, and be baptized with my baptism," said Jesus. "But it is not mine to say who shall sit on my right hand and on my left. Those places shall be given to those whom my Father has chosen for them."

By his cup and his baptism, Jesus meant his sufferings and his death; but this James and John did not know. When the other ten disciples heard of this they were very angry with the two brothers for trying to get ahead of them. But Jesus called them to him and said:

"You know that in the nations of this world their rulers lord it over them, and their great men make the people serve them. But it must not be so with you. Whoever among you has the will to be great, let him be a servant to the others; and whoever would be first, let him be even as a slave. For the Son of Man came not to be served, but to serve, and to give up his life that he may save many."

The river Jordan

Bartimeus, hearing that Jesus had sent for him, sprang up and flung his coat to the ground, and was led to Jesus.

The Blind Man at the Gate

CHAPTER 70

JESUS HAD now ended his work of preaching in the land of Perea, on the east of the Jordan. With his disciples and a great throng of people who were going up to the feast of the Passover at Jerusalem, he came to the river at another Bethabara, or "the place of the crossing," because like the Bethabara near the Sea of Galilee, the river though very wide was very shallow, so that people could wade across it. This Bethabara was opposite the city of Jericho, which had been built up and made beautiful by King Herod the Great, about forty years before.

More than a thousand years before Jesus stood beside the river, the Israelites had walked across it to enter the land; when God held back the water. Jesus could have walked on the water if he had chosen to do it; but he never caused a miracle for himself, though often he did for others. At that time some of the people going up to Jerusalem waded across the river, holding their clothes on their heads, while others crossed in a ferry-boat. We are not told in which way Jesus went across the river.

Six miles from the river Jordan, on the west, stood Jericho, toward which Jesus came with a great crowd of people around him. As he drew near Jericho, a blind man was seated beside the gate, begging for the small coins of those who passed by. This blind man's name was Bartimeus, a word which means "the son of Timeus." Hearing the tramping and the voices of a crowd, he asked why so many people were coming. They said to him:

"Jesus the Nazarene is passing by."

Bartimeus had heard of Jesus and his good works, curing many that were blind and lame and lepers. He had often wished that Jesus might pass his way and cure him. Now, when he heard that Jesus was really coming, he shouted out at the top of his voice:

"Jesus, son of David, have pity on me! Jesus, son of David, have pity on me!"

The people who were in front told him to be quiet; but he felt that this was the chance of his life, and he kept on calling, "Jesus, son of David, have pity on me!"

Jesus stopped, and said to those near, "Go, and bring this man to me."

Then they said to Bartimeus, "Be of good cheer; get up and go to Jesus, for he is calling you!"

Bartimeus was in such a hurry to get to Jesus that he sprang up, flung aside his cloak, and left it on the ground, while they led him to the Lord. When he came near, Jesus said to him:

"What would you have me do for you?"

"Lord," he answered, "let me have my sight again!"

"Have your sight," said Jesus, "your faith has made you well."

And at once his sight came back to him; and he joined the crowd following Jesus, giving praise to God with a loud voice. And all those who saw this wonderful work added their praises to God.

In the Rich Man's Home at Jericho

CHAPTER 71

BUT BLIND Bartimeus was not the only man in Jericho who was eager to meet Jesus. In that city was living a very rich man named Zacc eus, who was the head of all the tax collectors in that part of the country. He had heard that Jesus was unlike other Jews, in being friendly toward the tax gatherers, and he greatly desired to see him. But Zaccheus was a small man, and in the crowd he could have no chance to look at Jesus, so he ran on ahead and climbed up into a mulberry tree that stood beside the road, and from a place among its branches he could look down upon the passing multitude.

When Jesus came opposite to the tree, he stopped, looked up and saw Zaccheus, and said to him:

"Zaccheus, make haste and come down; for I must stop at your house today!"

He was surprised and glad that the great Teacher should choose his house, out of all the homes in Jericho, to stay in. He came down and walked with Jesus to his house. But all the people began to find fault, saying:

"He has gone to visit at the house of a man who is a sinner!"

For they took for granted because many of the tax gatherers were wicked men and robbed the people, that all of them were bad.

Zaccheus knew how they were feeling and what they were saying; so he came forward, and stood before Jesus and said:

"Hear me, Master! I will give half of all that I

Jesus called out to Zaccheus in the tree: "Make haste and come down, for I must stop at your house today!"

own to help the poor; and if I have robbed or cheated anyone, I will pay him back four times as much as he has lost!"

"Today," said Jesus, "in this house a man has been saved from his sins; since even Zaccheus here is a true son of Abraham our father. For the Son of Man has come to look after the lost ones and to save them."

As the people were listening, he went on and spoke a parable to them; for he knew that as he was going up to Jerusalem, they were looking for the kingdom of God to be set up at once. This was "The Parable of the Pounds."

"A certain prince," said Jesus, "was going to a city far away, to be made a king, and then to come back and rule over his own land. Before leaving, he called ten of his servants, and gave to each one five hundred dollars, and said to him, 'Trade with this until I come back.' Then he went away.

"But the people of his land hated him, and sent messengers to follow him to the distant city and to say, 'We will not have this man as our king.'

"However, the prince was made king and came home to reign over his land. Then he sent for his servants to whom he had given the money, so that he might learn how much each one had made by buying and selling. The first servant came and said:

"'My lord, the five hundred dollars which you gave me has gained five thousand dollars.'

"'Well done, you good servant,' said the king, 'because you have been so wise and faithful with a small amount, I will make you the governor over ten cities in my kingdom.'

"Then came another servant, who said, 'My lord, your five hundred dollars has made five times as much as you gave me. Here are twenty-five hundred dollars.'

" 'Very well,' answered the king, 'you may be the ruler over five cities.'

"Soon one of the servants came, saying, 'My lord, here is your five hundred dollars, just as you gave it to me. I have kept it safe for you, wrapped up in a napkin. For I was afraid of you; you are such a hard, selfish man. You pick up what you never put down; and you reap what you do not sow.'

" 'You worthless servant!' answered the king, 'out of your own words will I pass judgment upon you. You knew, did you, that I was a hard man, picking up what I never put down, and reaping what I did not sow! If you knew this, why then did you not put my money into the bank? Then when I came home I could have gotten interest upon it, the money gained by lending it.'

"Then he said to those standing by, 'Take away from him the five hundred dollars, and give it to the one who has five thousand dollars!'

" 'My lord,' they said, 'why, he has five thousand dollars already! Why give it to him?'

" 'That is the very reason why he should have it,' said the king. 'I tell you, that to him who has, more shall be given; and as for him who has not, even the little that he has shall be taken away from him.' "

" 'And now, for these enemies of mine,' the king went on, 'those men who sent word that they would not have me for their king, seize them, and bind them in chains and bring them here. Let them be slain in my sight!' "

With these words Jesus went onward up the mountain road leading to Jerusalem.

The Alabaster Jar

CHAPTER 72

FROM JERICHO to Jerusalem was a journey of fifteen miles up the mountains by a very steep road; a road often dangerous on account of the robbers who were hidden among the rocks by the wayside. But at the time of the Passover when thousands of people were going up to the feast, it was safe, through the crowds traveling together. Up this road Jesus walked with his disciples and a great throng of people, all on their way to the Passover. He did not, however, go directly to Jerusalem, but turned aside when near the city, and stopped at the village of Bethany for a visit with his friends, Martha and Mary and Lazarus. They were very, very glad to see Jesus now, for you remember that on his last visit, some months before, he had called Lazarus out of his tomb to live again.

It was on Friday, just six days before the Passover was to be held, that Jesus came to Bethany. There, at the house of a man named Simon, a supper was given in honor of Jesus. This Simon had been a leper, but had been cured by Jesus, so that he had his own reason for showing love and honor to Jesus. At the supper, the guests sat leaning on couches, with their heads toward the table and their feet away from it; and those who waited at the tables passed the food and drink around to the guests. Among those who were serving at the table was Martha, the sister of Lazarus.

On the couch standing at the head of the table was leaning in the middle Simon, who gave the feast. On his right hand, in the place of honor, was Jesus; and on

Mary anointing Jesus' feet with fragrant oil from the alabaster jar

his left was Lazarus. On the side tables were lying the disciples of Jesus and other guests.

Suddenly, into the room came Mary, the sister of Lazarus. She carried in her arms a jar made of marble, of the kind called alabaster. Its cover was sealed; but Mary broke the seal, and at once a rich perfume arose in the air and floated not only through the dining hall, but

Judas secretly bargaining with the chief priests for the betrayal of Jesus into their hands

the whole house, for the jar was filled with a very fragrant and costly oil. Mary walked up the aisle between the tables and the couches whereon the guests were lying. She came opposite to Jesus, and poured some of the oil upon his head; then walked around the couch, poured the rest of it upon his feet and wiped them with her long hair, hanging loose upon her shoulders.

Everybody in the room was surprised at Mary's act; and one of the disciples of Jesus said aloud:

"What a waste this is? Why, that jar of perfume was worth at least fifty dollars! It might have been sold and the money given to the poor!"

The one who said this was Judas Iscariot, the wicked disciple who was already planning to give up his Lord to his enemies, the chief priests and rulers. Judas was the treasurer for Jesus and his twelve disciples. They all lived as one family, kept their money in one purse, and in addition whatever money was given to Jesus by his friends. Judas kept this purse; but he was a thief, and stole some of the money, that he might use it for himself. When Judas saw all the precious oil poured upon the head and feet of Jesus, he was angry, for he looked upon it as so much money that he might have kept.

"Why do you find fault with this woman?" said Jesus. "It is a beautiful thing that she has done to me. You will always have the poor with you, but you will not always have me. As she poured this perfume on my body, she did it for my burial, which is soon to take place. I tell you, wherever in the whole world my gospel shall be preached, the act of this woman will be told, and she will be remembered on account of it."

All the friends of Jesus were expecting him soon to go to Jerusalem and set up his kingdom and rule. They did not understand his words about dying and rising from the dead. But Mary, among them all, knew that Jesus was soon to die, and it was not only to show her love toward him for bringing her brother to life, but in a very tender way to put into an act what she would not say in words, that her Lord would soon die and be buried.

After this supper, Judas Iscariot, the disciple who had spoken against Mary and her gift, quietly made up his mind to give Jesus over to his enemies. He saw that Jesus would not be such a king as he wished him to be, and he had begun to fear that his stealings were known, or at least suspected. He went secretly to the chief priests and the rulers and said to them:

"What will you pay me if I will give Jesus into your hands?"

They were glad to hear this, and said to him, "We will give you thirty pieces of silver."

This was a little less than twenty dollars in our money, and it was the price paid for a slave. Think of it, for the value of a slave, the Lord of all the earth was sold by one of his own chosen followers!

Judas was sharp in his dealing with the priests. He was afraid that, after he had given Jesus up to them, he might be cheated out of his money. So he said:

"Pay me the money now; and when the right time comes, I will show you how to make Jesus of Nazareth your prisoner."

They gave Judas the thirty pieces of silver; and from that moment Judas was looking for the chance to put Jesus into the hands of his enemies.

Jewish shekel

Palm Sunday

CHAPTER [illegible]

THE NEWS that Jesus was at Bethany went abroad, and very soon the village was thronged with people eager to see him. Many of these were men who had come from the country up to Jerusalem for the feast of the Passover; and most of them were ready to believe in Jesus as the Christ, the promised King of Israel. Some came to Bethany, not only to see Jesus, but to see Lazarus also, the man whom Jesus had raised from death to life. The rulers, who had already made up their minds to put Jesus to death and had paid Judas to give him up to them, said to each other:

"If we are to prevent these people from making Jesus of Nazareth their king, it will not be enough to kill Jesus; we must first kill Lazarus, for on his account many are following Jesus."

On the morning after the supper at Simon's house, Jesus decided to go into Jerusalem. He called two of his disciples and said to them:

"Go into the next village on the road to Jerusalem, and just on the edge of it you will find an ass tied, and with it a colt on which no one has ever ridden; untie them and bring them to me. If anyone asks you, 'Why are you doing that?' tell him, 'The Master needs them; and will send them back soon;' and he will let you take the ass and the colt."

The two disciples went to the village, and found in the street in front of a house an ass and a colt tied just as Jesus had said. They were untying them when the owner, who was standing by, said:

"What are you doing, untying the ass?"

"The Master needs it," answered the disciples; and when the man heard this, he allowed them to take the ass and the colt. They brought them to Jesus at Bethany; and on the ass-colt they laid their cloaks, to form a cushion for Jesus; and he sat upon the colt, which never before had been ridden upon. Then the crowd, seeing that Jesus was riding toward Jerusalem, walked with him, some going before and

The brook Kedron

some following after. Those in front spread their clothes upon the road before Jesus; others threw on the ground leaves from the field; while many waved branches of palm taken from the trees beside the road.

And before they came to the top of the Mount of Olives, which was between Bethany and Jerusalem, another crowd of people met them, coming from the city to see Jesus. And all the multitude shouted together:

"God save the King, the Son of David! Blessed is he who comes in the Lord's name! Blessed is the kingdom of our father David! Praises be to the Lord!"

For all this crowd of people believed that now, at last, the kingdom of God was to be set up, with Jesus as Christ and King. But in the multitude were some Pharisees, enemies of Jesus, who became very angry as they saw the crowd waving the palm branches and cheering for Jesus as King. These men came up to Jesus as he was riding and said to him:

"Teacher, tell your followers to stop this noise!"

"I tell you," answered Jesus, "that if these men should keep still, the very stones would cry out!"

Soon they came to the top of the Mount of Olives, and then the Temple and the city of Jerusalem were in sight before them.

As Jesus looked upon the city, the tears came into his eyes and he said:

"O Jerusalem, Jerusalem! If only you might know, even now, while yet there is time, what would give you peace! But no, it is hidden from your sight! The time is coming when your enemies will build walls and forts around you, and shut you in on every side; and trample you down into the dust, and your children with you. They will not leave in you one stone standing upon another—and all because you would not understand when the Lord was visiting you."

Jesus rode down the Mount of Olives, and across the valley of the brook Kedron. At the gate of the Temple he got off from the back of the colt, and sent it with the ass back to its owner. As he came into the city and the Temple there was a great stir, the people everywhere flocking to meet him.

"Who is this?" they said; and the crowds answered, "This is the Prophet Jesus, from Nazareth in Galilee!"

Many waved branches of palm, and all the multitude shouted together: "God save the King, the son of David! Blessed is he who comes in the Lord's name!"

The Pharisees said to each other, "We can do nothing! The whole world has gone after Jesus!"

Everybody, both the friends and enemies of Jesus, looked to have him take control of the city and act as a king. But Jesus only went into the Temple and walked around it. By this time it was evening, and Jesus returned with his disciples to Bethany.

Forty years after that time, the terrible things that Jesus declared were to fall upon Jerusalem, did come to pass. The Jews rose against the Romans and made war upon them. A mighty Roman army came, and swept over all the land, bringing ruin and death everywhere. The Romans laid siege to Jerusalem, and built a strong wall around it, so that no one could come out or go in. The people fought desperately, until they were starved and could fight no more. At last the Romans broke into the Temple, and set the city on fire. Both the Temple and all the city were utterly destroyed; untold thousands of the people were slain, and many thousands more were sold as slaves. And from that time, seventy years after Jesus was born, and forty years after he died on the cross, the Jews have not had of their own a land or a city.

After teaching in the Temple all day, Jesus went out in the evening over the Mount of Olives to the home of his friends in Bethany.

Monday on the Mount and in the Temple

CHAPTER 74

AFTER THE royal coming of Jesus to the city and the Temple, on the next morning—which was Monday—Jesus left Bethany very early, without waiting for his breakfast, and with his twelve disciples walked over the Mount of Olives toward Jerusalem. The walk and the early morning air made him hungry, and seeing a fig tree covered with green leaves in a field near the road, he went to it, hoping to find some figs upon it.

The laws of the Jews allowed any person passing by a field which was not his own, to take as much fruit or grain as he wished to eat, but not to carry any away; so that Jesus had a right to go to this tree and help himself to its fruit. Jesus knew that it was not quite the time for ripe figs, for they do not become ripe in that country before May or June, and that day may have been in March. But on the sunny slope of the Mount of Olives figs often ripen early in the season and as the figs always come before the leaves, wherever the leaves were abundant, there might be among them some ripe figs.

But when Jesus came to the fig tree, and looked at it closely, he found that upon it was no fruit, either ripe or green, but only leaves. Then a thought came to Jesus, and in the presence of his disciples he spoke to the fig tree.

"From this time let no fruit ever be picked from this tree forever!" he said.

This was not because Jesus was angry with the poor tree, which could not help not having fruit. It was because he saw in that tree a parable or picture of the Jewish people. They made a show of serving God, and were like trees covered with leaves; but they did not bring forth the fruit of good lives, of love to God and their fellow-men. They were fruitless trees, and trees which have been planted and kept for fruit are of no use without fruit.

As the traders looked upon Jesus and heard his stern rebuke, they became afraid and rushed out of the court before him

The twelve disciples who were with Jesus around the fig tree heard those words, and soon had cause to remember them.

From the Mount of Olives they walked, as on the day before, across the valley of the brook Kedron, and again came into the Temple. You remember that two years before when Jesus visited the Temple, he then drove out from its court all the people that he found buying and selling and changing money. But in the two years that had passed, they had all come back, and the Court of the Gentiles was again a place of business and of confusion. All around were oxen lowing and sheep bleating; their owners calling upon the people passing by to come and buy them; cages full of pigeons and doves were standing on every side; and from a row of tables might be heard the chink of silver, as the money of foreign lands was changed for that of Judea.

When these traders saw Jesus standing before them, some of them could remember how two years before he had driven them out of the Temple, and all saw in him the man whom only yesterday the people had welcomed as the coming King of Israel. There was a look upon the face of Jesus which made all these wrongdoers afraid of him; and when he spcke in the hearing of them all, "God's book says, 'My house shall be called a house of prayer; but you are making it a den of robbers,' " with one accord they rushed out of the court before him, driving out the sheep and oxen, carrying away the cages of doves, and even upsetting the tables of the money-changers.

Jesus saw that people who were coming from outside the wall were carrying goods and jars of water and of oil through the Court of the Gentiles as the nearest way to the city, so that the court was becoming merely a street between the city and the country. He put a stop to this carrying of loads through the Temple courts; and would not allow even a jar of water to be taken by way of the Temple into the city. This building in all its parts was the house of God, and Jesus as the Son of God gave commands that everywhere it was to be used only for the worship of his heavenly Father.

After casting out all these evil things from the outer court, Jesus walked up the steps to the inner court, called the Treasury. There he sat down, and for the rest of the day taught the people who crowded around him.

While he was in the Treasury, they led to him the

blind, and he gave them sight by a word; and the lame came in on crutches, or were carried in by their friends to his feet, and he gave them power to walk. Boys too were marching around the Temple and shouting everywhere, "May God save the Son of David!"

All these things made the priests and the rulers very angry; for they were only waiting for a chance to find Jesus alone and make him their prisoner, and they could do nothing while such crowds were around him, all believing that he was the promised Son of David and King of Israel. But these enemies of Jesus could not keep quiet amid all these praises.

"Do you hear," they said to Jesus, "what these boys are shouting? Why do you not tell them to be still?"

"Yes, I hear them," answered Jesus, "and have you never read what is said in the book of Psalms, 'Out of the lips of little children, even of babies in their mothers' arms, thy praises have been made perfect?'"

Jesus stayed in the Temple teaching until the evening drew near. Then he went with his disciples back to Bethany for the night. There among his friends he was safe.

Tuesday Morning in the Temple

CHAPTER 75

AGAIN ON Tuesday morning of that great week, the last week of our Saviour's life on earth, he went with his disciples out of Bethany to go to Jerusalem. As they were walking up the Mount of Olives, they came to the fig tree to which Jesus had spoken on the morning before. It was standing upon the hillside, but withered and dead, its dry leaves turned yellow, rustling in the wind.

"Master, look!" said Peter, "the fig tree to which you spoke those words yesterday is all withered!"

"Have faith in God," answered Jesus. "I tell you in truth, that if any one of you should say to this mountain before us, 'Be lifted up and thrown into the sea,' and should not have in his mind a doubt, but believes that what he says will come to pass, it shall be done. So I say to you, whatever you pray God for, believe that God gives it to you, and it shall be yours. But keep this also in mind, whenever you stand up for prayer, if there is anything that you have against anybody, forgive him. Then, and then only, will your Father in heaven forgive you your sins against him."

Again they came to Jerusalem, and walked across the Court of the Gentiles now quiet and free from the confusion of the morning before, no buying, no selling, and no carrying of loads through it to the city. They went into the Treasury, where Jesus had taught and cured on the day before; and they found it already full of people who had come together, hoping to listen again to the words of the great Teacher.

The chief priests angrily demanded of Jesus: "What right have you to come here and act as a ruler?"

But not only were there in the Temple people friendly to Jesus, and eager to hear him; the chief priests, the teachers of the law, and the members of the great council, were also there, ready to do all in their power against him. These men were very angry at Jesus for what he had done on the day before. They pushed their way through the crowds up to Jesus, and said to him, with an air of lordship:

"What right have you to come here and act as a ruler? Who gave you the right to do what you did yesterday?"

"I will ask you a question," answered Jesus promptly, "and if you will answer that, then I will tell you who has given me the right to do what I have done here in the Temple. What do you say about John the Baptist—did he speak the words of God as his messenger? Or did he speak his own words only, without authority or power from God? Answer me that question!"

They were taken aback at this answer of Jesus; and began talking together, while the crowd around looked on.

"What shall we say?" they whispered to each other. "If we say, 'John the Baptist spoke from God,' he will ask, 'Then why did you not believe his words and obey him?' No, let us say, 'He spoke only as a man, without authority or power from God.' But then, if we say that, the people will stone us, for they all believe that John was a true prophet of God."

So after a time these men said to Jesus, "We cannot answer your question. We don't know whether John spoke the words of God or his own words."

Then said Jesus, "No more will I tell you who has given me the power to do these things."

For Jesus well knew that if these men had not believed when John the Baptist said, "Thus saith the Lord," they would not believe him saying, "I do only what my Father tells me to do."

The pool of Mamilla, at Jerusalem

Three Parables of Warning

CHAPTER 76

IMMEDIATELY after answering the question of the priests and the rulers, Jesus gave three parables, one directly after another; and all aimed at his enemies. The first was "The Parable of the Two Sons."

"What do you think of this?" said Jesus. "There was a man who had two sons. He went to the older son, and said to him, 'My son, go and work in the vineyard today.' 'Yes, sir,' said the young man. 'I will go.' But although he had given his promise to go, he broke it, for he did not go.

"Then the father spoke to his second son, as he had spoken to the first. 'My son, go and work today in the vineyard.' This one said to his father, 'I will not go.' But afterward he was sorry, and went into the vineyard to work. Now tell me, which of these two sons did as his father told him to do?"

They answered him, "The second."

"I tell you truly," said Jesus, "that the tax-gatherers and the bad women are going into the kingdom of God instead of you, who believe yourselves to be better than others. For John the Baptist came and showed you how to live, and you would not believe him nor do as he said. But the tax-gatherers and the bad women believed him and turned from their evil ways to God. And even when you saw them turning from evil to good, you would not seek God after them and follow the words of John."

Then Jesus spoke to these rulers another parable, called "The Parable of the Wicked Vine-dressers."

"Listen to another parable," he said. "A man who owned some land planted upon it a vineyard of grape-vines. He put a fence around it, dug a wine-vat inside it, and built a tower in the middle of the vineyard, so that a watchman might be on the lookout against thieves. Then he let it out to vine-dressers, to take care of it, and at the time of ripe grapes to send him his share of the fruit or its worth in money. After leasing the vineyard, he went away to another country.

Vineyard and watch-tower in Bethlehem

"When the time for the vintage drew near, the time for gathering the grapes, he sent his servants for his share of the fruit. But instead of giving him what belonged to him, the vine-dressers seized his servants. One servant they flogged and drove away, another they killed, and a third they stoned. A second time the owner sent some other servants, more than before; and the vine-dressers treated them in the same way. And so it was with many others; some they beat and some they killed.

"The owner of the vineyard had one son, a young

man, whom he loved very dearly. Last of all he sent this son to them, saying to himself, 'They will surely respect my son, and will not treat him as they have treated the servants.'

"But those men said, as soon as they saw him, 'This is the one who is to own the vineyard when his father dies. Let us kill him, and then the vineyard will be ours.' So when he came, they seized him and killed him, and flung his body outside the vineyard.

"Now, I will ask you," said Jesus, "when the owner of that vineyard comes, what will he do to those vine-dressers?"

They answered, "He will utterly destroy those vile, cruel men, and will lease his vineyard to other vine-dressers, who will give him every year his share of the fruit."

"Have you never read this verse," said Jesus.

> "The stone which the builders refused
> Has now become the chief and corner-stone;
> This is the work of the Lord,
> And it is wonderful in our sight?"

"I tell you," added Jesus, "that the kingdom of God shall be taken from you and given to a people that brings to God its fruits. Yes, and he who falls on this stone shall be dashed to pieces; and whoever this stone falls on shall be ground to powder!"

As the chief priests and Pharisees and rulers heard these parables, they knew at once that they were spoken against them. They were eager to seize Jesus, but were afraid of the crowds around, for all the common people looked upon him as a prophet speaking God's word.

Jesus gave a third parable: that of "The Marriage of the King's Son." This, given in the Temple, was in some parts like another, "The Parable of the Great Feast," which he had already given in Perea; but other parts of it, as we shall see, were different from that parable.

"There was a certain king," said Jesus, "who gave a great supper at the marriage of his son. He sent out his servants to those who had been invited to the feast, but they would not come. Once again he sent some other servants, and told them to say to the guests:

"'Here is my supper all ready, the oxen and fat cattle have been killed; everything is ready; come to the feast.'

"But they paid no attention to his words, and went off, one to his farm and another to his shop. And some seized his servants, ill-treated them and even killed them. This made the king very angry. He sent his army, put those murderers to death and burned up their city.

"Then the king said to his servants, 'The marriage feast is ready; but those who were the invited guests were not fit for it. Go out into the streets of the city and the roads in the country, and ask everybody whom you meet to come to the wedding.' The servants went forth into the roads, and brought to the feast all whom they met, both the bad and the good. So the marriage supper had plenty of guests.

"When the king came in to meet the guests, he saw a man among them who was not wearing a wedding robe. For as each guest came to the house, a beautiful robe was given him, to be worn at the supper.

"'My friend,' said the king to this man, 'how was it that you came in here without a wedding robe?'

"The man stood silent, for he had nothing to say. Then said the king to his servants:

"'Tie this man hand and foot, and throw him out of doors into the darkness. There men will wail and gnash their teeth. For I tell you that many are invited, but few are chosen.'"

The Head on the Coin

CHAPTER 77

THE ENEMIES of Jesus thought that, perhaps, they might lead him to say some words against the Roman rulers over the land. If he would do this, then they could complain to the Roman governor and cause Jesus to be seized and put in prison, or even slain, as an enemy of the Roman state. These priests and Pharisees and rulers themselves hated the Romans, and would gladly throw off the Roman yoke if they dared to do it; but they were willing to pretend friendliness to their Roman masters, if only through them they could destroy Jesus.

The head on the coin

With this purpose in mind, while Jesus was in the Temple on that Tuesday morning, they sent to him some men whom Jesus had never met, men who seemed honest and true; for they knew that if they came themselves Jesus would at once see through their plans and be on his guard against them. They did not know that Jesus as the Son of God knew all things, could look into every heart of man and read all their thoughts.

So these men came to Jesus in the Temple and tried at first to speak flattering words to him to win his favor.

"Teacher," they said, "we know that you are honest and speak the truth; that you are not afraid of anybody and do not try to please men, but say only what is right. There is a question that troubles us, for we do not know how to meet it. For that reason we bring it to you, for we know that you will give us a right answer. Tell us now what you think about it. Is it right for our people to pay taxes to the Roman rulers over the land? Shall we pay, or shall we refuse to pay?"

Silver coin of Tiberius Cæsar

This was indeed a hard question to answer, especially to answer at once, without time for thinking about it. For if Jesus should say, "Do not pay the tax," the Romans would arrest him as an enemy to their rule, and might even put him to death, as they had seized and slain many for this very act of refusing to pay the taxes. At that very time hundreds of men were hiding from the Romans in caves and forests, trying to escape from paying this tax. On the other hand, if Jesus should say, "Pay the tax," all the common people would turn against him; for all the Jews hated this tax, which was a sign of the Roman power over them; and every man among them only paid it because he was afraid of the Roman governor and the Roman soldiers.

But Jesus saw through all their plots and plans, and he had his answer ready.

"You men of false heart, pretending to be honest!" he said, "why do you try to catch me in a snare? Let me see some of the tax money!"

They brought to him a piece of silver, a Roman coin. He looked at it closely and then asked:

"Whose head is this that I find upon the coin? What are the words around the edge?"

"Why, that is the head of the Roman emperor, Tiberius Cæsar, and those words are his title."

"Well, then," said Jesus, "give to Cæsar what belongs to Cæsar; and be sure to give to God what belongs to God."

There was nothing in that answer which they could make to appear either unfriendly or friendly to the Roman rule; nor yet was there anything that could be used against Jesus with the people. Wondering at the answer of Jesus, these men left him.

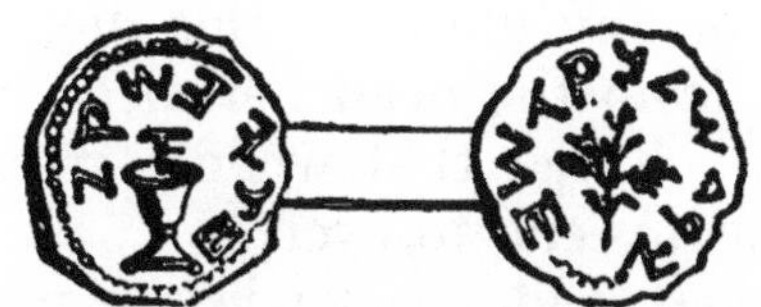

Jewish half-shekel, the coin in which the Temple tax was paid—"tribute money" (Matt. 17:27)—value, 32 cents

The Woman with Seven Husbands

CHAPTER 73

WE HAVE heard much in the story of the Pharisees, who were looked upon as leaders of the people in religion, because they regularly went to church, paid the church dues and obeyed all the rules, foolish as some of those rules seemed. These Pharisees, as you know, were bitter enemies of Jesus, and everywhere stirred up the people against him.

But there was another party among the Jews, the Sadducees, whom we have not mentioned up to this time. These people were equally opposed to the Pharisees and to Jesus. They were easy-living men, not paying much attention to the church rules; and in fact not going often to the church, which you know was called "the synagogue." But although they cared little for the churches in the different towns, they cared greatly for the Temple in Jerusalem, for most of the priests in the Temple were Sadducees, as also were many of the rulers in the great council of the Jews.

The Sadducees did not believe that there was any soul in man, nor any life after this life, nor any angels, nor any rising from the dead hereafter, nor any heaven or hell. They believed that when a man died and was buried, that was his end forever.

Some of these Sadducees tried to puzzle Jesus with a question. They came to him in the Temple that Tuesday while he was speaking to the people.

"Teacher," they said to him, "you remember that in the law of Moses it is ordered that if a man should die without any children, but leaving a wife, then the man's brother shall take the widow for his wife, and raise a family for his brother. Well, there were living seven brothers. The oldest of these married a wife, and after a time died, leaving no children. Then the second married her, and he too died without a child. The third took her and died, the fourth also, and all the rest of the seven died, leaving no children. Finally the woman herself died. Now, you have been teaching that there will come a day when the dead shall rise to life. When that day comes, and these seven men rise, all of whom were married to this woman, whose wife out of them all will she be, for every one of them in turn was married to her?"

"You make a mistake," answered Jesus, "because you do not understand the teachings of the Bible; nor do you know how great is the power of God, who can at a word call the dead up to life. In this world men and women marry because they live on earth only for a time, and must have families to live after them. But when the dead are raised up, they do not rise as husbands and wives, nor do they marry in that world to come, for they will have no need to raise up families to take their places. In that land all live forever, like the angels of God. And as to the resurrection, the rising from the dead, have you not read the words that God spoke to Moses at the burning bush?

" 'I am the God of Abraham, and the God of Isaac, and the God of Jacob.'

"Now God is not the God of dead men, but of living men. For in the sight of God all men are alive, even after they have died on earth."

While Jesus was answering these questions—that of the rulers of the Temple about his right to drive out those that were buying and selling; that of the Pharisees about the paying of taxes; and that of the Sadducees about the resurrection, the rising from the dead—the people were standing around listening. Although the rulers were enemies of Jesus the common people were friendly, and heard him gladly. They saw how ready and how apt his answers were, and they were greatly pleased to find the enemies of Jesus put to confusion before him.

The tomb of David as shown to-day in Jerusalem

The Greatest of All the Commandments

CHAPTER 79

WHILE JESUS was talking in the Temple and answering all these questions, a teacher of the law was standing near and listening. He saw how well Jesus answered all the questions put to him, and coming up to him, said:

"Teacher, what commandment stands first of all?"

We might suppose that he was speaking of the Ten Commandments and asking which of these is the most important. But that was not his purpose. He was thinking, not of the commandments given by God, but of the rules made by the scribes. One teacher would say that the rules about keeping the Sabbath were the greatest, another that the rules about washing were first; and so on, each scribe or teacher laying stress on one set of rules above another. Jesus looked upon all these little laws made by men as of no importance; and this was his answer to the scribe who had asked the question:

"The first and greatest of all the commandments is this, 'Hear, O ye people of Israel; the Lord our God is one Lord; and thou shalt love the Lord thy God with all thy heart, and with all thy soul, and with all thy mind, and with all thy strength.' And the second commandment is this, 'Thou shalt love thy neighbor as thyself.' There is no other commandment greater than these two."

To love God with all the heart is to do God's will, not because we must do it, but because we love to do it and find joy in doing it. And to love our neighbor means to feel an interest in our fellow-men and to do for them whatever we would wish to have them do for us.

"You are right, Teacher!" said the scribe in answer to Jesus. "It is true, as you say, that there is one God; and there is no other God besides him. And to love God with the whole heart, and with the whole mind, and with the whole strength; and to love one's fellow-man as one's self—this is far beyond all offerings upon the altar!"

Jesus saw that this man's words were true and good

Ruins at the place where Jesus foretold the destruction of Jerusalem

and that he had the right thought of our duty to God and to our fellow-man. He said to him:

"You are not far from the kingdom of God."

This was the last question put to Jesus. No one ventured to ask him any more, for they were afraid of his wonderful answers. The chief priests and the rulers were more and more angry at him, but the common people listened to him willingly.

While Jesus was teaching he in his turn asked a question of the Pharisees and teachers of the law.

"Tell me," he said, "what you think of the Messiah-Christ, the King of Israel, promised to come. Whose son is he?"

They answered at once, "David's son."

"How is it then," asked Jesus again, "that David in one of the psalms calls him 'Lord'?

> "The Lord said to my Lord, 'Sit at my right hand,
> Until I put your enemies under your feet.'

"If David calls this coming Christ 'my Lord,' how can he be David's son?"

This they could not answer, and they dared not ask Jesus any more questions. But we know, from the words of the New Testament, that while Christ as a man was sprung from David's line, as the Son of God he was David's Lord.

After this Jesus spoke strong words to the priests, the scribes, and the rulers, for their wickedness of life for their leading the people away from God's will, and for their unjust, cruel purpose to put him to death. He told them that for their sins and the sins of their people, the Temple should be thrown down, the city of Jerusalem should be destroyed, and the land should be made desolate. These were his last words, and when he had spoken them, he rose up to go out of the Temple.

The Greatest Gift; and the Strangers from Afar

CHAPTER 80

THE ROOM in the Temple where Jesus spoke on that Tuesday, the last day of his teaching in public, was called "The Treasury," because beside its walls were chests or boxes in which people who came to worship placed their money for gifts to pay for the offerings of poor people. As Jesus rose up to leave the room, he noticed the people dropping their money into these boxes. Some rich men made a show of giving large sums of money, letting it make a noise as they dropped it slowly, piece after piece, into the box.

There came in a poor woman, whose dress showed that she was a widow; and she dropped into the box two little copper coins, worth together only a quarter of a cent. Jesus saw her, and calling his disciples, he said:

"I tell you in truth, that in the sight of God this poor widow has put into the box more money than any of the others. All the rest have been putting in money that they could spare and did not need. But she in her need gave all that she had, her whole living!"

Then Jesus walked out of the Treasury through the door on the east, which was so richly decorated that it was called "The Beautiful Gate," his disciples with him. They stepped down into the Court of the Gentiles; and at the foot of the stairs met a number of men whose looks and dress showed that they were not Jews, but foreigners. These men were Greeks, from a land far away. They were waiting for Jesus at the foot of the stairs, for not being Jews they were forbidden to enter the inner courts of the Temple.

These Greeks stepped up to one of the twelve disciples, Philip, who had come from Bethsaida in the north of Galilee, and could speak their language.

The poor widow drops in two little coins

"Sir," they said to Philip, "we would like to meet Jesus."

Philip was not sure whether his Master would be willing to talk to these men; for Jews kept Gentiles or foreigners at a distance, would never eat with them, and would scarcely speak with them. Philip thought that Andrew, the brother of Peter, might know whether to bring these men to Jesus or not, so he spoke to Andrew, and Andrew took the lead in coming to Jesus with the Greeks.

"The time has now come," said Jesus, "for the Son of Man to be lifted up, and to die. For it is only by dying that I can bring forth fruit. When a kernel of wheat is dropped into the ground, unless its outside shell dies, it lives alone; but if it dies, then it becomes a seed and brings a harvest of many kernels of wheat. He who loves his life and keeps it, loses it; but he who takes no care of his life here shall have it forever. If any man is ready to serve me, let him follow me; and where I am going there shall my servant be with me. If any one is my servant, he shall have honor from my Father."

At that moment it came to the mind of Jesus that in less than three days he would be hanging dead upon the cross. For an instant the thought gave him pain. "I am deeply troubled, and have sorrow in my heart," said Jesus, "and what can I say? Shall I say, 'Father, save me from the hour that is coming so soon?' No, I will not say that, because it was for that hour of death on the cross that I have lived even until now. I will say, 'Father, give honor to thine own name!'"

Then a voice from heaven was heard, saying, "I have honored my name already, and I will honor it once more."

The people standing around said, "That was a peal of thunder just now."

"No," said others, "it was an angel speaking to this man!"

"It was not on my account that the voice came," said Jesus, "but on your account. Soon will come the hour when God will judge this world, and the prince of evil, who rules this world, shall be driven away."

Then Jesus thought of his coming death on the cross; what it was to bring to the world; how that everywhere after his death men should believe on him as their Lord and Saviour; not only Jews, but Greeks, and people of every land; and he said:

"And when I am lifted up from the earth, I will draw all men to me."

Soon after this Jesus walked out of the Temple, never again to set his foot within it.

Jesus Telling of Dark Days to Come

CHAPTER 81

JESUS WALKED across the Court of the Gentiles or Strangers, the large outer court of the Temple, toward the Mount of Olives. On that side of the court stood Solomon's Porch, a double row of pillars, having a roof above to shield it from the sun. Under this porch they stepped down a marble staircase to pass out of the Temple grounds through a gate called "The Golden Gate." As they drew near this gate the disciples called his attention to the great stones in the wall, the pillars and the splendid buildings around.

"Are you looking at these stones and buildings?" said Jesus. "I tell you now, that the time is coming, and not far away, when all of these stones shall be torn apart, and of these fine buildings not one stone shall be left standing in its place; all shall be thrown down!"

The disciples heard these words with alarm and sadness. They knew that their Lord spoke as a prophet; and whatever he said would be sure to come to pass. But they looked upon Jerusalem as the holy city, and upon the Temple as the house of God. To them, the fall of the city and the Temple seemed like the end of the whole world. They walked after Jesus in silence across the valley of the brook Kedron and up the steep sides of the Mount of Olives. On its top they sat down to rest, and looked over the valley at the city, its towers and roofs rising in their view. While they were sitting on the mountain, Peter and Andrew, with the brothers James and John, came to Jesus, and said to him:

"Tell us, Master, what your words mean, and when

these terrible things will come to pass? Are you going away, and then coming back again? How may we know when to look for you?"

Then, sitting on the mountain, with the twelve disciples around him, Jesus gave a long talk about the things that were to come. He began by warning them against following after men claiming to be Christ, the King of Israel.

"Take care," he said, "that no one lead you astray. For many will come saying, 'I am Christ, the King of Israel,' and they will lead away many people. But do not follow any of these false Christs.

The Golden Gate, on east of the Temple Area, Jerusalem (now closed)

"You will hear of wars that have come, and reports of wars that are coming; but do not be frightened. These must come, but they are not the end. Nation shall make war with nation, and kingdom against kingdom; and you shall hear of earthquakes in many places; and times shall come when there will be no bread for the hungry to eat. But all these are only the beginnings of the trouble; and the worst is yet to come.

"But before these take place there are some other sufferings that you must meet because you are my disciples. Enemies will rise up against you. You shall be brought before councils and courts to be tried; you shall be seized and beaten in the churches of the Jews; you shall stand before governors and kings to give account for yourselves as my followers. But when they seize you and bring you to be tried, do not be anxious as to what you shall speak; for the right words shall be given you in that hour of trial. It will not be you that speak, but the Spirit of God that speaks through you.

"In those times of trial fathers and mothers shall turn against their children, and brothers shall give up brothers who believe in me. Some of you shall be put

The Mount of Olives from Gethsemane

to death in those days. And all men shall hate you because you are my disciples. But if you are faithful to the end, even to death, you shall be saved to everlasting life."

Then Jesus told of the terrible times that were coming to Jerusalem and the land of the Jews. He said:

"When you see great armies encamped on these hills all around Jerusalem, then know that the time has come for the city and the Temple to be destroyed. Let this be a sign for everyone in Judea to hide among the mountains. If a man at that time is on the roof of his house, let him not go down to take anything out of his house; nor a man in the field go home after his cloak; but hasten away just as he is, with the clothes that are upon his back, and find a safe hiding-place.

"If anyone tells you in such times as those, 'Here is Christ!' or 'There he is!' do not believe it, for false Christs will come and false prophets will appear; and they will show signs and wonders, so as to lead astray even some of God's own people. I tell you truly that many who are now living shall see all these things come to pass."

Jesus had already told his disciples that he was soon going away to leave them, but in his own time he would come again. He now spoke about his "coming again."

"As to the coming of the Son of Man, no one knows about that day or hour; no man knows when it will be, nor the angels, nor even the Son himself, but only the Father. It will be then as it was in the days of Noah; they went on eating and drinking, marrying and being married, until the day Noah went into the ark; and they took no notice until the flood came and swept them all away.

"So will it be when the Son of Man comes. Then there will be two men working together in the field; one shall be taken and the other left. Two women will be grinding grain with the hand mill; one shall be taken and the other left. Keep on the watch then, for you never know what day the Lord will come. Be sure of this, if the owner of the house had known at what time in the night the thief would come, he would have been on the watch for him, and would never have allowed his house to be broken into. So be ready all the time, for when you least expect him, the Son of Man will come."

The Parable of the Ten Bridesmaids

CHAPTER 82

AT THE CLOSE of a long talk with the disciples, on the Mount of Olives, Jesus gave three parables. The first parable was to show that his followers must watch and be ready for his sudden coming. It is "The Parable of the Ten Bridesmaids."

"The coming of the Lord in his kingdom," said Jesus, "will be as when ten girls, the bridesmaids at a wedding, took their lamps and went out to meet the bridegroom with his friends, and go with them to the house of the bride. Five of these girls were foolish and thoughtless, and five of them were wise. The foolish young women brought their lamps, but never thought that they would need more oil to fill their lamps again. But each of the five wise girls carried a small flask of oil to refill her lamp when needed.

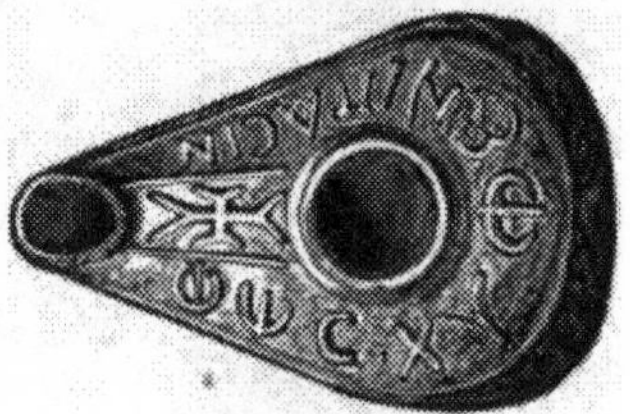

Oriental lamp

"As the bridegroom, the young man who was to be married, was late in coming, the ten bridesmaids grew sleepy, and finally all fell asleep. They slept until midnight, when suddenly they were awakened by the shout, 'Here comes the bridegroom! Come out to meet him!'

"Then all the girls got up and began trimming their lamps. The careless, foolish ones said to the wise and thoughtful ones:

" 'Come, let us have some of your oil. Our lamps are going out.'

"But the wise bridesmaids answered them, 'No, each one of us has brought just enough oil for her own lamp. If we should divide our oil with you, then none of us would have enough to keep her lamp burning and we should all be in the dark together. You must go to the store and buy for yourselves!'

"So, in the middle of the night, while the bride-

The coming of the bridegroom

groom was coming, those foolish women had to go to the town, and wake up the oil-sellers and buy more oil. While they were on their way buying oil, the bridegroom and his party came; and the bridesmaids who were ready went with them to the marriage-supper. When they were all inside the room, the door was shut to keep out strangers who had no right to enter.

"After a time, the rest of the bridesmaids came

and found the door shut. They called out to the bridegroom:

" 'Oh, sir, oh, sir! Please open the door for us!'

"But he answered them, 'I tell you, I do not know who you are!'

"So," said Jesus, "I say to you, keep on the watch, and be ready at all times, for you do not know either the day or the hour when your Lord will come."

Watch-tower

The Parable of the Talents

CHAPTER 83

THE SECOND of the three parables with which Jesus closed his long talk to his disciples on the Mount of Olives was "The Parable of the Talents." In some parts it was like "The Parable of the Pounds," given to the crowd at Jericho only a week before, but in other parts it was different. In that parable, there was a king, going to a distant city to have a kingdom given to him. In this parable, it was a rich man going on a long journey. In the parable of the Pounds, all the servants began with the same amount of money; in this parable, they received different amounts, one of them five times as much as another received. In the parable of the Pounds, one gained ten times, the other five times what had been given to him; and they obtained different rewards, one the ruler over ten cities, another over five. But in the parable of the Talents, each faithful servant doubled what he had received, and both had the same reward. But we will give the parable of the Talents, and you can see how it differs from the parable of the Pounds. Jesus said:

"When the Son of Man comes, it will be as when a man returned from his journey into a far country. Before starting out upon his journey, this man called together his servants and gave his money into their charge. To one he gave five talents, to another two, and to another one. Each talent was worth about two thousand dollars, so that the first servant had ten thousand dollars, the second four thousand dollars, and the third two thousand dollars. To each man was given as much as his master thought that he was able to take care of. They were to use the money and gain with it until their master should come home again; and then bring it with their gains to him. After dividing his money, the man went away.

"At once the servant who had the five talents or ten thousand dollars, went to trade with his money, and made with it ten thousand dollars more, or twenty thousand dollars in all. The second servant, who had two talents or four thousand dollars, also used his money carefully, and doubled it, making eight thousand dollars. But the third servant, to whom had been given one talent, or two thousand dollars, instead of making use of his master's money, went away and dug a hole in the ground, and put the talent into the hole and left it there.

"After a long time the master of the servants came home again, and called for his servants, to see what each had gained. The one who had received the five talents came with bags of gold in his arms. He said:

"'My lord, you gave me ten thousand dollars. Here they are, and ten thousand dollars more, which I have gained with your money.'

"'Well done, you good servant!' said his master. 'You have done well in small things; now I will give you great things; come and share your master's feast!'

"Then came the second servant, to whom had been given two talents.

"'My lord,' said he, 'you trusted me with four thousand dollars. See, here it is with four thousand dollars more that I have gained for you!'

"'Well done, you good servant,' said his master. 'You too have done well in small things; now I will give you great things; come and share the feast with me!'

"Then came the servant to whom had been given

one talent, two thousand dollars. In his hand was the same bag of gold that he had received, and no more.

" 'Sir,' he said, 'I knew that you were a hard man, reaping where you never sowed, and taking grain that you did not harvest. So I was afraid, and hid your money in the ground. Look, here is what belongs to you.'

"You lazy, worthless servant!" said his master

" 'You lazy, worthless servant!' said his master. 'You knew, did you, that I reap where I did not sow, and that I take grain that I did not harvest? If you knew that I am such a man as that, you should have put my money into the savings bank; and then at least I might have had my own money with some gain added to it.

" 'Therefore,' the master went on, 'take away the talent from this man, and give it to the one who has brought me the ten talents, the twenty thousand dollars; for that shows that he is fitted to take care of it. For to every one that has, more shall be given and still more. But from him that does not have, even that which he has shall be taken away.

"'And as for that good-for-nothing servant, turn him out of doors from the feast, into the darkness outside; there those who cannot come into the feast shall wail and gnash their teeth.'"

From this parable, as well as the parable of the Pounds, it is plain that by "every one who has," the Lord meant "every one who cares for and makes use of what he has"; and by "him who has not" he meant "the one who makes no use of what he has." Whoever uses rightly what he has, whether money, or knowledge, or powers of mind, or the chance to do good, will find more and more of it; and whoever neglects what he has will surely lose it.

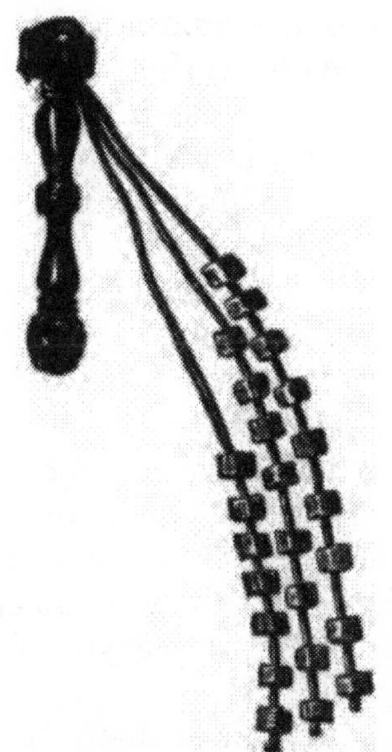

Flagellum or scourge

The Last Great Day

CHAPTER 84

AFTER THE two parables of "The Bridesmaids" and "The Talents," Jesus still with his disciples on the Mount of Olives, gave one more parable; a picture of "The Last Great Day." He said:

"When the Son of Man shall come again to earth, in all his glory as King, and with him all the angels of God, then he will take his seat upon his royal throne; and before him shall be gathered all the people of the world to be judged. At that time he will send out his angels and they shall divide the great multitude into two parts, as a shepherd divides his flock, putting the sheep on his right hand and the goats on his left. Then the King shall say to those on his right hand:

" 'Come, you who are blessed by my Father. Come, and take the kingdom made ready for you ever since the beginning of the world. For, when I was hungry, you gave me food; when I was thirsty, you gave me drink; when I was a stranger, you opened your doors and took me into your homes; when I had no clothes, you gave me clothing; when I was sick, you cared for me; when I was in prison, you came to visit me.'

"Then the good will answer, 'When was it that we found you hungry and gave you food? Or thirsty and gave you drink? When did we see you a stranger, and took you into our homes? Or without clothes, and gave you clothing? When did we see you sick, or in prison, and went to visit you?'

"And the King will answer them, 'I tell you, as often as you did any of these things to one of these my brothers who believe in me, even the least of them, you did it to me.'

"Then the King will turn to those on his left hand, and will say to them:

"'Go away from me, you whom God has cursed, to the everlasting fires which have been kindled for the Devil and his angels, the wicked spirits. There shall be your home forever! For I was hungry, but you never gave me food; I was thirsty, but you never gave me drink; I was a stranger, but you never opened your doors to me; I was in need of clothes, but you never gave me any; I was sick and in prison, but you never cared for me.'

"Then these will answer him:

"'Lord, when did we ever see you hungry, or thirsty, or a stranger, or without clothing, or sick, or in prison, and did not help you?'

"And he shall answer them, 'In very truth I say to you, that as often as you did not help in their need these my brothers who believe in me, even the very least of them, you did not help me.' So these will go away to suffer punishment forever; but those who have done the right will go to life everlasting."

It was now late on Tuesday afternoon, and Jesus with his disciples went down the Mount of Olives to Bethany. On the way he said to them:

"You know that two days from now is the Feast of the Passover. On that day the Son of Man will be given up to his enemies; and they shall put him to death upon the cross."

But, although he had spoken of this many times, even now they could not believe it. They went together to Bethany, to the home of Martha and Mary and Lazarus.

"You, my Lord, shall never wash my feet!" said Peter. "Unless I wash you," answered Jesus, "you are not one of mine."

Washing the Disciples' Feet

CHAPTER 85

TUESDAY HAD been a busy day for Jesus, as we have already seen; but Wednesday must have been a quiet day, for none of the four gospels tells us of any events taking place on that day. Jesus knew that in two days more his sufferings were to begin, and he needed Wednesday, his last full day, for rest and for talking with his Father in heaven. On Wednesday, therefore, Jesus was alone with God, not talking much with his disciples.

On Thursday evening was to be held by all the Jews the great Feast of the Passover. This kept in mind the day, more than a thousand years before, when the Israelites went out of Egypt and became a free people. At that time each Israelite family in Egypt killed a lamb, roasted it, and ate it, their last meal in Egypt; and with it they ate "unleavened bread," that is, bread made without yeast; somewhat like soda biscuit. In memory of that day, the families of Israel went up to Jerusalem every year in the spring and ate a dinner of roasted lamb with unleavened bread, which they called "The Feast of the Passover," because on that night in Egypt the angel of death "passed over" the homes of the Israelites, while he brought death to the families of Egypt.

On Thursday morning, Peter and John came to Jesus in Bethany and said:

"Master, where shall we make ready the passover feast for you?"

"Go into the city," answered Jesus, "and you will meet a man carrying a jar of water; follow him, and into whatever house he goes, say to the man living there, 'The Teacher says, I must eat the passover at your house tonight with my disciples—where is my room?' And this man will show you a large room upstairs; there make ready all things for the supper."

Peter and John went from Bethany into the city as they were told; they met the man with the water jar and followed him to the house. There they found the owner of the house, and spoke to him as Jesus had said. This man may have been a follower of Jesus, glad to have his Master take a meal at his house. He led Peter and John upstairs into a large room, with tables standing, and around them couches for the guests.

Then the two disciples went into the market and bought a lamb. This they carried upon their shoulders to the Temple. There it was killed and its blood was poured out at the foot of the great altar. The lamb was then roasted in an oven; and after sunset it was brought to the supper room and placed upon the table. Beside it were the flat biscuits of unleavened bread, and also some vegetables of a slightly bitter taste, to be eaten with the lamb.

Late on Thursday afternoon Jesus and the rest of his disciples left Bethany. Jesus alone knew that this was his last farewell to that home and its loving people; but he said nothing, not wishing to alarm them. Among his followers on that afternoon was Judas Iscariot, knowing that he had sold his Master to his enemies, and that the thirty silver pieces were even then in his money bag. Jesus knew it, too, but he said not a word of it, either to Judas or the disciples.

They went around the Mount of Olives, crossed the valley, and came through one of the gates into the city; then found their way among the streets on Mount Zion to the house where in the upper room the supper was all ready for them. Here, as many times before, arose a little quarrel over the question as to which of the twelve disciples should sit at the guest table with Jesus, for that table was the place of honor. Jesus stopped the dispute by saying to them what he had said before:

"He that would be greatest among you, let him take the lowest place; and he who would be chief, let him become your servant. But there is no need for you to be anxious about places. You have stood by me through all my trials, and I will give you all high places in my kingdom, for you shall sit on twelve thrones, each of you over one of the tribes of Israel."

But Jesus in teaching his disciples lowliness of mind and unselfishness of spirit, did not stop with words. He taught them by an act which made them wonder. Just before the supper, he rose from the couch where he was lying, took off his robe and outer garments, then tied a towel around his waist, poured water into a basin, and began to wash the feet of the disciples as they were reclining around the tables, their heads toward the tables, their feet away from them. Jesus came first to Simon Peter, and stood at his feet, holding the basin of water. Peter looked up at him, and saw that the Saviour was preparing to wash his feet.

"What, Master!" said Peter. "Are you going to wash my feet?"

"You do not understand now what this means," said Jesus, "but you will learn after a time."

"You, my Lord, shall never wash my feet!" said Peter.

"Unless I wash you," answered Jesus, "you are not one of mine."

"Then, Master," said Peter, "if that be so, wash not only my feet, but my hands and my head!"

"He who has already bathed," said Jesus, "is clean,

and needs only to wash his feet. And you are clean—but not every one of you."

In those words "not every one of you," he was thinking of Judas, the traitor, who was there with the others.

So Jesus washed Peter's feet and wiped them dry with the towel around his waist; and he went around the couches, washing the feet of every disciple, even the feet of wicked Judas. When he had finished, he took off the towel, and put on his outer clothes, and took again his place at the table.

After taking the piece of bread, Judas at once went out into the night

"Do you understand the meaning of what I have done to you?" said Jesus. "You call me your Teacher and your Lord, and you are right, for I am both Teacher and Lord. Well, if I, who am your Teacher and your Lord, have washed your feet, you ought to wash each other's feet. I have set you an example, that you should do what I have done to you. I tell you truly, a servant is not greater than his master, nor is a messenger greater than the one who sends him. If you know all this, you are happy if you do them."

Then Jesus went on, saying, "When I say 'you' I do not mean all of you; for there is one of you eating with me now who will give me up to my enemies. Truly, truly, I tell you one of you shall betray me!"

As Jesus said this his face showed that he was in

Then Jesus took up the cup and blessed it, and gave it also to his disciples.

deep trouble. The disciples looked at each other, not knowing of whom Jesus was speaking. They too were filled with sorrow, and began to say to him, all around the table, "Is it I, Lord?"

"One of you that puts his hand into the same dish with me," answered Jesus, "is the traitor. The Son of Man goes from earth, as has been written of him in the Scripture, but woe, woe to that man who betrays his Lord! It would have been well for that man if he had never been born!"

Next to Jesus at the table was reclining one of the disciples, John, whom Jesus loved greatly. Simon Peter made signs to John, which meant, "Find out who it is that he is speaking of."

So John leaned back on Jesus' shoulder and whispered:

"Who is it, Master?"

"It is the one," answered Jesus, "to whom I shall hand this piece of bread, after dipping it in the dish."

Jesus dipped the bread into the dish holding the roasted lamb, and handed it to Judas Iscariot. At that moment the spirit of evil went fully into the heart of Judas. Jesus said to him:

"What you are going to do, do at once."

But no one at the table understood what these words meant. As Judas kept the purse for the company, they thought that Jesus was telling him to buy some things for the feast, or perhaps to give some money to the poor. After taking the piece of bread, Judas at once went out into the night.

The Lord's Supper

CHAPTER 86

WHILE THEY were eating the passover meal, Jesus took a loaf of bread, and holding it in his hand, with his eyes lifted to heaven, spoke a blessing upon it. Then he broke it and gave a piece of it to each of the disciples. As he gave it to them, he said:

"Take this, and eat it; this means my body which is given for you."

Then he took a cup of the wine, and blessed it, and gave this also to his disciples, saying:

"Drink from this, all of you; this means my blood, the blood of the new covenant, which is poured out for many, to take away their sins. I tell you, from this time I will never again drink the juice of the grape, until that day when I drink it new with you, in the kingdom of my Father."

In the old times, an agreement or promise was called "a covenant," and when it was made a lamb or a goat was killed for an offering, and laid upon the altar to be burned. The blood of the offering was poured out on the altar; and this was called "the blood of the covenant." Jesus meant to tell his disciples that soon his blood would be poured forth as the sign of God's promise to take away sin from those who believed in him.

You have seen at some services in the church a table covered with a white cloth. When the cloth has been taken away, you have seen plates of bread and cups of wine. The minister gives the bread to the people, and repeats the words of Jesus, "Take, eat; this is my body which is given for you." And afterward as the wine is taken, he says, "Drink ye all of this; for this is my blood shed for you." This service is called "The Lord's Supper," and it is held to keep in our minds the thought of the last meal that Jesus ate with his disciples.

"My dear children," said Jesus after the supper, "I am to be with you only a little longer; then you will look for me, and as I told the Jews I tell you now, where I am going you cannot come. I give you a new commandment, to love one another. As I have loved you, you are to love each other. By this every one will know that you are my disciples, by your loving each other."

"Lord," said Simon Peter, "where are you going?"

"I am going," answered Jesus, "where you cannot follow me now; but you shall follow me after a time."

"Why cannot I follow you now, Master?" asked Peter. "I am ready to lay down my life and die for you!"

"Will you lay down your life for me?" said Jesus. "I tell you truly, Peter, before the cock crows twice tomorrow morning you will three times declare that you have never known me."

But Peter again said most earnestly, "If I must die with you, I will never deny you."

And all the disciples who were present said with Peter that they would never forsake their Lord, even unto death.

The Vine and the Branches

CHAPTER 87

JESUS SAW that his disciples were greatly disturbed at his words, as he spoke of going away to some place where they could not go with him, and leaving them alone among people who were his enemies; especially as he told Peter that he would soon disown his Master, and that all the rest of the disciples should leave him to suffer alone. Jesus tried to comfort them in their fears and their sorrows.

"Do not be troubled in your hearts," he said to them; "trust in God, and trust in me, and in my words. In my Father's dwelling-place there are many homes. I am going to prepare a place for you; and when I have prepared it, I will come back and take you to be with me there, so that you may be where I am. And you know the way to the place where I am going."

"Master," said Thomas, "we do not know where you are going; and how then are we to know the way?"

"I am the way, and the truth, and the life," answered Jesus. "No one ever comes to the Father in any way except through me. If you knew me, you would know my Father also. You know him now, and have seen him; for you have seen me."

"Master," said Philip, "let us see the Father; that is all that we want."

"Have I been with you all this time, Philip," answered Jesus, "and yet you do not know me? Whoever has seen me has seen the Father. What do you mean by saying, 'Let us see the Father'? Do you not believe that the Father and I are one, that I am in the Father and the

Father in me? The words that I speak are my Father's words; and the works that I do are my Father's works. I tell you truly, that whoever believes in me shall do the very works that I do; and he shall do even greater works than these. I am going to the Father, and whatever you ask the Father in my name that I will do, that the Father may be honored in the Son. If you ask anything in my name, I will do it.

"If you love me," Jesus went on, "you will do whatever I have told you to do; and I will ask the Father to give you another Helper to be with you always. That Helper is the Spirit of Truth. The people of this world cannot have the Spirit, because they do not see him nor know him. But you know him, because he is always with you, and is within you. I will not leave you alone in your sorrow; I am coming to you. A little while longer, and the world will see me no more; but you will see me, for I am living, and you will be living, too. He who has my commands and keeps them in his heart is the one who loves me; and he who loves me will be loved by my Father; and I will love him and I will make myself known to him."

Then said one of the disciples named Judas—not Judas Iscariot the traitor (he had gone out), but another Judas, the brother of James—"How is it, Lord, that you are to make yourself known to us and not to the world?"

"If any one loves me," answered Jesus, "he will obey my word; and my Father will love him; and we will come to him and make our home with him. He who does not love me will not obey my words; and the word to which you are listening is not my own word, but the word of the Father who sent me. I have told you all this while I am still with you, but the Helper, the Holy Spirit, whom the Father will send to you to take my place, he will teach you all that you need to know and he will bring to your mind all that I have said to you. Peace be with you! My own peace I give you. I do not give my peace to you as the world gives its 'peace.' Do not let your hearts be troubled; do not be afraid.

"You heard me say that I was going away and soon afterward coming back to you. If you loved me fully, you would be glad that I am going to the Father, for the Father is greater than I am. I have told you all this—that I am going away—before it happens, so that when it does happen, as it will very soon, you may still believe in me, and believe that I am coming again."

"I am the vine, and you are the branches"

Then Jesus gave to his disciples another parable, "The Vine and the Branches." He said:

"I am the true vine, and my Father is the vine-grower, the Master of the vineyard. You, my disciples, and all who believe in me, are the branches of the vine. If the vine-grower finds on his vine any branches that bear no fruit, he cuts them off, for they are of no use. If he finds branches that bear fruit, he trims them and cleans them, so that they may bear better fruit. You are already clean through the word that I have spoken to you. Keep united to me, the vine, and I will keep united to you. Just as a branch cannot bear fruit by itself when separate from the vine, no more can you bear fruit unless you stay united to me.

"Remember, I am the vine, and you are the branches. He who keeps himself in union with me, and keeps me in union with himself bears rich fruit. But apart from me you can do nothing. If any one does not stay united to me, he is thrown away, just as a branch would be, and he withers up; then the worthless, withered branches are gathered and thrown into the fire and are burned.

"If you stay united to me, and my teaching stays in your hearts, you may ask whatever you wish, and it shall be yours. As you bear rich fruit and prove yourselves my disciples, my Father is honored. As my Father has loved me, so I have loved you; stay in my love. If you keep my commands in your hearts, you will stay in my love, just as I have kept my Father's commands in my heart and dwell in his love."

The Last Words of Jesus to His Disciples

CHAPTER 88

JESUS WENT on giving his last talk with his disciples, in the room after the supper. Among other things, he said:

"This is my last command to you. Love one another as I have loved you. No one can give greater proof of love than by laying down his life for his friends. You are my friends if you do what I command you. I do not any more call you 'servants'; for a servant does not know what his master is doing; but I have called you 'friends,' for all things that I have learned from my Father I have told you. It was not you who chose me, but I have chosen you, and appointed you to go and bear fruit that shall last, so that the Father may give you whatever you ask in my name.

"This is what I command you, to love one another. If the world hates you, remember that it hated me first. If you belonged to the world, the world would love its own; but because you do not belong to the world, since I have chosen you out of the world, the world hates you. Remember what I said to you, 'A servant is not greater than his master.' If they have tried to do me harm, they will try to do you harm too. If they hold to my word, they will hold to yours also. It is written in the Holy Book, 'They hated me without any cause,' and that word has come true in me; for they have indeed hated me when there was no cause for it. But when that Helper comes, he whom I will send to you—the Spirit of Truth who comes from the Father—he will speak for me; yes, and you shall speak for me, for you have been with me from the very first.

"I have said these things to you now, so that in the times to come, knowing these things you will not be discouraged nor fail. They will put you out of their churches; yes, there is coming a time when if anyone kills you he will think that he is pleasing God. They will do these things because they have not really known my Father, nor known me. But I am telling you of these things now, that when the time comes, and you find the rulers and the people your enemies, you will remember I told you, and will be ready for these things.

In a little while your sorrow shall be turned into joy, and your joy shall never be taken away from you

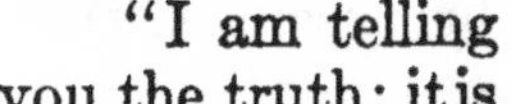

"I am telling you the truth; it is best for you that I go away; for if I do not leave you, that Helper, the Spirit of God, will not come to you; but if I go away, I will send him to you. When he the Spirit of Truth comes, he will lead you into all truth; and he will make known to you what is to come. In a little while you will not see me any longer: then after another little while you will see me again."

These words seemed to the disciples hard to understand. They said to each other:

"What does he mean by telling us, 'In a little while you will not see me: then after another little while you will see me'; and 'I am going to the Father'? What does he mean by 'a little while'?"

Jesus knew that they wanted to ask him: and he said to them, "Are you trying to find out what I meant in saying 'a little while and ye shall not see me, and then a little while and ye shall see me'? I tell you truly, that in a very little while you will be weeping and sorrowing, while the world around you will be glad. Then in a little while again, your sorrow shall be turned into joy, for you shall see me again, and your joy shall never be taken away from you."

Jesus meant them to understand that in a few hours he would be taken from them and placed upon the cross to die; that he would be buried, and all these things should give them pain and sorrow. But in a few days he would rise again from the grave, and then they would be glad and happy, with a happiness that should never pass away, even though he should again, after that, leave them and go to the Father.

After saying these things, Jesus lifted up his hands to God and prayed. In his prayer he gave thanks to God that he had been able to finish the work that had been given him to do. He prayed also for his disciples, that they might all be one in heart, and love each other, and that they might be kept faithful to the end. He prayed, too, not only for those his disciples, but for all who through their words should come to believe in him as the Saviour of the world; that they all might be of one heart, loving each other; one with Jesus, and one with his Father.

When Jesus had finished his prayer, they all sang a hymn together, and went out of the supper room into the silent streets of the city. They walked toward the Mount of Olives, as if expecting to return to Bethany, the place from which they had come in the afternoon.

With the disciples, as they went out of the house, was a young man whose name was John Mark. He may have been the son of the man at whose house Jesus and his disciples had eaten the supper. If that be so, then his mother's name was Mary, just like the name of Jesus' mother, though she was not the same woman. Long afterward, this John Mark wrote one of the four gospels, telling of the life of Jesus, "The Gospel of Mark."

Olive tree and oil press

Jesus, leaving his three disciples to watch at the entrance to the Garden of Gethsemane, went farther inside to pray.

In the Garden of Gethsemane

CHAPTER 89

DURING THE week of the Passover, while the city of Jerusalem held three or four times as many people as usual, the gates in its walls were kept open day and night, although during most of the year they were closed at sunset. It was near midnight on Thursday when Jesus and his disciples, coming from the supper room, passed through a gate in the eastern wall just north of the Temple. They went down into the valley of the brook Kedron, and crossed the brook upon a bridge. On the further side of the valley, they came to an orchard of olive trees, called the Garden of Gethsemane. Jesus had often visited this garden, for it was a quiet place; and he loved to pray under the shadow of its olive trees. The orchard had a wall around it; and at its gate Jesus said to his disciples:

"Sit here, while I go and pray inside the garden."

He took with him three of his disciples, Simon Peter, James, and John his brother, and with these three went into the garden. The disciples began to notice that their Master was now showing the signs of deep sorrow, as if full of grief. He said to the three disciples:

"My heart is sad; sad even to death; stay here and watch."

Then he went forward a little way, and fell with his face upon the earth, and prayed to the Father:

"Oh, my Father! My Father!" he cried. "Thou canst do anything! Take this cup away from me, I pray! Yet I do not ask to have my own will, but only what is thy will."

The "cup" of which Jesus spoke was the terrible suffering that was very soon to come upon him. In these last moments as he saw his trial and death drawing near like a black cloud his spirit shrank. So earnest was his prayer, that the sweat stood upon his face in drops of blood. Just then came an angel from heaven, standing by his side to cheer and help him.

Ancient olive tree, in the garden of Gethsemane

He rose up, and walked to the place where he had left the three disciples. They had fallen asleep, being overcome with the trouble which they felt in knowing that soon they were to lose their Master. Jesus spoke to Peter,

"Simon, are you sleeping? Could you not watch with me for a single hour? Watch and pray, all of you, that you may be kept from being tempted. I know that your spirit is willing, but your bodies are weak."

Again he went away, and prayed in the same words:

"My Father! My Father! Thou canst do anything! Take this cup away from me! Yet, I would not have my own will, but thy will."

Coming back, he found them again asleep, for their eyes were heavy and they could not keep them open. When awaked, they did not know what to say to him, for they were ashamed of being found asleep a second time. Jesus left them, and prayed for the third time. In this prayer he said:

"Oh, my Father, if this cup cannot be taken away; if I must drink it, then thy will be done!"

He went once more to the three disciples, and found them asleep, just as before. He now said to them:

"You may as well sleep on now, and take your rest; for it is too late for you to help me. My time has come! The Son of Man has been given into the hands of wicked men. Come, get up, here is the traitor close at hand!"

And at that very instant, while he was speaking these words, the traitor, Judas Iscariot, burst into the garden, with a crowd of men, armed with swords and clubs. These men had been sent by the chief priests and the rulers to seize Jesus. Spies had been watching near the house while Jesus was talking after the supper, and others watching at the gate when Jesus passed out of it. Word had been sent to the chief priests that Jesus was in the garden, and while he was praying to his Father, these men, led by Judas Iscariot, were hurrying to that place to make Jesus their prisoner.

The men who had come to seize Jesus were not sure that in the night time, even though the full moon was shining, they would know him among his disciples. They said to Judas:

"How can we tell in the dark, under the trees, who is the one for us to take hold of as prisoner?"

"You watch me," said Judas, "and when I go up and kiss a man, seize him, for that one whom I shall kiss will be the man you are looking for."

Judas Iscariot, burst into the garden with a crowd of men, armed with swords and clubs.

So Judas went into the garden, where by this time all the other disciples were gathered around Jesus. He came rushing up, saying "Master! Master!" and kissed him, just though he were glad to see him.

"Judas," said Jesus, "do you betray the Son of Man with a kiss?"

Then he went forward to the band of men who were standing with their lanterns and torches, their swords and spears.

"For whom are you looking?" he said to these men.

"For Jesus of Nazareth," they answered him.

"I am he," said Jesus. At the instant when he said this, they went backward, as if frightened, and fell upon their faces on the ground. Again, after a moment, he asked them:

"For whom are you looking?"

And again they answered, "Jesus of Nazareth."

"I have already told you," said Jesus, "that I am he. If you are looking for me, then let these men go away."

For even in that hour Jesus was thinking not of his own safety, but of his disciples. The delay of a few moments gave to the disciples some courage. They began asking:

"Master, shall we strike with the sword?"

Simon Peter, not waiting for an answer from Jesus, drew a sword which he had brought with him, and with it struck one of the high priest's servants; a man named Malchus, and cut off his right ear; for by this time the band had risen to their feet and were drawing near. Jesus said:

"Let me at least do this;" and he touched his ear; and at once his ear was made well again.

"Put up your sword," said Jesus to Peter. "Those who take the sword shall die by the sword. Do you not know, that with a word I could call upon my Father, and even now he would send me twelve armies of angels to keep me safely? The cup which my Father has given me, must I not drink it?"

Then he turned to the band of men who had come to take him.

"Do you come out to arrest me as if I were a robber, with swords and clubs? Day after day I was with you in the Temple, and you did not lay your hands upon me. But now your time has come, and the dark Power has its way."

Then the disciples, finding that they could do nothing to protect Jesus, ran away and left him alone. The men of the band put chains upon Jesus, and led him away.

But John followed the company, and Peter also, anxious to see what would be done with their Lord. The young man John Mark was also following him, when one of the band tried to seize hold of him by his clothes. He left the linen cloth wrapped around him in the hands of the man, and slipped away with only his undergarments upon his body.

Jesus Before Annas

CHAPTER 90

THE MEN who took Jesus as their prisoner were the policemen of the Temple, led by their chief. With them were some of the priests and officers, and a crowd of the lowest people, who had been gathered from the streets by the rulers. All these formed together a noisy and disorderly mob, dragging Jesus out of the Garden of Gethsemane and into the city on Mount Zion. Two of the disciples, Peter and John, followed, keeping close to the crowd, but outside of it, their hearts filled with alarm for their Master.

The Temple policemen brought Jesus, all tied with ropes and chains, to the house on Mount Zion, inside the wall of the city, where lived one of the chief priests named Annas. Annas had once been the high priest, that is, the great priest at the head of all the priests; but the Roman rulers of the land had taken his office away from him, and made Caiaphas, whose wife was the daughter of Annas, high priest in his place. Many of the people believed that the Romans had no right to take his office away from Annas, and still looked upon him as the true and rightful high priest. Annas was a man of great power, feared by many; and therefore the men who had seized Jesus brought him first to the house of Annas. In the house were met a number of the chief rulers and members of the great council of the Jews. Jesus was brought in before them all. Annas asked Jesus to tell him what he had taught, and who were his disciples. Jesus answered him:

"My teachings have never been in secret; I have

always been open and public in my words. I spoke everywhere in the churches and in the Temple, where the people go to worship. Why do you ask me what I have said? Ask the people who heard me; they know what I said."

As Jesus spoke these words, one of the police officers

Priests and officers taking Jesus from the Garden of Gethsemane

standing by struck Jesus a hard blow with his hand, saying:

"Is that the way that you answer the high priest?"

Jesus answered him calmly, "If I have said anything that is not true, prove it; but if I have spoken the truth, why do you strike me?"

When Jesus was taken into the house of Annas, John followed the crowd inside, for John knew the high priest, and he was not afraid to go into his house.

But Peter stood outside in the street. Then John spoke to the woman who had charge of the door, and asked her to let in the man standing outside, and she opened the door for Peter. The rooms of the house stood around an open court, and Peter stood in the court among the servants and policemen. It was cold, and they had made a charcoal fire in a brazier—that is an iron pan standing upon either three or four legs. Around this fire the people gathered; and Peter stood in the court among them, holding his hands over the fire to warm them. The woman who kept the door looked sharply at Peter, and said:

"Are you not one of this man's disciples?"

Peter was alone among the enemies of Jesus, for John had gone into the room where Jesus was standing before Annas and the other rulers. Peter felt a sudden fear come over him, and to this woman's question, he answered:

"No, I am not!"

Poor Peter! Already he had begun to deny his Lord!

Annas knew that he had no right to act as judge upon Jesus. All that he could do was to examine Jesus, listen to what he might say, and try to find in his words some ground for his enemies to bring charges against him. So after a little, Annas sent Jesus, all bound as he was, to Caiaphas, who was the high priest by law.

Jesus brought for trial before Caiaphas, who in anger tore his clothes and flung up his arms, denouncing Jesus because he declared himself to be the son of God.

Jesus Before Caiaphas

CHAPTER 91

THE HIGH PRIEST Caiaphas, before whom Jesus was now brought for a regular trial, had been in office many years. He was a shrewd, sharp man, caring very little about right or wrong, but always ready to do whatever would please the Jewish leaders, without giving offence to the Roman rulers.

You remember that after Jesus raised Lazarus to life, and many people were believing in Jesus, it was this Caiaphas who said, "No matter whether Jesus is innocent or guilty, whether he is good or bad, the easiest way for us to avoid trouble is to kill him; and that we must do." That showed the spirit of Caiaphas the high priest.

The houses of Annas and Caiaphas were not far apart, and may have been in the same group of buildings on Mount Zion. The officers and policemen took Jesus into the large hall in the high priest's house where all the members of the Jewish council that could be brought together so suddenly were gathered. It was a little after midnight when Jesus was made prisoner in the garden, and it must have been between four and five o'clock on Friday morning when Jesus stood before Caiaphas and the council.

Peter had come with the crowd, and was in the court of the high priest's house. John was not there, but had gone to the house in Jerusalem, where Mary the mother of Jesus was staying, to bring to her the terrible news that her Son was in the hands of his enemies, and to try to give her comfort. So again Peter

was left alone in the midst of a throng opposed to Jesus.

By the law of the Jews, no one could be put to death unless two persons could be found to tell of a wicked act that they had seen him do, or wicked words that they had heard him speak; and also, the accounts of these two witnesses must agree. The rulers looked for witnesses to come and speak against Jesus of what they had seen and heard. They did not care whether these witnesses speaking against Jesus spoke the truth or spoke lies; all they wanted was to have them agree in their words. There were many who spoke falsely against Jesus, but what they said did not agree. After a time two men stood up, and said:

"We ourselves heard this man say in the Temple, 'I will destroy this Temple made by the hands of men, and in three days I will build another made without hands.'"

But even those witnesses did not agree in their account of what Jesus had said. You remember, that three years before, in the Temple, Jesus had said, "Destroy this temple and in three days I will raise it up." But he was speaking not of the Temple of the Jews, but of himself as the temple of the Lord, and of his own death and rising from the tomb. You see how these men changed the words of Jesus in the telling of them.

Now, the Jews had agreed that for any man to speak of destroying the house of God was very wicked; and that whoever should speak of such a thing must be put to death. So in the words of these two men, even though they did not agree, and were false, Caiaphas and the council saw a chance to carry out their purpose of putting Jesus to death.

The high priest Caiaphas stood up, and said to Jesus in a very loud and fierce manner:

"What have you to say of the things spoken by these witnesses? Have you no answer to give?"

But Jesus stood silent and would not speak a word. He knew that speaking would not help him, for their minds were made up to kill him, whatever he might

Judas filled with remorse returns the thirty pieces of silver

say. After a moment of waiting Caiaphas spoke again.

"Are you the Christ," he asked, "the Son of that Blessed One?"

Then Jesus spoke out, once for all:

"I am," he answered, "and what is more, you will all see the Son of Man sitting on the right hand of Almighty God, and coming in the clouds of heaven!"

At this the high priest became furious. In his anger he tore his clothes, and flung up his arms and cried:

"What awful, awful words!" shouted the high priest. "Why this man makes himself equal to Almighty God! We need no more witnesses; he has spoken his own doom. What shall be done to a man who calls himself God?"

Then with one voice all the council said, "He deserves to die," and the sentence of death upon Jesus was given.

Then they began to spit in his face and to strike him. They threw a covering over his face, and after striking him, would say, "Are you a prophet? then tell who it was that struck you!"

The potter's field

All this time Peter was in the court of the building, and through the open door he could see Jesus standing in the inner room. One of the young women servants looked closely at Peter, and finally said:

"You were one of those with Jesus, the Nazarene!"

"I don't know what you are talking about," said Peter in answer; and he went away from the group into the hall outside. Just then the cock crew, and Peter heard it.

Again the woman who had noticed him began to tell those standing near, "That fellow is one of them!" But he denied it again. After a little another man said to Peter:

"You surely are one of this fellow's men! Why,

As Peter was speaking, which was his third denial of his Master, the cock crew for the second time. At that moment Jesus turned and looked on Peter, who instantly repented and went out and wept bitter tears.

your very accent shows that you come from Galilee! You speak your words like a Galilean!"

Then Peter began to curse and to swear: and he said, "I don't know the man you are talking about, and have never seen him!"

As Peter was speaking, the cock crew for the second time. And at that moment the Lord Jesus in the inner room turned and looked on Peter, standing outside the open door. Then all at once flashed upon Peter's mind what his Lord had said on the evening before, "Before the cock crows twice tomorrow morning you will three times deny that you have ever known me." And Peter went away, and as he thought upon it all, he was full of sorrow and wept bitter tears.

But Simon Peter was not the only man in trouble that morning. There was one whose trouble was far deeper. That man was Judas Iscariot, who had sold his Lord for money. When he found that the chief priests and the council had given sentence of death upon Jesus, Judas saw how wicked he had been, and that through his guilty act, Jesus was to be slain. He brought back to the Temple the thirty pieces of silver that had been given him, and threw them down upon the floor, saying:

"I have done wrong in betraying an innocent man! Take back your money!"

"What difference is that to us?" answered the priests. "That is your affair, not ours."

Judas went away, and in his sorrow became wild and hung himself. The next day he was found hanging dead. The chief priests did not know what to do with the money that he had brought back. They said:

"It would never do to put that money among the gifts of the people to the Temple, for it is the price of blood."

They finally decided to take the money; and with it bought a piece of ground as a burial-place for strangers in the city. They bought it of a man who made pots and jars of earthenware; and it was named "The Potter's Field." But by all the people it was called ever after "The Field of Blood."

"The Field of Blood." Purchased with money Judas received.

Pilate came down and sat upon his throne as a judge, and said: "What is the charge which you bring against this man?"

Jesus Before the Roman Governor

CHAPTER 92

ALTHOUGH the high council of the Jews had given sentence upon Jesus that he should be put to death, they could not kill him without the consent of the Roman governor, Pontius Pilate; for long before this the Romans had taken away from the Jews the right to put any man to death. So, very early in the morning, before sunrise, the chief priests and rulers brought Jesus to the castle where the governor was staying. His home was in the city of Cæsarea, nearly sixty miles away, on the sea-coast; but at the time of the Passover, when the city was crowded with people from every part of the land, he usually came to Jerusalem to see that it was kept quiet and in order; and at this time he stayed in a castle north of the Temple, called "The Castle of Antonia."

The Jews had condemned Jesus to die, because, as they claimed, he had said that he was the Son of God; and that claim according to their laws was a high crime, deserving of death. Jesus *was* the Son of God, and as God's Son they should have honored him and obeyed his teachings. But they knew very well that Pilate would not care for their law, and would not order Jesus put to death merely because Jesus had said that he was the Son of God. So they undertook to find something against Jesus which was contrary to the laws of the Romans; and the charge which they resolved to make was that Jesus had spoken against the Roman rule, and had declared that he himself was the King of the Jews. He was, indeed, a king, but not such a king as would be against the Romans or their government.

The Jews came to the castle, and standing outside, called for Pilate to come from the room where he was sleeping, and give judgment upon a law-breaker whom they had brought to him. They hoped that Pilate would do as they wished, without looking closely into the matter. He came down, and sat upon his throne as a judge, and said:

"What is the charge which you bring against this man?"

"If he were not a wicked man, one who has broken the laws, we would not have brought him to you," they answered.

"Well," said Pilate, "if he has broken the laws of the land, take him to your own court and punish him."

"We found this man," said the Jewish rulers, "everywhere leading the people away from their rulers. He forbids them to pay the tax to the Roman emperor, Cæsar, telling the people that he is Christ, the King of the Jews. He ought to be put to death for stirring the people up against the government, and we ask you to give sentence against him."

Pilate began at once to be very suspicious of these Jewish rulers. He knew that they themselves hated the Roman power, and that they would never wish to have anybody punished for opposing it. He looked at Jesus, standing bound and helpless among them, and he thought that this man could not be a dangerous enemy. Pilate said to them:

"Bring this man to me. I wish to speak with him."

Jesus was led up to the foot of the steps to Pilate's judgment throne; and Pilate asked him,

"Are you the King of the Jews?"

Jesus answered the governor, "Do you ask this of your own accord, or did others tell you that I am a king?"

"Do you take me for a Jew?" asked Pilate. "Your

Jesus was led to Pilate, who questioned him privately: "Are you the King of the Jews?"

own people and the priests have brought you before me, saying that you have claimed to be a king. Now tell me, what have you done?"

"My rule as a king does not belong to this world," said Jesus. "If my kingdom were of this world, my men would fight to keep me from being given up to the Jews; but my kingdom is not here on the earth."

"Then you are a king!" said Pilate.

"You speak the truth, I am a king," said Jesus. "I was born for this: I came into the world for this, that I should speak in behalf of the truth. Every one who is on the side of truth listens to my words."

"Truth! What is truth?" said Pilate. Then he went out of the hall and spoke to the Jewish rulers:

"I do not find anything wrong in this man."

This decision of Pilate made the Jews very angry, for they had hoped that he would approve their sentence without asking many questions; and now they found that he was willing to set Jesus free. Pilate thought that Jesus was a harmless man, perhaps not quite right in his mind in believing that he was a king.

But the rulers would not cease their charges against Jesus. They said to Pilate, "This man stirs up the people everywhere, and makes trouble. He began in Galilee; and now he has come here."

"What," said Pilate, "does this man come from Galilee? Then he belongs to the rule of King Herod; and Herod is now here in Jerusalem. Take him to Herod, and let Herod decide his case."

This Pilate said merely because he wished to avoid deciding it himself. He knew that Jesus had broken no law, and should be set free; but he did not wish to displease the Jewish rulers, and he thought to rid himself of the matter by sending Jesus to be tried before Herod, the ruler of Galilee.

Jesus Before Herod

CHAPTER 93

HEROD, to whom Jesus had been sent by Pilate, was the ruler of Galilee, the northern part of the land, and of Perea, on the east of the river Jordan. Jesus had lived in Galilee nearly all his life; and lately had been through Perea, preaching, so that Herod had been the ruler over Jesus for years. Herod was not really a king. His title was "Tetrarch," which means, "the ruler of a fourth part of a kingdom"; and he was so called because when his father, Herod the Great, died, he received as his share one-fourth of his father's kingdom. But he was generally called "King Herod," because the people knew that it pleased him to be looked upon as a king, rather than "the quarter of a king." This was the Herod who had caused John the Baptist to be killed, on account of his promise to the young girl who danced at his feast. That shows what sort of a man Herod was—weak of will, fond of pleasure, and caring very little whether his acts were right or wrong.

Like thousands of other people, high and low, King Herod had come to Jerusalem to take part in the Feast of the Passover; for Herod was a Jew, and kept the Jewish feasts; while Pontius Pilate, the governor of Judea, was a Roman, and worshipped the idols of Rome. Herod was highly pleased to have Jesus sent to him for trial, partly because Pilate and Herod, rulers of lands next to each other, had not been friendly, and this act, the sending of Jesus for trial, showed that Pilate wished to have Herod as his friend. Also, while Jesus was living in Capernaum and teaching all through Galilee,

Herod had heard much about him. You remember that some time before this, when they told King Herod of the many wonderful works of Jesus, how he made the sick well, gave sight to the blind, and even raised the dead, Herod said, "This must be John the Baptist whom I killed, come to life again."

Although Herod did not live in Jerusalem, but in Galilee, he owned a fine house in that city, called a palace; and in this palace he stayed while in Jerusalem. Into the great hall of this palace Jesus was brought by the soldiers of Pilate; and the high priest Caiaphas came with them, also many of the Jewish priests and rulers, to speak against Jesus. Herod was very glad to see Jesus, the prophet and wonder-worker of whom he had heard so much. He wished to see Jesus work a miracle, and commanded him to do it, for he supposed that Jesus, being in his power, for life or death, would be very desirous of pleasing him.

But as you know, Jesus never worked his miracles merely for people to look at them. He would make the sick people well or give hearing to the deaf, because he pitied them in their trouble; but when Herod spoke to him, calling upon him to do some wonderful work, Jesus stood still, and would do nothing. Herod asked Jesus many questions, but Jesus would not answer them, and remained silent. The king did not know what to do with such a prisoner, who would not speak a word, even to save his life.

All this time, while Jesus was silent, the priests and the rulers stood around him, charging Jesus with wickedness of all sorts, disobedience to the laws of the land, and trying to make himself a king in Herod's own country. But Jesus answered nothing to all their charges against him.

Herod thought to make sport of Jesus. As they said

falsely that Jesus claimed to be "King of the Jews," Herod sent for a splendid mantle, such as kings wore, and had it placed on Jesus. Then they bowed low before him, and called him "king," mocking him as one who pretended to royal power. But in the midst of the crowd of mockers stood Jesus, calm and still, paying no attention and looking as though his thoughts were elsewhere.

Herod knew very well that Jesus had done nothing worthy of death; that he was a good man, and harmless. He would not do what the priests and rulers urged him, over and over again, to do, to command that Jesus should be put to death. So, after holding Jesus up to contempt for some time, he sent him back to Pilate, all dressed as Jesus was in the royal robe.

Jesus Sentenced to Death

CHAPTER 94

WHEN PILATE sent Jesus to King Herod, he felt relieved, for he was unwilling on one hand to order Jesus, an innocent man, to be put to death; and on the other hand, he did not wish to offend the Jewish rulers by setting Jesus free. He thought that he had gotten rid of his difficulties, when suddenly he found Jesus brought back to him, and the priests clamoring as before, that he should be put to death.

Pilate very unwillingly sat down again upon his throne, compelled to hold the trial of Jesus once more, and unable to avoid making a decision upon his case. Just as he was about to begin the new trial of Jesus, a message from his wife came to him, which added to his anxiety and his alarm. Pilate's wife sent this word to him:

"My husband, I ask you not to allow any harm to come to that good man; for this day I have been very unhappy on account of a dream about him."

This message made Pilate all the more desirous not to yield to the Jews and put Jesus to death. He thought of a new plan to save the life of Jesus; and with this in mind he said to the chief priests and the leaders:

"You brought before me this man charged with the crime of trying to lead the people to rise up against the government, and I have looked into his case, and have found the charges false. He has not done the things that you accuse him of; and there is nothing wicked in his acts, so far as I can see. Nor has Herod found any

The soldiers took Jesus into the guard room, tied him to a pillar, and beat him with heavy whips.

fault with him, for he has sent him back. He has done nothing that demands death. But he deserves some punishment for causing all this excitement and stir. I will order him to be well beaten, and then set free."

But with one voice, they all cried out, "Away with this fellow! To the cross with him! Don't release him: release to us Barabbas!"

It was a custom that at the Feast of the Passover, as a sign of the gladness of the time, to set free some prisoner, whatever man in prison the people should call for. There was at that time in the prison a man named Barabbas, who had led a party of Jews against the Roman rulers, and in the fight had killed a man. He had been condemned to die, but the people did not think any the less of him because he had fought against the Romans, whom they also hated, and whom they would gladly drive out of the land if they were not afraid of their power. The crowd began calling out to Pilate to do as had been done every year, and set free some prisoner.

"Are you willing," asked Pilate "that I should free this man Jesus, the King of the Jews?"

But the chief priests and the Jewish rulers went around among the crowd, and persuaded them to ask, not for Jesus, but for Barabbas. And the people shouted out, as if they were all one man:

"We will not have this man; we will have Barabbas!"

This was not what Pilate had looked for. He had thought that according to the custom of the feast he might set Jesus free and still please the people. He said to the crowd:

"What then shall I do with Jesus, the man whom they call Christ?"

"Send him to the cross! Let him die on the cross!" they roared with all their might.

They put on Jesus a cloak of scarlet and wove together a wreath of thorns and pressed it on his head until the blood streamed out; they beat him with the reed, and in mockery bowed before him saying: "Long live the King of the Jews."

"Why, what wicked thing has he done?" asked Pilate of the crowd. "I find nothing on his part that deserves death. I will have him beaten, and let him go!"

Then, at Pilate's command, the soldiers took Jesus into the guard room. They stripped off all his clothes, tied him to one of the pillars, and beat him with heavy whips, which tore into his flesh. To mock him, as one who called himself "King," they put on him a cloak of scarlet color; they wove together a wreath of thorns, and pressed it on his head until the blood streamed out; they placed in his hand a reed, as if it were a scepter held by a king; they fell down on their knees before him, and said to him: "Long live the King of the Jews!" They struck him with their hands, over and over again; they beat him with the reed; and they spat in his face.

Pilate thought that if the people could see Jesus as he was, crowned with thorns, and covered with blood, they would feel pity for him, and not call for him to be put to death. He said to the Jews:

"I will bring him out for you to see; but understand, I cannot find anything wrong in him."

Then they brought Jesus out on the steps of the palace. His face was stained with blood; on his head was the wreath of thorns; and on his shoulders was the scarlet cloak. And Pilate said to the crowd:

"See, here is the man!"

But if Pilate hoped that the sight of Jesus, so woeful and sad, would arouse the pity of the people, he soon found himself mistaken. Led by the chief priests and their officers, they cried out with loud voices:

"To the cross with him! Let him be crucified!"

To be crucified was to be fastened with nails on a cross, which was then stood up, and left standing until the suffering man was dead. This was what the crowd of Jews before Pilate's palace called upon him to do with Jesus who had done no harm, but only good!

Pilate answered them: "You can take him and crucify him, if you choose. I will have nothing to do with it; for I can not find that he has done anything wicked."

The rulers of the Jews answered Pilate: "But we have a law; and by our law he must die, because he has made himself out to be the Son of God!"

When Pilate heard that, he was still more afraid, for there seemed to him something strange in this man Jesus. He did not know what to do. He went inside the palace and took Jesus with him.

"Where do you come from?" said Pilate to Jesus.

Jesus gave him no answer. Pilate said to him:

"You will not speak to me? Don't you know that it is in my power either to set you free, or to send you to the cross, just as I please?"

"You would have no power over me," answered Jesus, "if it had not been given you from one who is above. God gave you that power to use for the right and not for the wrong. There is one man whose sin is greater than yours; and that is the high priest who brought me to you!" Jesus meant to have Pilate understand that he was only a weak man, yielding to the will of the high priest, and that he as the governor should have a mind of his own and do only what was right in God's sight.

All this made Pilate the more anxious not to put Jesus to death, but to set him free. But the rulers of the Jews shouted aloud to him:

"If you set this man free, who has called himself a king, you are no friend to Cæsar, the emperor at Rome! Anyone who calls himself a king sets himself above the emperor who is over us all!"

Pilate washed his hands, and holding them out, called to the people: "My hands are clean from this good man's blood! This is your doing, not mine!"

Pilate knew that Cæsar the emperor was very jealous and would be very angry if he knew that any man was trying to make himself a king. Very unwillingly, Pilate made up his mind that it would be safer for himself to let Jesus be put to death, rather than to make the emperor at Rome his enemy. So Pilate again took his seat upon the throne, and had Jesus brought before him. It was now the time of sunrise, six o'clock in the morning. Pilate said to the Jews:

"Here is your king!"

"Kill him! kill him!" yelled the Jews. "Crucify him! Crucify him!"

"This fellow is not our king," shouted the priests and rulers. "We have no king but Cæsar the emperor!"

Pilate tried to show the Jews that the act of putting Jesus to death was their deed, not his. He sent for a basin of water, and in presence of them all washed his hands. Then holding out his hands, he called out to the people:

"My hands are clean from this good man's blood! I tell you that he has done nothing to deserve death! This is your doing, not mine!"

"This blood be on us, and on our children who come after us," answered the Jews.

Then Pilate, sitting on his throne, gave sentence that it should be as they wished, that Barabbas, a robber and a murderer, should be set free, and that Jesus, who had done no harm, but only good, should be sent to the cross.

Denarius of Cæsar

Jesus Led to Calvary

CHAPTER 95

IN OUR TIME, and in all well-governed lands, when a man has been sentenced to death, he is taken to prison and kept there safely for a few days, that he may prepare to die. No one is allowed to do him harm; good food is given him to eat, and he is allowed to live his last days in peace. But in the old times, when Jesus was among men, prisoners appointed to die were treated with the greatest cruelty. They were mocked and beaten and spit upon for an hour or more, and then they were led away to death.

So it was with Jesus on that day. After the soldiers had treated him shamefully, they took off the scarlet robe and put on him his own clothes. Then they laid upon his wounded shoulders the heavy beam of his cross, and led him from Pilate's palace through the streets of Jerusalem toward a hill outside the city wall. This hill was called in the Hebrew tongue, the language of the Jewish people, "Golgotha," a word meaning "Skull-place." In the language of the Romans, the word meaning "Skull-place" was "Calvaria," and from this word the place where Jesus was crucified has been called "Mount Calvary."

It is not certain where was the true Mount Calvary, the place of Christ's cross. For a long time it was believed to be a little hill on the west of the city; and over that hill was built in the after years a great church, called "The Church of the Holy Sepulchre," because inside that church they show not only the place where people thought that the cross stood, but also the tomb or sepulchre in which Jesus was buried. To this church thousands of people go every year, thinking that they can see the very places where the Saviour died and was buried.

But most of those who have studied carefully all that can be known about the city of Jerusalem and the hills around it, have believed that the true Calvary was not where the great Church of the Holy Sepulchre now stands, but at some other place. Many think that it was a rounded, grass-covered little hill just outside the city on the north. The side of this hill looking toward the city is very steep, and in it are two great caves. As one stands on the city wall and looks at this rounded hill, with the two holes in it, he thinks of a skull—which is a man's head without the skin and the flesh, and with two eye-holes. This hill may have been called "the skull-place," because it looks so much like a skull. On this skull-like hill it may be that Jesus was crucified.

Church of the Holy Sepulchre, sometimes claimed to be built upon the site of Calvary

Jesus walked through the streets of the city loaded down with the heavy beam of his cross on his shoulders. The soldiers were dragging him on, and some were driving him forward with blows, when suddenly, worn out with

Turning to the women weeping over him, Jesus said: "Women of Jerusalem, weep not for me but weep for yourselves and your children!"

suffering, and fainting from loss of blood and want of food, he sank down upon the ground, unable to carry his load any further. Just then a man coming from the country into Jerusalem, met the soldiers and the crowd with Jesus. This man was named Simon. He was not Simon Peter, the disciple of Jesus, but another Simon, who had come from a city far away in Africa, called Cyrene. The soldiers seized this man, and made him help Jesus in carrying the cross, until they came to Calvary.

Following the soldiers who had been commanded to crucify Jesus, was a crowd of Jewish priests and scribes, the teachers of the law, and a multitude of the lowest of the people, all shouting aloud their rejoicing that Jesus was to be put to death, just as if he had been the wickedest man in all the land. But among these were a few friends of Jesus, and some of the women who had known him and loved him, and were now weeping over the wrongs done to him.

Jesus turned and spoke to these women:

"Women of Jerusalem, do not weep for me, but weep for yourselves and your children! For the time is coming when they shall say, 'Happy are those who have no children to suffer and to die.' In those days they shall call out to the mountains, 'Fall on us,' and to the hills, 'Hide us.' If this is what they do now in the beginning, what will they do then in the end?"

Even in those terrible moments Jesus was not thinking of himself and his own sufferings, but the sorrows that would soon come upon others.

There is a story told of Jesus on the way to Calvary, which is not found in any of the gospels, and may not be true. It is said that a good woman, named Veronica, was standing by the street when Jesus went by. Seeing his face covered with sweat, and dust, and blood, she went to him and wiped his face with a napkin. When she

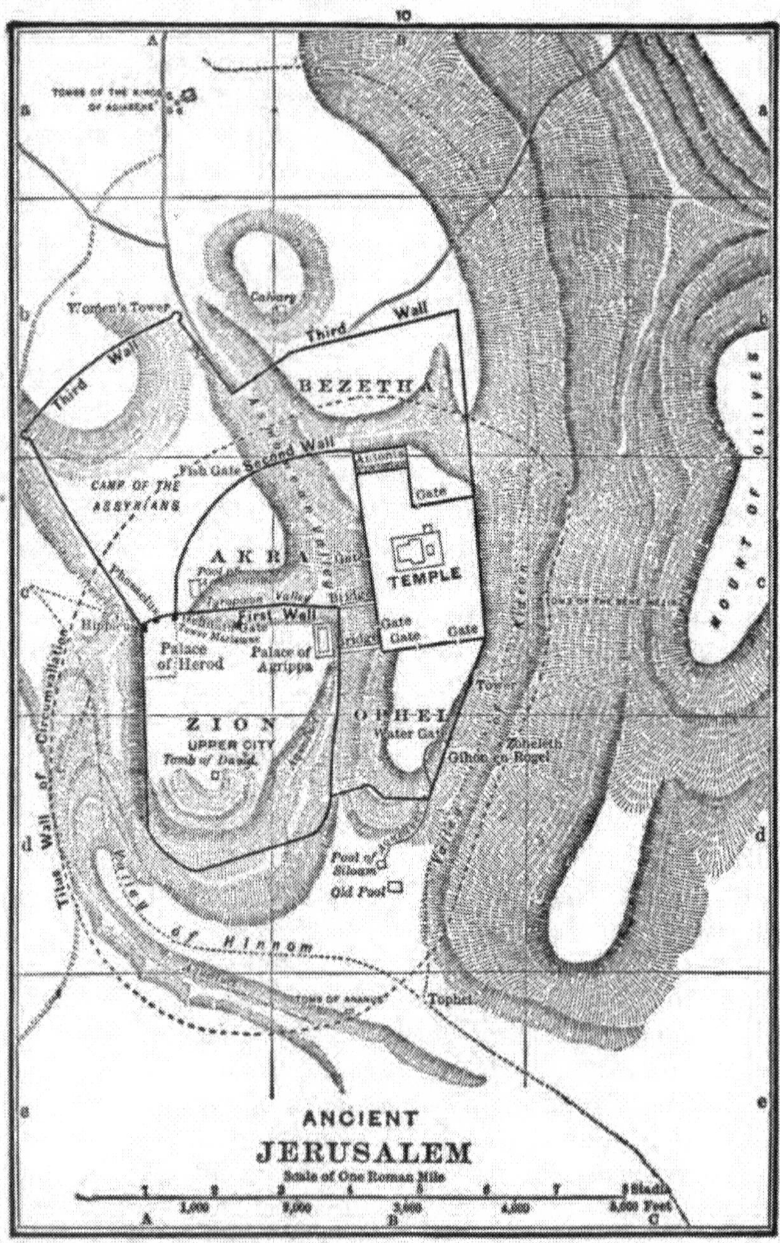

Tombs of the Kings
Women's Tower
Third Wall
Calvary
BEZETHA
Second Wall
Fish Gate
CAMP OF THE ASSYRIANS
Antonia
Gate
AKRA
TEMPLE
Phasaelus
Hippicus
First Wall
Palace of Herod
Palace of Agrippa
Bridge
Gate
Tower
ZION
UPPER CITY
Tomb of David
OPHEL
Water Gate
Zoheleth
Gihon En Rogel
Pool of Siloam
Old Pool
Titus Wall of Circumvallation
Valley of Hinnom
Tophet
Kidron
MOUNT OF OLIVES
ANCIENT
JERUSALEM
Scale of One Roman Mile

looked at her napkin, she found that on it had been printed the portr t of Jesus; and she kept it ever afterward as her greatest treasure.

They led Jesus out of the gate in the city wall, and up the side of the hill Calvary, wherever that hill was. There they laid the cross upon the ground and stretched Jesus out upon it. They drove nails through his hands and feet to fasten his body to the cross. Then they lifted it up with Jesus upon it, and dropped the lower end of it into a hole so that it would stand upright.

With Jesus they had brought two other men, who had been robbers, and sentenced to die by the cross. These two men they crucified with Jesus, one on his right hand and the other on his left, and Jesus between them, as if he had been the most wicked man of the three.

Jesus knew that the Roman soldiers who fastened him to the cross were not his enemies, as the Jews were, but were only obeying the orders that had been given them by their officers. He prayed to God for them.

"Father," said Jesus, "forgive them, for they do not know what they are doing!"

It was nine o'clock on Friday morning when Jesus was placed upon the cross; and he hung there living for six awful hours, until three o'clock in the afternoon.

When Jesus saw his mother, and beside her the disciple whom he loved, he spoke from the cross to her: "Woman, there is your son." Then he said to John: "Son, there is your mother."

Jesus on the Cross

CHAPTER 96

IT WAS the custom of the Romans when they put to death any man upon the cross, to place on the cross above his head a writing, telling what the man's crime was. Pilate commanded that the writing above the head of Jesus should be

THIS IS JESUS OF NAZARETH
THE KING OF THE JEWS.

It was written in the language of three different peoples; in Hebrew, the tongue spoken by the Jews; in Latin, the language of the Romans; and in Greek, the language spoken by all in that part of the world who were not Jews. These words told a great truth, that Jesus was a king, and they told it to all the earth, although very few people believed it then. Now, all over the world are millions upon millions of people who serve Jesus as Lord and King.

When the priests and rulers of the Jews read this writing upon the cross they were greatly displeased, for they did not like to have Jesus called a king. The priests went to Pilate in his palace and said to him:

"Will you not change the writing upon the cross of that man? Let it not be, 'The King of the Jews.' Please change it to, 'He said, "I am King of the Jews."' "

But Pilate answered them, "What I have written, I have written." He meant that whatever he had placed upon the cross must stand there unchanged.

It was also the custom of the Romans when a man

was crucified to give his clothes to the soldiers who fixed him on the cross. Four soldiers were in charge of the cross. These men divided the clothes of Jesus among them, each taking one garment. But one garment was left over, the shirt of Jesus. This was all woven in one piece, not sewed together; so the soldiers said:

"Let us not tear it, but cast lots to settle whose it shall be."

They threw upon the ground little square pieces of ivory having spots upon them. These squares were called dice. Each soldier threw one ivory piece; and they counted the spots on the side that was uppermost. The soldier whose piece showed the highest number took the shirt of Jesus as his own. One of the disciples of Jesus was standing near, and saw the soldiers dividing the clothes of Jesus, and he thought of the words in the twenty-second psalm, as a prophecy or foretelling of what should happen to Christ. These were the words of the psalm, written many hundred years before:

"They shared my garments among them,
And over my clothing they cast lots."

The soldiers having done their work, sat down around the cross to watch it. A great crowd of the priests and scribes and people stood around the cross, looking at Jesus hanging there. Some of them spoke spitefully to Jesus, shaking their heads at him, saying such words as these:

"Ah! you would destroy the Temple and build it again in three days, would you? Then come down from the cross and save yourself if you can!"

And some of the priests and scribes called out, "He saved others; but he can not save himself! If he is, as he said, 'Christ, the King of Israel,' let him now come down from the cross in our sight. Then we will believe on him."

"He trusts in God," said others; "now let God help him, if he chooses; for he said, 'I am the Son of God.' "

One of the two robbers who were hanging on the crosses beside Jesus called out to him, joining in the abuse:

"Are you not the Christ, the King of Israel? If you are, why don't you save yourself and save us with you?"

But the crucified man on the other side of Jesus rebuked him:

"Have you no fear of a just God?" he said. "You are suffering the same sentence as this man. And you and I are suffering only what we deserve for our deeds; but this man has done nothing wrong."

Then this man from his cross said to Jesus, "Jesus, do not forget me when you come into your kingdom."

And Jesus answered him, "I tell you truly, this very day you shall be with me in the heavenly land."

At this time, near the cross of Jesus, was standing John, his disciple, the one disciple that Jesus loved, and with him was Mary, the mother of Jesus, also her sister and two other women named Mary—Mary the wife of Clopas, and Mary Magdalene, or Mary of Magdala. When Jesus saw his mother, and beside her the disciple whom he loved, he spoke from the cross to her:

"Woman, there is your son."

Then he said to John:

"Son, there is your mother."

And from that time Mary, the mother of Jesus, lived with the disciple John, as though he was her own son.

It was now noon, and Jesus had been upon the cross three long, terrible hours; the sun beating with its rays upon his head. Just at noon a sudden darkness came over the sky and the earth, and the darkness did not pass away until three o'clock. This darkness alarmed the people, and those who had been speaking to Jesus words of contempt, now stood still, full of fear.

At about three o'clock, Jesus called out with a loud voice these words:

"My God! My God! Why hast thou forsaken me?"

These are the opening words of the twenty-second psalm, written many hundred years before as a prophecy of what Christ should suffer. It may be that Jesus spoke those words to show that all his suffering had been foretold long before. Jesus in speaking those words used the old Hebrew tongue, the language in which the psalm was written. In the old Hebrew the words, "My God! My God!" were "Eloi! Eloi!" But the language had changed so greatly since the psalms were written that the people who heard him did not understand the words. Some said, "He is calling upon Elijah the prophet to help him!"

Then Jesus spoke again and said:

"I am thirsty."

There was standing by a jar full of vinegar. One of the men took a sponge, soaked it in the vinegar, fastened it on the end of a stick, and placed it on the lips of Jesus. This also had been foretold in the sixty-ninth psalm, in the words,

> "In my thirst they gave me vinegar to drink."

As soon as Jesus tasted the vinegar, he said:

"All is finished."

Then, after a moment's pause, he spoke with a loud voice to God:

"Father, into thy hands I give up my spirit!"

And with those words his head dropped forward, and Jesus was hanging dead upon his cross.

Just at the moment when Jesus died, suddenly there was an earthquake; the ground was shaken, the rocks were torn apart, and many of the tombs around Jerusalem were opened. In the Temple on Mount Moriah, a wonderful event was seen. The great veil

The people on Mt. Calvary looking at the dying Jesus were filled with fear, and went back to the city in terror at the darkness and earthquake.

that hung between the Holy Place and the Most Holy Place was suddenly torn from the top to the bottom, as if by a mighty unseen hand, so that the priests in the Temple could see what none of them, except the high priest, had ever seen before, the inside of the Holy of Holies.

The people who were standing on Mount Calvary, looking at the dying Jesus, were filled with fear. They beat upon their breasts with their hands, and went back to the city in terror at the darkness and the earthquake. The Roman captain, who was in charge of the soldiers around the cross, said:

"Surely this was a good man, a son of God!"

You know that the Sabbath among the Jews was kept on the seventh day of the week and that it always began at sunset on the evening before. It was on Friday that Jesus was crucified, and three o'clock on that afternoon. The Jews did not wish to have the men upon the three crosses hanging there upon the Sabbath, for that day, the Passover Sabbath, was kept especially holy.

The Jewish rulers came to Pilate and asked him that the men should not be left upon the cross over the Sabbath, but that they should be killed and their bodies taken away. They did not know at that time that Jesus was already dead. Pilate gave orders to the soldiers to have the men killed. This they did by breaking their legs, as they hung upon the crosses. As they saw that Jesus was no longer alive, they did not break his legs. But one of the soldiers, to be sure of his death, drove his spear into the side of Jesus, to strike his heart. John the disciple was still standing there watching beside the cross to the very last, and he wrote in his gospel many years afterward that he saw both water and blood pour forth from the side of Jesus, out of the wound made by the spear.

The Tomb in the Garden

CHAPTER 97

YOU REMEMBER that from the garden of Gethsemane, very early on Friday morning, Jesus was brought before the high council of the Jews for trial, and that by the council it was ordered that Jesus should be put to death as one who falsely claimed that he was Christ, the King of Israel. But not all the members of this council were enemies of Jesus. A very few of them were his friends, but in secret, not daring to speak for him or to vote for him, for fear of the rulers and the people.

One of these secret friends of Jesus was Nicodemus, the ruler who had come to see Jesus at night three years before, on his first visit to Jerusalem. Another was a good man named Joseph, a rich man, who lived at a place called Arimathea, some miles out of Jerusalem, in the country. This man, Joseph of Arimathea, did a very bold thing. He went to Pilate in his palace, and asked Pilate to allow him to take down from the cross the dead body of Jesus, and to bury it. To us this may not seem a brave act, but it was, for the Roman rulers were very suspicious of anybody who appeared to be the friend of one who had been condemned to death. Some time before this, when a man asked the governor for the body of a man who had been put to death, the governor ordered that his friend should also be slain as an enemy of the Romans and the governor's enemy. It might be said that Joseph of Arimathea "took his life in his hands" when he asked Pilate for the body of Jesus.

But Pilate was not angry with Joseph; and at heart he was not an enemy of Jesus. Pilate was sur-

In the side of a rocky hill was a cave which Joseph of Arimathea had hollowed out for his own tomb, and there they laid the body of Jesus.

prised to learn that Jesus was already dead, for sometimes upon the cross men lived several days of terrible pain. He sent for the Roman captain who had been in charge at the cross, and asked him if Jesus the Nazarene was dead. When the captain told him that Jesus was dead, he allowed Joseph to take away the body and do with it as he pleased.

Then Joseph, with some of the disciples of Jesus, carefully and tenderly took down from the cross the body of Jesus; and after the manner of Jewish burials at that time, wrapped it round and round with long strips of linen cloth. They also tied a napkin over the face of Jesus. Nicodemus came to help in the burial, bringing with him the weight of a hundred pounds in fragrant and costly spices, aloes and myrrh, which they laid in the linen cloth around the body.

Near the place where Jesus was crucified was a garden belonging to Joseph of Arimathea, and in the side of the rocky hill was a cave which Joseph had hollowed out for his own tomb. No dead body had ever been buried in this tomb; and there they laid the body of Jesus. Then they rolled a great stone to the door of the tomb, and left it.

Near by, at this time, were some of the women who had come with Jesus from Galilee; looking on while the body of Jesus, whom they had loved so fondly, was laid in the tomb. One of these women was Mary Magdalene, or "Mary of Magdala" by the Sea of Galilee, a woman from whom Jesus had driven out evil spirits more than a year before. Another woman was Mary, the wife of Clopas; and another was named Salome, who may have been the mother of the disciples James and John, and the wife of Zebedee the fisherman. These women noticed carefully the place where the body of Jesus was buried.

On the next morning, which was the Jewish Sabbath day, the chief priests and leading men among the Jews came to Pilate and said to him:

"We remember, sir, that while this man who deceived the people was alive, he said, 'After three days in the tomb I will arise again.' Now, then, give orders that the tomb where he is buried be kept under guard for three days. For if it be not watched, his disciples may come and steal his body out of the tomb and hide it; then they will tell the people, 'He is risen from the dead,' and the last false report will do more harm than the first, that he was the King of Israel."

"Take a guard of soldiers," said Pilate, "and make it just as sure as you can."

So they went and made the tomb secure by putting a seal on the great stone at the door. Also they placed a guard of soldiers in front of the tomb, with orders to stay there for three days.

On one side of the rounded skull-like hill which may have been Calvary, where Jesus was crucified, there has been found a very ancient tomb, which may have been the place of the Saviour's burial. No one can be sure of this; but we may be certain that either in this tomb, or in one like it, not far away, Jesus was buried.

The Risen Christ and the Empty Tomb

CHAPTER 98

IT WAS FRIDAY evening at sunset, only three hours after Jesus had died upon his cross, when the stone at the door of the tomb was rolled against the door, and the body of Jesus was left alone in its resting place. All day on Saturday, the Jewish Sabbath, and through that night, the body lay in the tomb, watched by Roman soldiers. But early on Sunday morning, before the sun rose, something wonderful took place such as had never been seen from the beginning of the world and never has been seen since that day.

There was a great earthquake, shaking the ground around the tomb, as an angel from heaven came down. His face and his form shone with dazzling brightness like lightning, and his clothing was white as snow glittering in the sun. The soldiers on guard trembled as they saw the angel, and fell down on the ground as if they were dead; and after a little while rising up, crept away in their fear, and left the garden.

The bright angel laid his hand on the stone at the door of the tomb, paying no attention to the seal upon it, and rolled the stone away. As he stood at the open door of the tomb, the Lord Jesus Christ walked out from it, no longer dead but living, and living never to die again. The grave clothes were not now wrapped around his body, and the napkin had been taken from his face.

If the Roman soldiers were still there, they could not see Jesus, for a change had come over him, and he was now seen only by those whom he wished to see him and

The women at the empty tomb listened in fear and wonder to the words of the angel: "He is not here; he has risen!"

by no others. And he could suddenly appear and disappear as he chose. He could be seen suddenly in one place, and then a moment after could be seen just as suddenly in another place miles and miles away. He could pass through closed doors just as if they were wide open; and after being seen by his friends could vanish out of their sight.

A few moments after the earthquake, and after the risen Christ had come from his tomb, a few women came from the city to the tomb, bringing some more spices and perfumes to place around his body. Those women were Mary Magdalene, and Mary the wife of Clopas, and Salome, and a woman named Joanna, and perhaps others. They may have felt the earthquake shock, but they did not know the wonderful things that had taken place, and supposed that the body of Jesus was in the tomb. As they came near, they said to each other:

"Who will roll away for us the great stone at the door of the tomb?"

But when they came to the tomb, they found the stone already rolled away, and the tomb open. Mary Magdalene came a little before the others, and was the first to see that the tomb was open, and looking inside she saw that it was empty. She took but one glance, and then, without waiting for the others, ran away to tell some of the disciples of Jesus that the tomb had been opened and the body of Jesus taken away, for she did not know that Jesus had risen and was living.

A moment after Mary Magdalene had gone away, the other women came to the tomb. They, too, saw that the stone had been rolled away, the tomb was open and the body of Jesus was not there. But these women saw what Mary Magdalene had not seen, a young man with shining face and long white robe, seated on the right side of the place where the body of Jesus had been laid. They were frightened as they looked upon him, for this young man was the angel who had rolled away the stone. But he calmed their fears, saying to them:

"Do not be afraid, you are looking for Jesus the Nazarene, who has been crucified. He has risen; he is not here! Look! this the place where his body was laid; and you can see it is empty! But go, find his disciples, and Peter, and tell them that he will go before you into Galilee, to the mountains. There they will see him, as he said to them before he died."

So these women, like Mary Magdalene only a few minutes before, went away from the tomb to find some of the disciples. They found Peter and John, and told them the news that the angel had given to them.

Peter and John at once hurried to the tomb. John was younger than Peter, and came to the tomb first. He saw the stone rolled away and the tomb open, and stood at the door, hesitating, uncertain whether to go into the tomb or not. But Peter, who came a moment afterward, did not hesitate. He rushed past John into the tomb, and saw that it was empty. It was like John, the thoughtful one, to wait at the door of the tomb; and it was like Peter, the quick and hasty one, to rush straight into the tomb. After Peter walked into the tomb, John followed him inside. They saw that the grave-place was empty; but they saw no angel. John noticed that the grave-clothes were lying in a heap on the floor, just as if Jesus had slipped out of them, without unrolling the long bands; and that the napkin which he had seen bound about his face had been carefully folded and was lying by itself. All these things showed that the body had not been taken away suddenly or in haste.

Peter and John hurried to the tomb; seeing that it was empty they were convinced that Jesus had risen.

Peter, the excitable, was not a thinker, and just looked at these things and wondered. But John, the thoughtful disciple, looked at these things—the stone rolled away with its seal broken, the empty tomb, the grave clothes in an orderly pile, and the napkin folded carefully. Then it flashed upon his mind for the first time that his Lord had risen alive from the tomb! And at that moment came to him the words of Jesus spoken more than once, that he must die, and on the third day would rise again from death to life. Of all the eleven disciples of Jesus—for now that Judas was dead, they were no longer twelve, but eleven—John, the disciple whom Jesus loved the most, was the first one to believe that Jesus had risen, and he believed it before he had seen his living Lord.

As yet no one had seen Jesus living. Two disciples had looked into the empty tomb, and the women, except Mary Magdalene, had seen the angel, but none of them had seen Jesus; and all of them, save Mary Magdalene, went away, wondering and scarcely knowing what to think.

Jesus and Mary Magdalene

CHAPTER 99

ALL THE FOUR gospels agree in saying that the first person who saw Jesus Christ living after his death on the cross was Mary Magdalene; that is, Mary of Magdala, a town on the Sea of Galilee; a woman from whom a year before Jesus had driven out evil spirits; and who in love for what Jesus had done to her, followed him, and helped him with her gifts, for she was a rich woman.

When the other women, with Peter and John, went away from the tomb, Mary stayed there, weeping and sobbing; for she had not seen the angel who said that Jesus had risen, and did not know that he was alive. As she stood weeping at the door of the tomb, she looked inside. There she saw two angels sitting at the empty grave-place, one at the head, the other at the feet, where the body of Jesus had been lying.

"Woman," said one of the angels, "why are you weeping?"

"Because they have taken away my Lord," answered Mary, "and I do not know where they have laid him."

Just then something caused her to turn around, and she saw a man standing near her. It was Jesus, but she did not know him; for after rising from his grave Jesus showed himself in differing forms, and people could not know him until he allowed them.

"Woman," said Jesus to her, "why are you weeping? Who is it that you are looking for?"

Mary thought that this strange man was the gardener. She said to him:

"Oh, sir, if you have carried him anywhere, tell me where you have laid him, and I will take him away myself."

"Mary!" said Jesus.

And as he spoke her name, she knew him; and fell at his feet, clasping them in her hands.

"My own Master!" was all that she could say, in her joy at seeing him alive once more, whom she had last looked upon dead, hanging on the cross.

"Do not hold me," said Jesus, "for I have yet to arise and go to my Father in heaven; but go to my brothers, my disciples, and tell them that I shall soon rise up from the earth and go to my Father and your Father, to my God, and your God."

Mary Magdalene went and found the disciples, and said to them, "I have seen the Lord!" telling them also what he had said to her.

After Mary Magdalene had gone away from the tomb, the other women—Mary the wife of Clopas, Joanna, and Salome—came back from having seen the disciples, and having told them what the angel had said, that Jesus had risen. As they drew near the tomb, Jesus went to meet them.

"Welcome!" he said to the women. They ran up to him, fell on their faces, and clasped his feet, just as Mary had done, for they felt joy and fear mingled as they saw him.

"Do not be afraid," said Jesus, "go tell my brothers to go to Galilee and they shall see me there."

So these women went again to find the disciples and give them the news that Jesus was really living, and that they had seen him. All this was on Sunday morning—the first Easter-day.

On that morning, when the soldiers who had fled from the tomb recovered from their terror, they went

Mary Magdalene turned and answered the strange man whom she thought was the gardener: "Oh, sir, if you have carried him anywhere, tell me where you have laid him." "Mary!" said Jesus. And as he spoke her name she knew him.

to the chief priests and told them about the earthquake and the angel who had rolled away the stone. The priests had a talk with the rulers of the city; then they gave a large sum of money to the soldiers, and told them to say to everybody:

"The disciples came at night, while we were asleep, and broke open the tomb, and stole the body of Jesus."

They knew that a soldier had no right to sleep while on guard; and the rule of the army was, that any soldier who slept on his post should be put to death. But the rulers said to them:

"If the governor hears about this, we will satisfy him, and see that no harm comes to you."

So the soldiers took their money and did as they were told. And the story that the body of Jesus was stolen from the tomb, was told among the Jewish people and believed by them.

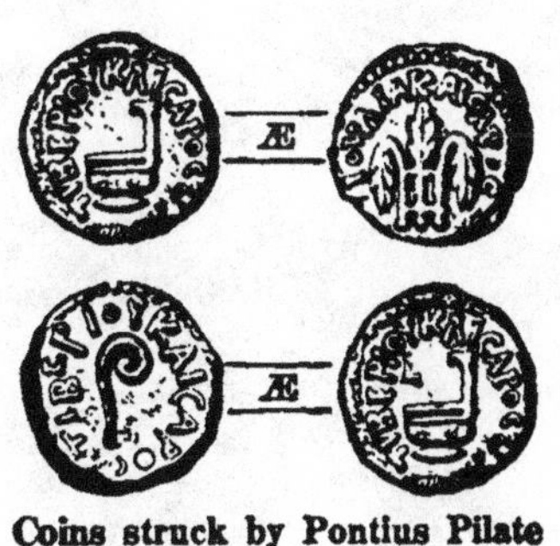

Coins struck by Pontius Pilate

Then Jesus began to show them in all the Old Testament books, how all the prophets had foretold the things that should take place with Christ when he should come.

A Walk with the Risen Christ

CHAPTER 100

WHEN JESUS was seen after he rose from the tomb, it was called an "appearance" because Jesus appeared to someone. His first appearance, as you have read, was to Mary Magdalene; his second appearance was to the other women; and his third appearance was to two men walking out into the country on that first Easter morning.

Those two men were not among the twelve disciples of Jesus; but they had believed in him as the Christ, the King of Israel. One of them was named Cleopas; the name of the other has not been given in the gospel by Saint Luke, where this story is told. The two men on that morning were walking out from Jerusalem to a village called Emmaus, which was six or seven miles from the city. As they walked, they talked together of Jesus, of his death, his burial, and of a report which had just come to them, that he was living again.

While they were walking and talking, they suddenly saw another man walking with them. This stranger was Jesus, but they did not know him; just as Mary Magdalene did not know Jesus when first she saw him. He said to them:

"What is it that you are talking about, as you walk along?"

They stood still, with sorrowful faces; and Cleopas answered this stranger.

"What!" said Cleopas, "do you live all alone in Jerusalem, since you seem not to have heard of the things that have taken place there in the last few days?"

"What things do you mean?" asked the stranger.

"Why, about Jesus of Nazareth," they answered. "Have you never heard of him? He was a wonderful prophet, to whom God gave power in his words and his deeds before all the people. But the chief priests and our rulers seized him, and gave him up to be sentenced to death, and crucified him. But it was our hope that he was to be the one to set Israel free from its enemies, and reign as our King. And now, this is the third day since he died, and this morning some women of our company have brought to us news that greatly surprised us. They went to the tomb at daybreak, and found it open, but did not find his body within it. They told us that they had seen some angels, who said that Jesus was alive! At once some of our men went to the tomb, and found it just as the women had said, the tomb thrown open and the body gone; but they did not see Jesus."

"O, foolish men, with hearts so slow to believe, after all that the prophets have said in the Holy Book!" said the stranger, who was the risen Jesus. "Do you not know that Christ was bound to suffer all these things before he could enter his glory as the Son of God?"

Then he began to show them in all the Old Testament books, how Moses in the law, and David in the psalms, and all the prophets in their writings, had foretold the things that should take place with Christ when he should come; and that all these things had come to pass with Jesus, showing that Jesus of Nazareth was in truth the Son of God and the King of Israel.

While they went on talking together, they drew near the village of Emmaus, to which the two men were going. The unknown Jesus seemed as if he was going further; but they urged him to stop.

"Stay with us," they said to him, "for it is getting toward evening; the sun is already about to set."

After his resurrection Jesus appears to Simon Peter.

And Jesus went with them to the village and into the house. They sat down to supper; and the stranger took the loaf of bread, blessed it, broke it, and gave it to them. In that instant, their eyes were opened, and they knew who he was, Jesus their Master! But in that moment he vanished out of their sight.

"How our hearts burned within us," they said to each other, "while he was talking to us on the road and explaining to us what is said in the Holy Book!"

Then they immediately rose up from the table, and went back in haste to Jerusalem. They found some of the disciples and others in the upper room at Jerusalem, where Jesus had taken his last supper with his disciples. Before Cleopas and his friend found a chance to tell their story, those in the room said to them:

"The Lord has really risen, and has appeared to Simon Peter!"

Then the two men from Emmaus told how the stranger had walked with them on the road, and had told them many things out of the Old Testament; and how they had suddenly known that he was Jesus, while he was blessing and breaking the bread.

These were the third and fourth appearances of Jesus, the third to Simon Peter; but what Jesus said to him has not been written; and the fourth, to Cleopas and his friend on the road to Emmaus.

Two Sunday Evenings with the Risen Christ

CHAPTER 101

THE MEETING place of all who believed in Jesus, after his death on the cross, seems to have been the upstairs room, where Jesus had his last supper. There they met from day to day; and it was to this place that the two men came from Emmaus with the report of their meeting with Jesus. On the evening of Sunday, the first Easter day, the followers of Jesus were gathered together in this room. Ten of the eleven disciples of Christ were there, Thomas being absent; and with them were the women and a number of others who were believers in Jesus.

The doors leading to this room were shut and locked, for they feared the Jewish rulers and people. They were talking together of these reports that had come to them of Jesus having risen and having been seen, when all of a sudden they saw Jesus himself standing in the middle of the room. He said to them:

"Peace be to you!"

At the first sight of him, they were frightened, for they thought it was not Jesus alive whom they saw, but the ghost or spirit of Jesus dead.

"Why are you so startled?" said Jesus to them, "and why do doubts come to you? Look at my hands and my feet. It is I, myself. Feel me, and look at me; a spirit has not flesh and bones, as you see that I have!"

With these words he showed them his hands and his feet, with the holes left by the nails on the cross still in them. Even yet, they felt the sight of Jesus

Jesus looked at Thomas and said to him: "Look at my hands and put your finger there, and look at my side and thrust your hand into it."

was too good to be true, and could scarcely believe that it was their Lord living. He said to them:

"Have you here anything to eat?"

They brought to him a piece of broiled fish; and he ate it while they looked on. This was not because he was hungry and needed food, for he no longer needed anything; but simply to show them that he was really living.

Then at last they were afraid no longer, and believed fully that their Lord was with them living; and their hearts were full of joy. Jesus said to them again:

"Peace be with you; as the Father sent me forth, even so I send you forth."

Then he breathed on them, and said, "Receive the Holy Spirit of God! I give you power that if you take away the sins of men, they are taken away from them, just as if I myself forgave them; and if you do not take away their sins, then the guilt of their sins shall stay upon them."

After talking with his followers for a time on that evening, Jesus disappeared as suddenly as he had come. This was his fifth appearance on that day, the day of his rising from the tomb.

But, as we have seen, Thomas, one of the twelve disciples of Jesus, was not with the others on that evening, and being absent did not meet the risen Jesus. The other disciples said to him:

"We have seen the Lord!"

But Thomas would not believe them. He thought that they were all mistaken, and said:

"Unless I see in his hands the mark of the nails on the cross, and put my finger on those marks of the nails; and unless I can put my hand into the wound made by the spear in his side, I will not believe that he is alive!"

A week later, on the next Sunday evening, they all met again in the upper room; and at this time, Thomas was present. Though the doors were shut, Jesus came again, and stood among them, with the words as before: "*Peace be with you!*"

He looked at Thomas and said to him:

"*Look at my hands, and put your finger there; and look at my side, and thrust your hand into it. Do not longer refuse to believe that I am alive, but believe in me.*"

Thomas answered him: "My Lord, and my God!"

"Is it because you have seen me that you have believed in me?" said Jesus. "Blessed are those who have not seen, and yet have believed!"

You remember that John, the beloved disciple, believed that Jesus had risen when he looked into the empty tomb, and before he had seen him alive.

This meeting with the disciples on the second Sunday evening was the sixth appearance of Jesus after rising from the dead.

The Breakfast by the Sea

CHAPTER 102

ON THE NIGHT before the death of Jesus, at the supper he had said to the twelve disciples, "After I have risen from the dead, I will go before you to Galilee." And after rising from his tomb, he had said to the women, "Go and tell my disciples that I will meet them on the mountain in Galilee." This mountain was Kurn Hattin, near the Sea of Galilee, where in the year before, he had preached his great "Sermon on the Mount."

The word that Jesus would show himself to all who believed on him, on this mountain in Galilee, led the followers of Jesus from all parts of the land to go to Galilee and to this mountain. They waited near that place for some days without seeing Jesus.

One morning seven of the eleven disciples of Jesus were on the shore of the Sea of Galilee. These seven men were Simon Peter, James and John, Thomas, Nathanael (who was also called Bartholomew, which means "son of Tolmai"), and two other disciples, whose names have not been given.

While they were standing by the lake, Peter felt a longing for his old work as a fisherman, and he said to the others:

"I am going fishing."

He thought that while they were waiting for Jesus to come, they might also do some work. The other six men said:

"We will go fishing with you."

They went out in the boat, and fished all night, but

At daybreak they saw a man standing on the shore, who called to them: "Throw out your net on the right side of the boat and you will catch some fish."

caught nothing. The next morning, just as the day was breaking, they saw a man standing on the shore.

"Boys," called out this man, "have you caught anything?"

"No," they answered him.

"Throw out your net on the right side of the boat," said the stranger, "and you will find some fish."

They threw out the net as the man told them, and at once it was filled with large fish, so full that they could not at first haul it in. Then John, the disciple whom Jesus loved, said to Peter:

"That is our Lord!"

When Simon Peter heard that this man on the shore was the Lord Jesus, he slipped on his coat—for he had taken it off while working—and leaped into the water to swim ashore. The other disciples came ashore in a smaller boat, dragging the net, full of fish; for they were not more than a hundred yards from the beach.

When they landed on the shore, they saw a charcoal fire burning, with some fish cooking upon it and some bread beside it. Jesus said:

"Bring some of the fish that you have caught."

Peter went to the boat and pulled the net ashore, full of large fish. They counted them afterward, and found that they numbered one hundred and fifty-three; but although there were so many, the net was not torn anywhere. Jesus said to them:

"Come and have breakfast."

They sat down on the beach beside the fire; and Jesus passed the bread around to them, and also the broiled fish. This was now the third time that Jesus was seen by his disciples after rising from the dead; for he had already appeared to them on two Sunday evenings in Jerusalem; and in all, this was the seventh appearance of Jesus after his rising from the dead.

After they had eaten their breakfast, and were still sitting together, Jesus said to Simon Peter:

"Simon, son of Jonas. do you love me more than the others?"

"Why, Master," answered Peter, "you know that I am your friend."

"Then," said Jesus, "feed my lambs."

There was a moment's pause, and then Jesus a second time asked Peter:

"Simon, son of Jonas, do you love me?"

"Yes, Master," he replied; "you know that I am your friend."

"Then," said Jesus, "be a shepherd to my sheep."

Then, a third time, Jesus asked him:

"Simon, son of Jonas, are you my friend?"

Peter felt hurt that his third question was "Are you my friend?" and not "Do you love me?" and he answered:

"Master, you know everything! You know that I am your friend!"

"Then feed my sheep," said Jesus; and he went on, "I tell you in truth, when you were young you put your own girdle around your waist, and went wherever you chose. But when you grow old, you will stretch out your hands for someone else to put a girdle around you, and you will be taken where you do not wish to go."

Then Jesus added, "Follow me."

As Peter on the night of his Master's trial had three times denied that he knew Jesus or was his disciple, so now Jesus wished him to say three times before them all that he was his friend. And when he had spoken this three times, the Lord said to him, as he had said long before by the Sea of Galilee, "Follow me." Thus Simon Peter was again given his old place among the disciples of Jesus.

What Jesus said to Peter about stretching out his hands and being carried where he did not wish to go, was spoken as a prophecy or foretelling of the manner by which Peter should die for the sake of Christ. Nearly forty years after that time, when Peter was an old man, he was put to death at Rome by being crucified as Jesus had been. It is said that when he was about to be fastened upon the cross, he said to the soldiers, that one who had denied his Master as he had, was not worthy of dying in the same manner as Jesus had died; and he begged them to set up his cross with his head downward toward the ground; and thus Peter died.

But to go back to that breakfast by the Sea of Galilee, after those words had been spoken by Jesus to Peter, he looked at John, who was standing near. Peter and John, though very different in their natures, loved each other greatly. In the story of Jesus and his disciples, and in the days that came after, we find that almost always Peter and John were together. Seeing John, Peter said to Jesus:

"Master, you have told me about myself; now tell what this man shall do."

But Jesus said to Peter:

"If I choose that he shall wait until I come back to earth, what has that to do with you? Do you follow me, as I said."

John, the disciple whom Jesus loved, lived a long time after that day. When all the rest of the twelve disciples of Jesus had died—nearly all of them were slain by enemies of Christ—John was still living. And from these words of Jesus many thought that John would not die. But Jesus did not say that John would not die. He only said that if he chose to let John live until he, Jesus, came again, it was not Peter's matter, but the Lord's.

He rose into the air, higher and higher, until a cloud covered him from their sight, and Jesus the Lord of glory was seen no more.

Jesus Rising up from Earth to Heaven

CHAPTER 103

SOON AFTER the appearance of Jesus to the seven disciples by the Sea of Galilee, a great meeting was held of many who believed in Jesus, on the mountain, in Galilee, where Jesus had told them to come together. It is said that at this meeting more than five hundred people who were followers of Jesus gathered in one place. There Jesus showed himself to the whole company. When they saw him they bowed down to the ground before him; but even then some of them were in doubt whether they had really seen the Lord.

At that time Jesus drew near to this company and said to them:

"All power as the Son of God, and the King of God's Kingdom in heaven and on earth has been given to me by my Father. I command you, therefore, to go and preach the gospel to all the world, and make disciples of all nations and in all lands. Those who believe on me, baptize in the name of the Father, and the Son, and the Holy Spirit; and teach them to obey all the commands that I have given you. Whoever believes on me as his Saviour shall be saved from his sins; but whoever will not believe, shall suffer the guilt of his sins. And these powers shall be given to those who believe; in my name they shall drive out evil spirits; they shall speak with new tongues; they shall take up poisonous snakes in their hands and shall suffer no harm; if they drink any poison it shall not hurt them; they will place their hands on sick people, and they shall become well. And

I will be with you all the time, even to the very end of the world."

After this there was a ninth appearance of Jesus to James; not James the brother of John, but another James who was the son of Joseph and Mary, and a younger brother of Jesus. What was said at that appearance has not been told, but from that time James was one of the foremost followers of Jesus, and for many years a leader in the church at Jerusalem. Long after this, James wrote one of the books in the New Testament, the Epistle of James.

Jesus was seen from time to time during forty days by his disciples and followers. We know of ten times in all when Jesus appeared; but there may have been other times of which no mention is made in the gospels or in the other writings of the New Testament. His tenth appearance, as far as we know, and his last, may have been at the upper room in Jerusalem, forty days after he had risen from his tomb. At that time he said:

"When I was with you, I told you this, that everything written of me in the books of Moses, and the psalms and the prophets must come to pass."

Then he opened their minds to understand what was written in the Old Testament.

"Thus," he said, "it is written that Christ the King of Israel must suffer, and die, and rise again the third day, just as has come to pass. And now you are to go forth and preach that men must everywhere turn from their sins to God, and be forgiven of their sins through the power given to me. And you are to begin your preaching here in Jerusalem, the very place where I have been crucified. I will soon send down on you the Holy Spirit whom my Father has promised. But wait in this city until the power comes upon you from on high."

Then the risen Christ led them out of the city to

"Where two or three are gathered together in my name, there am I in the midst of them."

the Mount of Olives. No one except those who believed in him could see him, for he was unseen to all other people. As he drew near Bethany he lifted up his hands and blessed his followers. While they were looking at him, and his hands were held out, he rose into the air, higher and higher, until after a time a cloud covered him from their sight, and Jesus the Lord of glory was seen no more.

While they were looking upward, two men dressed in shining white, angels of God, were seen standing beside them. These angels said to the followers of Jesus:

"Men of Galilee, why are you standing here looking up towards the heavens? This Jesus, who has been taken from you, will come again to earth in the very same way that you have seen him go up to heaven."

So Jesus Christ was taken up to heaven, and there sat down on his throne at the right hand of God. He sits there still, watching over his people until the day shall come for him to return to earth.